Shooting

Mr. J. H. FitzGerald

Shooting

by

J.H. FitzGerald

*Firearms Expert, Lecturer, and Instructor in
Target and Defense Shooting*

-

Member New York State Police
Inspector-Instructor, N.Y. State Police School for 11 Years
Member Portland, Oregon, Police Department
Life Member National Rifle Association
Member National Identification Association
Member N.Y. State Police Chiefs' Association

**Vincennes University
Shake Learning Resources Center
Vincennes, Indiana 47591-9986**

Published by

Wolfe Publishing Company
6471 Airpark Drive
Prescott, Arizona 86301

Roam where you will, meet whom you may,
  There is one who will brighten the darkest hour,
Whose assistance and kindness will pave the way,
  Through sickness and sorrow, through darkness and power.

TO MY WIFE

Whose kindness and assistance has helped me
in my many years of active work in the courts,
on the ranges, and in my home life,
this book is dedicated.

Originally published in 1930 by The G.F. Book Company

ISBN: 1-879356-211-X

Reprinted in January 1993
by
Wolfe Publishing Company
6471 Airpark Drive
Prescott, Arizona 86301

CONTENTS

Page

SECTION 1. REVOLVERS, PISTOLS, AND THEIR USES.. 1

SECTION 2. TARGET SHOOTING.................. 12
  Illustrations: Fitz Luck Target, .22 Caliber
    Fitz Luck Target, .38 Caliber
    25-yard Rapid Fire Target
    50-yard Standard American Target
    George Marshall and Claude Shaylor

SECTION 3. POSITION FOR TARGET SHOOTING...... 27
  Illustrations: Major H. L. Harker
    Captain Max B. Wendlandt
    Captain J. H. Young
    Captain Joseph Sonnenberg
    Mr. George Marshall
    Mr. Harry C. Almy
    Dr. H. R. Brunton
    Mr. Adolph P. Schuber
    Dr. John L. Bastey
    Major Joseph J. Marek
    Lieut. Paul A. Shepherd
    Mr. C. M. Corbin
    Col. Norman B. Schwarzkopf
    Dr. Claude A. Warner
    Capt. Edward A. Langrish
    Capt. Jacob Lienhard
    Lieut. Lewis A. Hohn
    Lieut. Raymond T. Presnell
    Lieut. William Whaling

SECTION 4. TRIGGER SQUEEZE................... 46

v

		Page
SECTION 5.	FLINCHING............................	51

SECTION 6. THE REVOLVER GRIP................ 55
   Illustrations: Thumb above Latch
               Thumb below Latch
               Little Finger under Grip
               Cocking Hammer Straight Back
               Revolver with Gadget or Addition

SECTION 7. SHOOTING IN THE WIND.............. 65

SECTION 8. MATCH SHOOTING................... 67
   Illustrations: Camp Perry Firing Line
               Old Timers at the Big Camp
               Col. John J. Dooley
               Royal Canadian Mounted Team

SECTION 9. DON'TS FOR TARGET SHOOTERS........ 75
   Illustrations: Loading the Revolver
               Closing the Revolver
               Unloading the Revolver

SECTION 10. DRY SHOOTING...................... 80
   Illustration: Eastman Clock

SECTION 11. EYES AND EYESIGHT................ 84
   Illustrations: Sketch of Sight Errors
               Lining Up Sights

SECTION 12. LEFT-HANDED SHOOTING AND AVERAGE
               SCORES..................... 88
   Illustration: Left-Handed Firing Position

SECTION 13. HOLDING THE BREATH................ 92
     Description by Dr. Schuyler McCuller Martin

SECTION 14. TESTING REVOLVERS AND PISTOLS FOR
THE TRADE 97
Illustration: Testing Table

SECTION 15. ADJUSTABLE AND STATIONARY SIGHTS . 104
Illustrations: Three Degree Angle Rear Sight
Proper Method of Sighting for 6 o'Clock Hold

SECTION 16. GRIP MATERIAL AND CHECKING....... 111

SECTION 17. THE AUTOMATIC PISTOL.............. 115
Illustrations: The .45 Colt's Government Automatic
The .22 Woodsman Automatic
The .38 Super Colt's Automatic

SECTION 18. SHOOTING HISTORY................. 121
Illustrations: Mrs. J. H. FitzGerald—Firing Position
Miss G. L. Kenyon—Firing Position
Miss Mildred Harker—Firing Position
Miss Arlayne Brown—Firing Position

SECTION 19. THE REVOLVER CLUB................ 130
Illustrations: The St. Louis Range

SECTION 20. RANGES AND TARGETS 136
Illustrations: The New Target Paster
The Caswell Ranges
The Toledo Police Range

SECTION 21. QUESTION DEPARTMENT.............. 160

SECTION 22. MISFIRES.......................... 174

SECTION 23.   THE TWO-INCH REVOLVER BARREL....176
   Illustration: Detective Special .38 Revolver

SECTION 24.   OBSTRUCTIONS IN THE BARREL........179

SECTION 25.   CARE AND CLEANING.................181

SECTION 26.   BEING YOUR OWN REPAIRMAN.........184
   Illustrations: Fitz at Camp Perry
              Correct Trigger Pull, New Service Revolver

SECTION 27.   PAST MASTERS AND PRESENT.........193
   Illustration: Colt's Patterson Model 1836

SECTION 28.   SPECIAL ARMS FOR QUICK-DRAW WORK. 198
   Illustration: New Service Two-inch Barrel Remodeled
             Police Positive Special Two-inch Barrel Remodeled

SECTION 29.   QUICK DRAW........................203
   Illustrations: Hardy Belts and Holsters
              Cross Draw—Start
              Cross Draw—Finish
              Cross Draw Upsidedown—Grip
              Cross Draw Upsidedown—Finish
              Brunton Suspender Holster
              Fitz Two-Gun Leg Draw Tied Down—Finish
              Side Draw High on Belt

SECTION 30.   TRICK AND FANCY SHOOTING..........227
   Illustrations: Gun-Bugs, Fitz and Hardy
              Shooting Lying on Back
              Shooting with Looking Glass

SECTION 31. HUNTING WITH THE HAND GUN........237
   Ballistic Tables

SECTION 32. COMPARING VARIOUS BULLETS AS MAN
              STOPPERS..................248

SECTION 33. SINGLE AND DOUBLE ACTION SHOOTING. 253

SECTION 34. THE SHOOTER'S SECTION.............256
   Building a Championship Team, by Captain J. H. Young
   Camp Perry, by Major H. L. Harker
   Illustration: P. J. O'Hare at Camp Perry

SECTION 35. EVIDENCE AND EXPERT TESTIMONY....269
   Illustrations: Bullet Comparison Pictures
                Captain Jones and His Comparison Microscope
                Mr. Albert Foster, Jr.

SECTION 36. HOW TO BECOME A FIREARMS EXPERT. 285
   Illustrations: Spencer Comparison Microscope
                Contact Shots
                One-fourth Inch Distance Shots

PREFACE TO POLICE AND BANK SECTIONS..........301

SECTION 37. PRACTICAL POLICE AND DEFENSE
              SHOOTING..................302
   Illustrations: Disarming Holds by Captain Langrish and
                Lieutenant McGann

SECTION 38. THE MAGIC OF KNOWING THAT YOU
              CAN SHOOT QUICK AND STRAIGHT....314

	Page

SECTION 39. POLICE REVOLVERS..................318
  Illustrations: .38 Official Police Model
       .38 Officer's Model

SECTION 40. INSPECTION OF POLICE REVOLVERS....324

SECTION 41. Match Shooting and Police Work.....326
  Illustrations: Captain Edward J. Langrish and His Target
       Langrish Limbless Target

SECTION 42. THE COLT'S SILHOUETTE TARGET......334
  Illustration: Colt's Silhouette Target

SECTION 43. THE NEW YORK STATE POLICE REVOLVER COURSE IN SHOOTING....339
  Illustration: Officials of the School

SECTION 44. THE INSTRUCTOR....................345

SECTION 45. OUTGUESSING THE CRIMINAL..........349

SECTION 46. DOUBLE-ACTION REVOLVER VERSUS AUTOMATIC.................353

SECTION 47. PRONE SHOOTING....................355
  Illustration: Captain Albert B. Moore

SECTION 48. CARRYING A REVOLVER WHEN RUNNING 358
  Illustration: Captain Albert B. Moore

		Page
SECTION 49.	STOP WHEN FIRING	360

Illustration: Captain Albert B. Moore

SECTION 50. TWO-HAND SHOOTING..............362
   Illustration: Two-Hand Shooting

SECTION 51. NIGHT SHOOTING..................364

SECTION 52. RIGHT AND LEFT HAND SHOOTING.....365

SECTION 53. USING TWO REVOLVERS.............367
   Illustration: Sergt. William E. Cashin, New York State Troopers

SECTION 54. DRAWING FROM THE SIDE OR FRONT POCKET..................370

SECTION 55. FITZ TRICK HOLDS AND PERSUADERS...372
   Illustrations: Positions for Searching
       Revolver Muzzle against Stomach
       Revolver Muzzle against Back

SECTION 56. SHOOTING FROM MOTORCYCLE OR HORSE....................387

SECTION 57. SHOOTING FROM A MOTOR CAR........390

SECTION 58. THE SCIENCE OF USING A REVOLVER AS A CLUB.................393

xi

	Page
SECTION 59. BADGES AND PROTECTIVE POLICE COAT..	394
SECTION 60. TELEGRAPH MATCHES FOR POLICE AND BANKS......................	395
SECTION 61. BANK PROTECTION—THE INSTRUCTOR..	397
Bank Protection, by Mr. Harry C. Almy	
SECTION 62. THE ARMORED CAR, PASSENGER CAR AND GUARDS................	409
Illustration: Armored Car	
SECTION 63. MY DAD AND I.....	413
SECTION 64. OUR FRIENDLY TALK................	416

PREFACE

After more than thirty-five years of shooting experience I find my study filled with manuscripts relating to the different pistols, revolvers, ammunition, and their uses.

My years of experience in instruction work with the New York State Troopers (of which I am a member), on the different target ranges, and in banks and police departments; the pleasant years spent as expert in charge of the testing department of the Colt Patent Fire Arms Manufacturing Company of Hartford, Connecticut; my association with the shooters, lectures and expert testimony, both in the United States and Canada, have left me with a wealth of data on all the different branches of revolver and pistol shooting.

It has been my ambition for many years to place all this in book form and in the following pages I will not describe all the different makes of small arms, properly called the One-Hand Gun, but will, instead, speak of the arms which I use in the different kinds of shooting explained in this book.

It is my hope that this book will prove to be a reference book for the beginner and a help to him throughout his shooting career, a reference book to police departments and banks, and all who are interested in pistol and revolver shooting.

In the following pages I have eliminated all data on obsolete arms and refer to only the latest models. I have owned over twelve hundred rifles, revolvers, and pistols in my shooting career and have used the same brand of side arms for over thirty years. No comparison is made of the different kinds of arms now on the market, as I feel that this space may be better used in explaining how to handle guns properly.

The arms pictured in this book are the ones I use in demonstration and lecture work. I have also used a great many pictures in the book because I feel that while they take up an entire page they save much explanation, for the position or stance may be more readily understood when it is illustrated.

To all my friends who have assisted in compiling the material contained in this book I wish to express my deepest appreciation. Only by association with experts who deeply study a chosen subject may any man hope to give to the public all the latest and best data on any subject.

SECTION 1
REVOLVERS, PISTOLS AND THEIR USES

Many people have compared shooting with other sports such as baseball, tennis, etc. To my mind it is vastly different from any of the other outdoor sports; for instance, in baseball the muscles are tensed for the instant when a certain amount of strength must be exerted and this is true of most of the other sports. In shooting this is not so; shooting requires perfect control over the nerves and muscles of the body and quietness instead of tenseness. From the time the revolver or pistol is raised with the intention of firing a shot, this control or mastery over the body must be maintained until the shot is fired.

Shooting may be compared more correctly with the work of doctors, dentists, and surgeons, and incidently in the above professions we have hundreds of expert revolver shots. A very noted surgeon told me that he never operated without first taking a pen in each hand and with the arms free brought the points together. (Try it.) In the medical profession this body control is necessary and it is just as necessary in shooting. It is lack of this control which discourages the beginner and only by practice can it be attained.

We have several legitimate uses for the hand gun, and first, and most important, is—protection. Police departments, banks, trust companies, mills, factories, the home, and, in fact, everywhere that anything of value is stored the revolver and automatic pistol play a very important part. In fact, it would not be a very safe procedure for any officer or guard to advertise the fact that his revolver was at home on the piano.

The remark is often heard, "Down with the 'Gun-Toter.' We should have a law to stop gun-toting." I wonder if the reader can recall an instance where a habitual "Gun-Toter" (one who carries a revolver around in his pocket or traveling bag because of his love for firearms) ever got into any serious trouble with it. Of course if he should get good and plastered, as one of our misleading ladies of recent fame would put it, I wouldn't even trust him with a sash weight. Personally, I can see no reason why a respectable citizen should not be allowed to carry a revolver if he wishes. I do believe, however, that if anyone is going to carry a revolver he should know how to use it, because if he does not know how to handle the arm safely and how to use it properly, it is far better that he should leave it at home until such time as he shall have become proficient in its use.

And here is where the Pistol and Revolver Club becomes useful. Practice makes perfect, and practice will enable the firearm lover to enjoy his pets. Target practice is the foundation for protection as it is for hunting and fancy shooting. Many good prospects are lost to the sport because they did not get the proper start. The purchase of a pistol or revolver, and a few shots fired from it with no knowledge or instruction, is bound to bring forth the remark: "It is of no use, I never would be able to shoot." The man might become a world beater if given the proper instruction, but he will never know it unless he starts properly.

If the good citizens of our country knew how to handle firearms properly crime would decrease by half. Our present firearm laws in many states so restrict the use of firearms that the honest, law-abiding citizen does not care to comply with the regulations and the red tape required to own a revolver or pistol, yet how else can he protect his home? What greater assurance does a crook need than the fact that he knows not one house in fifty is protected. He carries a revolver to protect himself against the honest citizen and the police, and he will continue to carry a revolver as long as he has his liberty regardless of any law that will ever be passed. Many of our known gangsters are carrying around permits to carry firearms. "How come" that our respected citizens cannot get permits as easily as the crook? However, that is another story.

Protection and target shooting are two very good reasons for learning to shoot. Then trick shooting is a very pleasant sport not indulged in by the majority of shooters. This may be explained by lack of open space at the ranges and lack of competition. All shooters have a desire to beat some one, therefore the love for competition and target shooting.

Hunting with the revolver is a very fascinating sport and not so hard after the art of target shooting is mastered. This brings up the question as to what is the extreme range of the revolver, which all depends upon the ability of the shooter. I have seen a good per cent of hits made up to three hundred yards and even at a greater distance; however, three hundred yards is out of the question in hunting, for many shooters, even with a rifle. Deer are usually killed at a distance of thirty to fifty yards, which is well inside the range of the average revolver shot. The one little fly in the ointment is shooting at moving game.

Another use for the revolver or pistol is as a vacation recreation. Tin cans, sea shells, and thousands of other targets are waiting to be punctured, so taking everything into consideration murder is not the only thing that the much abused revolver is capable of.

As I am writing I glanced at the *New York Daily News*, which every day tells the amount of deaths in greater New York; from January 1, 1928, until October 15, 1928: guns—251; booze—428; automobiles—835. You can readily see that guns are a poor third and many of those are shots fired by the police to preserve law and order.

This same average will be found to exist all over the country.

There are many cases of "I didn't know it was loaded," not only by children but by those who are old enough to know better. However, I have visited many families where the father is a gun crank and found that the little ones in the family are taught to keep their hands off guns laid on tables or benches. Many of the youngsters not over six or seven could pick up the arm, unload it and load it again when they were through looking at it, and could take it to the cellar range and shame some of the grown-ups.

Several years ago I visited the home of Major Harker in Baltimore and, of course, the first place we visited was the cellar range. Miss Ellen and Miss Mildred Harker went with us. Miss Mildred was then just able to hold up a .22 Colt Police Positive Target Revolver, but she could hit the bull's-eye and gave her older sister a battle for first honors. That same little girl visited Camp Perry in 1929 and captured honors many of the older shooters might well envy. She is, without doubt, the best shot with pistol, revolver, and rifle for her age in the United States. This shows what a little interest and the proper training will do.

On the other hand I have visited police departments to instruct the new men, many of whom have told me they never fired a revolver. These men at the end of the school were to be placed on the street. In my instruction I may probably see each man about two hours and in that time he must learn not only how to handle a revolver safely but learn how to shoot to protect his life. A lecture to a body of men who have never used firearms will not teach them how to shoot. They must have the practical experience, get on the range and shoot, and after the school is over they should shoot at least every month or every two weeks if possible.

One of our greatest troubles is getting banks and trust companies interested in shooting. One reason for this is that usually some retired peace officer of twenty years ago is in charge of the guards and he was an officer at the time when revolvers were not as important to protection as they are today. Times have changed and we must change with them.

Never in the history of the United States has the knowledge of firearms, and good firearms themselves, been so essential as it is today. Even in this day of machine guns, steel vests, and other playthings, the revolver expert has the edge. He doesn't have to spill a peck of bullets down the street to salivate one lone pilgrim. He fires one shot and says: "There, damn you, I guess you'll be good now."

While we have been so interested in revolver shooting we have neglected to mention the pistol. I am often asked what use a pistol is to a revolver shooter and this is it. It teaches the revolver man how to squeeze the trigger and to quit flinching. Learn the pistol thoroughly and you can do tricks with the revolver after practice sufficient to accustom yourself to the change of grip, recoil and trigger pull. My good friend, Sergeant J. H. Young of the Portland (Oregon) Police Department, will put his O. K. on this. He says if a man cannot shoot a pistol he is hopeless. And he is right. When the pistol is mastered you are ready to give a good account of yourself with the revolver in slow fire. Then comes the hardest of all, which is rapid fire, but still the pistol has taught you to hold and you can speed up and still hold.

To the men who have shot very little or to those who have not shot at all, I can hardly describe the sense of security you will feel when you know that you are capable of protecting your home, or the pleasure you will get out of target shooting when you begin to make your share of bull's-eyes at the target range. Shooting in the United States today is showing a big increase over even a year ago. Why not join the multitude? If you were to gaze on the solid firing line at Camp Perry you would say there must be something in it after all.

If one is to take up this fascinating sport the first essential is to purchase the best arms obtainable. It is money thrown away to purchase a cheap pistol or revolver for target shooting, for how may one determine his own ability if he is using an arm which will not shoot accurately. The best shot in the world can only prove himself to be such by using an arm that is extremely accurate. The man cannot correct his own shortcomings if the arm he is shooting is inaccurate. If he is shooting a .22 caliber pistol the sights must be of a size and shape best suited to his eyes, with proper amount of light and proper depth of rear notch, and sighted so that he may hold, at a point on the target, sights just touching the bull's-eye, or with a wide or narrow white line between the top of sights and bull's-eye, or as some shooters prefer to hold in the center of the black. Whatever ideas the shooter may have, can be carried out after he has acquired the skill necessary to make a fair score and to name his shots.

High-grade target pistols and revolvers are furnished with target showing where the arm grouped the shots at the factory and, while shooter's eyes may differ, the arm should group in some part of the bull's-eye when received. The range usually used for testing is fifteen yards and the arm at this distance should be held in at the bottom of the nine ring on a twenty-yard target. If it is to strike center at twenty yards, hold at the bottom of the black.

The .22 pistols or heavy .22 revolver are recommended for beginners because of the slight recoil, for if the beginner should start with a heavy caliber revolver he would be very liable to develop flinching, which would spoil his score. For rough and tumble police shooting it is not necessary to start with the pistol, for speed is more essential than placing the bullet inside a one-inch circle.

I believe we shooters are all handicapped because we set ourselves up as one hundred per cent perfect, while gun and ammunition are all to blame. I believe with our present perfection of arms and ammunition that all persons who aspire to become good shots may safely lay all alibis on the shelf and place the trouble where it belongs. I may mention a case where I personally targeted eight revolvers for a police department and a few days later I was notified that all the arms shot to the left, three to five inches at twenty yards. I visited the department and they told me their troubles. I asked each one of the men to shoot a target for me and the first man to shoot verified my suspicions; he shot with the right hand and the thumb at right angles with the revolver. With the proper instruction as to thumb pressure this officer made a good score and the arm did not shoot to the left. The others were all corrected in the same way.

No one revolver or pistol may be named as an all-round weapon. For a light target arm, where excessive noise may annoy the neighbors, and for camping trips the following arms are best suited: .22 target pistol; the .22 target revolver, both light and heavy models, and the .22 automatic pistol. For a medium-power hunting and target arm the .38 caliber revolver, with adjustable sights and 6″ or 7½″ barrel, the police revolver, with stationary sights and 4″, 5″, and 6″ barrels, have no equal. For a heavy target revolver and hunting arm the .45 caliber, .44 Special 7½″ target revolver with adjustable sights, and the new service revolvers with stationary sights, 5½″ barrels in the .45, .44/40, .38/40 and .44 Special calibers may be used. The new Super .38 and .45 caliber automatic pistols have earned an enviable position in the heavy caliber arms.

If a trip to Camp Perry is contemplated the following arms may be used: The .22 single shot pistol; the .22 automatic pistol; .38 caliber revolver, 6″ barrel, with stationary sights; the .38 caliber target revolver, 6″ or 7½″ barrel, and the .45 Colt automatic pistol.

For police work and protection the scene changes to the lighter weight arms, with shorter barrels for the men on foot, such as .32 and .38 caliber with 2″ or 4″ barrels. For the mounted men, the heavier arms, .38 caliber, with 4″, 5″, and 6″ barrel, and .45 caliber, with 5½″ barrel.

The small caliber arms, such as the .32, are fast being discarded for the heavier calibers, .38 or larger. The reason is that bootleggers and gunmen, in general, are now carrying .38 and .45 caliber arms, and the officer is badly handicapped if armed with the smaller calibers, for unless the bullet is placed in a vital spot the prisoner or prospective prisoner is still dangerous and capable of returning a larger caliber bullet in exchange.

The pocket model automatics, .25, .32, and .380, are extensively used for home protection and for pocket use. They, of course, must live down the feeling created by arms of cheap foreign make that jam, but this trouble has been overcome in the well-made American automatics of late years. Troubles may now be traced in many cases to a cartridge becoming oil-soaked by an excess of oil in the chamber, thereby causing a misfire, or by the bullet stopping in the barrel, or by the point of the bullet becoming jammed in the runway. Another cause of jams in the automatic pistols is rust or corrosion in the chamber. If the arm is cleaned thoroughly and fresh ammunition is used very little trouble will be encountered.

Soft point bullets are of no advantage in any of the low-powered pistols because the velocity of 900 feet or less is not great enough to spread or mushroom the bullet; therefore greater surety of fire and corresponding striking force can be obtained from the metal-cased bullets.

We could not get along without the automobile now; neither can we get along without the revolver and pistol if we are to protect life and property. We can increase our chances in case we are at any time called upon to protect our own lives or the lives and property of others by learning to use the weapons which are our only means of escaping with life and property from the gentleman who prefers to live upon the efforts of others instead of working for a living.

How helpless a man must feel who is awakened in the middle of the night by a noise in the lower part of the house, his wife and family to protect, and no revolver or automatic at hand. The old alibi given at many police stations, "No, you don't need a permit to buy or carry a revolver; if you have any trouble call us up," does not apply. In the first place ninety-five out of every hundred telephones are downstairs and, in the next place, give the crook of today credit for having some sense. The first thing he will do on entering a house is to cut the telephone wires and he will not enter a house until the officer is at the other end of his beat; then where do we get help? We must stand on our own feet and help ourselves.

How can we accomplish this unless we know how to shoot and have something to shoot with. A householder may have the courage to throw out his chest and boldly walk downstairs to be killed by some cigarette-sucking, dope-crazed crook, and his friends will say, "Wasn't John brave and doesn't he look natural." I call such a man the biggest kind of a damn fool or any man who will walk toward a man with a revolver and his own hands empty. The householder has the advantage if he is armed and moves quietly for he knows the lay of the house, position of lights, stairs, etc., but the last ten or fifteen feet is best covered by a bullet if the crook cannot be taken alive.

Instead of discouraging this practice of home protection one hundred dollars reward should be given by the town or city to any householder who will turn over, dead or alive, a burglar caught in the act of robbing a house. This would soon discourage many of our present-day amateur crooks.

Valuable heirlooms, silver, and money may be saved by the outlay of a few dollars and a few hours of practice. Many times I hear from some of my gun-loving friends: "Well, Fitz, I was awakened by a noise the other night and you know that pair of .38 revolvers of mine; I took one in each hand and started downstairs to find it was only the cat, but I sure would have salivated anyone I found trying to walk off with any of my goods." I then might write and ask: "How about leaving your wife upstairs alone?" The answer will come back like this: "Oh! she was all right; she had my pocket revolver and she can shoot as well as I can; she can take care of herself." And this is the story of a well-protected home and of a woman who need not fear if she is left alone either day or night.

I have found that it takes very little encouragement to interest every one in the art of shooting. Whether man, woman, or child, they are all interested if the subject is properly submitted to them and they enjoy it as much as the gun-addict. Protection of self, family, and property is a very good reason why every American citizen should learn to shoot. The fear of revolvers and pistols arises from ignorance of their manipulation and use; fear of accidents with firearms arises from the same source. The man who knows how to use a revolver has no fear of it and feels a sense of security in his home that cannot be derived in any other way.

Should the time ever come when the law-abiding citizen, those in good standing at their local police department, could obtain a permit to carry firearms, and the crook caught with a revolver or pistol in his possession in the commission of a crime was due for a life sentence, what a wonderful world this would be. However, so much pleasure may be derived from target shooting that we forget the serious side of shooting and look only upon the recreation side and we get a great deal of satisfaction in knowing that we can shoot quickly and accurately. We have a certain feeling of pride in the fact that our nerves and body are in a condition that will make this result possible.

SECTION 2
TARGET SHOOTING

Ever since the invention of small arms, or at least dating back to the early efforts of Colonel Colt, it has been the ambition of every red-blooded American to be a good shot with pistol and revolver. Thousands of professional and business men have taken up the sport of target shooting and have been well repaid for their efforts for they have found that shooting quickens the eye and teaches the control of every nerve and muscle in the body.

After a strenuous day at the office take a little hand bag with two or three of the favorite hand guns, cartridges, and cleaning outfit, and go to the range. With a few good fellows present to match their skill with yours and talk around the cleaning table, not forgetting the alibis (and this is the part of the shooting game that the shooter never has to learn), a few scores to compare with the ones you shot the last time you were at the range, then you have reached the end of a perfect day.

I do not believe that more lasting or greater friendships are formed in any fraternal order or wherever men gather than on a shooting range. It is a pleasure to spend an afternoon or evening on a range with the members and listen to their troubles and successes. I find that the men who succeed in becoming extra good shots are the ones who ask questions and try out different positions, etc., eliminating those which do not improve their scores, and who stick to one, two, and not over three, hand guns.

There is an old and true saying, "Beware of the man with one gun," and I have seen this proven on many ranges. The man who tries to use six or eight different revolvers and pistols the same day is going to be disappointed with the results. The same thing applies to the man who spends half his shooting time on whittling out different grips, changing the sights and in other ways trying to have the revolver or pistol do what he must do himself. Revolvers and pistols now on the market are so perfect in grip and balance that the shooter can easily adapt himself to the arm as issued.

Many and varied are the attachments and improvements that are tried out on the various arms; but the attachment which will place more holes in the ten ring than any other is the attachment which the shooter may have for actual shooting instead of trying to force a point or two more out of his revolver which is doing more than its share anyway. But with all our troubles and all our disappointments target shooting is to many people the finest sport in the world.

In the following pages will be found several pictures of the position or stance of well-known target shooters. Note the difference, and each one is a very good position.

Each individual will, as he advances, develop a position slightly different from the others. The build, development of certain muscles, eyesight, etc., all tend to develop a certain position and, when a comfortable position is found, the new shooter should practice doing the same thing in the same way every time. First, he should be sure that the arm is sighted correctly for his eyes. If he has not had experience in this work he should ask some of the older members to help him out. If the arm shoots center with them and shoots somewhere else with him, he should ask the instructor to watch him and try to find out what is wrong. Perhaps he is shooting to the left, due to insufficient thumb pressure, or perhaps he is flinching, which will account for low shots. If he is shooting high it may be due to seeing too much of the front sight. Many things enter into the making of good scores, which neither the revolver nor ammunition can correct.

As many kinds of shooters are in evidence at a well-patronized range as there are models of arms and kinds of ammunition. I believe you will recognize in the following a few of the shooters you have met.

First, the man who joins the club, buys a good target arm, uses it a few days, then, because some other member with another model is making good scores, he buys one like that and in a short time repeats the performance until he has six or eight of the finest guns to shoot, but because he finds he must work hard to become a good shot, that money and a fine collection of revolvers and pistols will not make him so, his enthusiasm cools as fast as it is kindled and he gives up the sport. We may think that such a man is God's gift to the revolver manufacturers, but he is not because he does not stick to the game. I meet in my travels each year thousands of shooters who have followed the sport for ten, twenty, and sometimes thirty, years, men who in that time have owned hundreds of firearms. These are the true boosters who have in their time encouraged and assisted hundreds of others to become good shots.

We have the beginner, who joins a club and gathers up all the information possible from his fellow shooters and, in a short time, is making good scores, winning a few matches, and a little later the big club matches, everything going smoothly until some other shooters come along and shooter number one commences to finish second. Then shooter number one finds other amusements and the shooting game has lost a good member. Stick to the game, boys; a few beatings will do you good and will help the other fellows, too.

Another of the specie, is truly called "the grip and sight specialist." He will work for days to perfect the one perfect pair of stocks or grips for his favorite arm and, after a thorough try-out, starts out in quest of more wood to conquer. This goes on and on until finally the artist discovers that stocks as issued are not so bad. The sight question is another breeder of sleepless nights, and after many experiments the same conclusion is reached that the sights as issued are not so bad. What wonderful target men we would have if all this effort was expended in trying to hit the ten ring, but if we all have fun and follow out our own ideas whose business is it, I ask you?

Another class of members which I must mention are those who come to the club every shooting night, but who shoot very little; they get their enjoyment from sitting around the lounging room talking to their friends. You will find, that even though they shoot very little, they know the game, if they have belonged to shooting clubs for any number of years, because they are observers of the mistakes and successes of others. They are all good fellows together ready to lend a helping hand to the beginner.

I believe the greatest assistance that any beginner can receive is the installing of a short range of twelve yards and using the twenty-yard target. The shooter must learn to creep before he can walk, and it is far better to start on the short range and hit the bull's-eye five shots out of ten and the other five on the paper, then to start at twenty yards and only get three or four shots on the paper. It is easy to change to the longer range at any time. Many things may be learned on the short range that it would take months to learn on the longer range. If the sights are right for the twenty-yard range they should be held three-quarters of an inch above the bottom of the black for twelve yards, or if they are adjustable sights they may be changed to hold at six o'clock with a white line or just touching the black. Care must be taken with every shot, otherwise the shooter will acquire a careless habit that will cause many wild shots.

To the beginner it seems a simple thing to hold out the arm, line up the sights, and squeeze the trigger. But assuming that the body and feet are in proper position it still takes months to train that arm, and to control the muscles to work in conjunction with the eye. Only a short time is required with normal eyesight to line up the sights; however, the trigger squeeze is a different proposition and requires much study.

Nearly every shooter after reaching a certain stage, from one to three months, reaches a slump and for a short time will be unable to make a satisfactory score, but with a little perseverance he will emerge from this shooting better than ever. He may even reach another slump after five or six months and, emerging from this one, he may expect average scores if he practices faithfully. When the average scores on the twenty-yard target at twenty yards reach ninety per cent or better, then the shooter is at peace with the world, and, if still looking for more worlds to conquer, change the .22 pistol for the target revolver.

The knowledge gained from the pistol will be of great assistance in conquering the revolver and this slow-fire revolver work is the proper foundation for the faster shooting to follow. If the shooter cannot make good scores at slow fire it is of no use to try the thirty, twenty, fifteen, and ten second time; speed does not improve the scores.

The most satisfactory system, if the twenty-five yard Camp Perry target is to be used at twenty-five yards, is first to practice slow fire until scores of ninety-five per cent or better are reached; then commence firing five shots in thirty seconds, taking more time at first, if necessary. The sights should be in line with the bull's-eye and the shot should not be fired until one is reasonably sure it will be in the bull's-eye. It is nothing to worry about if it takes forty seconds each the first few times to get a score of ninety-five or better for two five-shot strings. A little practice and without seemingly trying to lessen the time, the same scores will be made in thirty seconds that it formerly took forty seconds to make.

When the scores are satisfactory in thirty seconds try for the twenty second mark, but the time should not be lowered until it can be done without injuring the score. Twenty seconds is not excessive speed and the slow-fire score should not be over three points higher for ten shots. I know many target shooters who can make as good a score on this target in twenty seconds as they can at slow fire.

Below twenty seconds the scores will commence to fall. When trying for the fifteen second mark the same course should be followed; fifteen seconds should not be reached until it can be done without lowering the average scores below ninety-two. The real test comes when one has a ninety-six per cent slow fire, ninety-three per cent in twenty seconds, which makes the score down eleven points, and the place in the match depends on the ten second score. It is necessary to practice very carefully for the ten second stage. It should not be reached until ninety per cent is averaged, and when this is added to the above score it makes a total of two hundred and seventy-nine. This score is based on fair weather, no wind, and good light condition. Adverse conditions will lower this score from five to fifteen points, but regardless of conditions ten second scores will nearly always decide the match.

Care should be taken in this course to use up at least nine seconds of the time. I have sometimes found it necessary to speed the men up by starting at fifteen yards on this same target and holding the time to ten seconds, gradually working back a yard at a time until twenty-five yards were reached. This has proved to be very satisfactory.

The score I have named of two hundred and seventy-nine, with a decrease of five to fifteen points for adverse conditions, may seem a little high to the beginner, but is the point that must be reached and even higher to win matches. I cannot place too much emphasis on this: *The ten second time must be mastered or fine scores at slow fire and twenty second time will be of little use.* Matches of this kind always go to the ten second experts.

Perhaps the timed and rapid shooting does not appeal to some of the shooters; if not, I believe the reason is that they have never tried it or, if they have, it is only to fire one or two scores in ten seconds without the preliminary practice necessary to make it a success.

One very fascinating branch of target shooting is the long range shooting at from one hundred to three hundred yards. Many fine matches may be shot and scores will be high. At one hundred yards, shooting on a fifty-yard Standard American target, the scores will drop from ten to twenty points. At one hundred yards, using the A Military two or three hundred yard target, five ring ten inches blacked for sighting bull, four ring twenty-six inches, three ring forty-six inches, two ring balance of target, many fine scores can be made. The Military Target B used for rifle shooting at five hundred and six hundred yards makes an excellent target for two hundred yard shooting with revolvers and pistols. The five ring is used as a sighting bull which is black and twenty inches in diameter, four ring thirty-seven inches, three ring fifty-three inches, two ring balance of target six feet square. The Colt Police Silhouette target may be used with the K zone to count. Military Target C for eight hundred and nine hundred and one thousand yards with a rifle may be used at three hundred yards with a revolver. The five ring is thirty-six inches, black, for sighting bull, four ring fifty-three inches, three ring six feet square. The Colt Police Silhouette target may also be used at three hundred yards.

At the National Shoot held at Camp Perry, Ohio, in 1930, during an exhibition given by Captain A. H. Hardy, Peters Cartridge Company representative, volunteers were called upon by Captain Hardy to shoot three hundred yards at a Colt Silhouette target. George Marshall and Claude Shaylor of the Portland (Oregon) Police Team came forward and gave the best exhibition of long range shooting that I have ever seen or heard of. Each officer fired five shots and seven hits out of the ten shots were registered in the man target. The shooting was done with a .38 caliber Colt Officer's Model 7½" barrel, with a high rear sight (.635), no other change in the arm, and one-tenth inch Partridge sights were used. Neither man had ever fired that particular revolver before that day. This exhibition demonstrates not only the reliability of the revolver for long ranges, but the perfection that can be attained by men in perfect physical condition who take their practice seriously.

Many interesting matches may be shot at the long ranges, but skill and good judgment are necessary to make a success of this branch of shooting, for it would not be a practical match to shoot in a heavy wind at two hundred or three hundred yards. The only added equipment necessary for this shooting is an adjustable rear sight. The difficulty may be overcome very easily by filing an Officer's Model rear sight flat and brazing, or soldering the folding adjustable top of a rifle sight on it, or it may be attached by screws. The Company making the revolver may be induced to make the sight.

When proper sight adjustments are found for the different distances and targets, the sight should be marked so that it may be accurately replaced for each range. The Officer's Model allows for a reasonable amount of windage, and for the long range work the 7½" barrel is the favorite in the .38 caliber. The .44 Special and .45 Colt cartridges are well adapted for long range shooting and also for short range shooting if added weight and recoil are not a handicap.

The practicability of long range revolver shooting was demonstrated several years ago by the long shooters of Kentucky, who shot at the silhouette of a turkey at three hundred yards and many averaged three hits out of fifteen shots. Captain Hardy and several other shooters, including myself, duplicated this score and four and five hits were registered. The turkey was, of course, several sizes smaller than the targets I have mentioned, so a fair score can be made with correct sights after a few trials. I have spent a great deal of time on the long range work and I believe all shooters who try it will find it a pleasant diversion.

An outdoor novelty match which is a favorite with the shooters is the Clay Pigeon Match. Hang clay pigeons on a board twenty yards away from the shooters; two shots allowed to hit the pigeon; the successful ones move back to twenty-five yards and the ones who fail to hit the pigeon in two shots are out of the match. Two shots are allowed at twenty-five yards and the performance is repeated, moving back five yards each time until only one, the winner, remains on the line. This and many other novelty matches may be worked out to keep the club members interested and as a revenue to the club. The Hamilton Club in Chicago has installed moving targets such as are used in the commercial shooting galleries.

Do not become discouraged if others are making better scores than you are. Perseverance and study of each shot fired will finally overcome this handicap. The center shot requires no study; you know that it was caused by one of two things, either from a correctly fired shot or from one of those lucky shots which sometimes occur (usually in practice). If it occurs from a correctly fired shot there is nothing to learn, only remember to fire the next shot in the same manner.

Every shot fired creates a new problem; if it does not strike the ten ring, why did it go to right or left, high or low? There is a reason for every wild shot and in nearly every case it can be traced to the shooter and not to the arm or ammunition. I have been informed by several target shooters that they had a very peculiar revolver. It would make fine scores in slow-fire shooting, but would not group in ten or twenty second work. As soon as they could be convinced that they, themselves, and not the revolver, were to blame, they began to improve in the faster shooting.

Then we have the hurry-shooter. He hurries to the range, hurries to the firing line, and hurries through his match or practice. His scores are far below those that he is capable of making and his expected advance toward better scores will be slow to materialize.

Another handicap to winning scores is the man who feels that there are several in the club who can easily beat him and who will say, as he enters a match, "I know I won't win anything, but I'm going to enter anyhow." He is half-beaten before he shoots. His is not the spirit of a winner. A match is seldom won until the last shot is fired and your competitor, whom you feel is a better shot than you are, may get one or two wild shots. Such things have happened.

Now we have another class who count backward while in a match. Thus in the Camp Perry Match of 300 points they figure on 300 points minus, of course, the few points they will lose in thirty shots. When the sevens and eights come along and they add the points together they have lost in the first ten shots, their courage takes flight and a poor score is the result. Shoot the first shot thirty times and cease to worry about the final score or the scores that others in the match are making and the match is half won then.

In target shooting the nerves and muscles must be at rest. Do not expect good scores until you have rested fifteen minutes after running upstairs or getting excited in an argument. When the arm is unsteady lay the revolver or pistol down for a few seconds and rest; this can be repeated as often as necessary. If the noise of others shooting bothers you, use cotton in the ears to deaden the noise and do not wait for other men to fire; attend strictly to your own shooting. Do not bother other men by talking to them on the firing line and do not let them bother you; the best cure for them is not to answer their questions. A hat or cap should be worn that will shade the eyes and if shooting outdoors button coat or other garment to avoid its flapping in the wind and be sure that it does not bind the body or arms. All movements should be free, but a wrist strap may be used to advantage by men of slight build. Wrist watches and stoned rings are safer in the pocket, as shooting does not improve either one.

I think the best proof of the popularity and fascination for target shooting with the pistol and revolver is the hundreds of men who visit Camp Perry every year, coming from all parts of the United States, and who leave at the end of the matches with the avowed intention of coming back the next year.

FITZ LUCK TARGET

1	3	5	9	1	3	5	9	1	3
5	9	1	3	5	9	1	3	5	9
1	3	5	9	1	3	5	9	1	3
5	9	1	3	5	9	1	3	5	9
1	3	5	9	1	3	5	9	1	3
5	9	1	3	5	9	1	3	5	9
1	3	5	9	1	3	5	9	1	3
5	9	1	3	5	9	1	3	5	9
1	3	5	9	1	3	5	9	1	3
5	9	1	3	5	9	1	3	5	9

CONDITIONS

Three (3) shots, off-hand.

If shooter misses the numbered square, another shot allowed. (Object is to give all contestants an equal chance.)

High score to count.

If a bullet strikes on the cross lines all squares where the white is broken count for the shooter.

If the bullet strikes on the line between two squares, breaking the white in both squares, both are counted.

All ties to be settled with three shots on new target; high score to count.

Name.. Distance....................................

Date.. Score..

(T-5)

COLT
FITZ LUCK REVOLVER TARGET

1	3	5	9	1	3	5	9
5	9	1	3	5	9	1	3
1	3	5	9	1	3	5	9
5	9	1	3	5	9	1	3
1	3	5	9	1	3	5	9
5	9	1	3	5	9	1	3
1	3	5	9	1	3	5	9
5	9	1	3	5	9	1	3

CONDITIONS

Three (3) shots, off-hand.

If shooter misses the numbered square, another shot allowed. (Object is to give all contestants an equal chance.)

High score to count.

If a bullet strikes on the cross lines all squares where the white is broken count for the shooter.

If a bullet strikes on the line between two squares, breaking the white in both squares, both are counted.

All ties to be settled with three shots on new target; high score to count.

Name_____ Distance_____

Date_____ Score_____

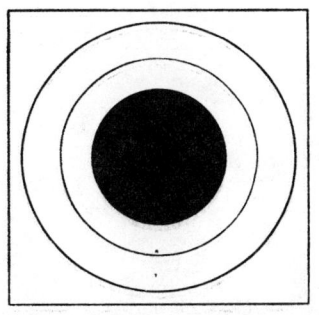

COLT'S 25-YARD REGULATION
POLICE TARGET

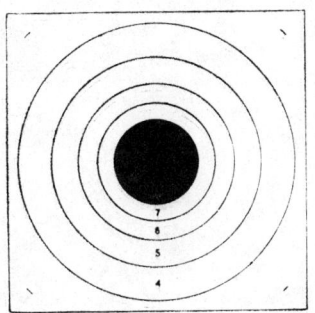

STANDARD AMERICAN 50-YARD
SLOW FIRE TARGET

300-Yard Target

GEORGE MARSHALL—CLAUDE SHAYLOR
Portland (Oregon) Police Department

SECTION

POSITION FOR TARGET SHOOTING

While standing behind the firing line at Camp Perry and many other ranges I have noticed the positions of the hand-gun experts and a difference may be noted in the position of each revolver contestant.

Some shooters hold the arm very rigid, with the shoulder thrown up and the chin resting on the shoulder, and I have seen some very good scores made in this position, but only a few of the shooters use it. In my own case it causes a tremor of the hand which destroys the accuracy and I have never been able to make good scores in this position. Another position is with a pronounced bend at the elbow and this is a position I could use very easily. The only trouble which I found with it was that a wild shot seemed to slip out further than I expected.

My best success has been obtained by holding the arm out fully extended or nearly so without a particle of muscle strain, the revolver gripped lightly in the hand, feet fifteen to eighteen inches apart, weight evenly divided upon both feet, standing at a forty-five degree angle from the target, by all means a comfortable position. One should be sure not to take the arm down or relax just as the trigger is pulled or a wild shot will be the result. The arm should be held and the shots called before taking down the arm.

It is well enough to try out all the different positions which you see, but as soon as possible settle down to one position and do not change it. Success in shooting is obtained by constant practice and by doing the same thing the same way every time.

The following photographs, I believe, will explain the position of some of the leading revolver shots in the

United States better than any written description. You will note that no two take the same position. Your own may be different from any of these, but the scores are what count and a comfortable position is the one best suited to good shooting.

When a desirable position is attained, the next important step which each shooter must master is to tend strictly to his own shooting. He should never interest himself in the scores of his next door neighbors, neither should he feel that the success of his team mates and the score rest only upon his shoulders. Let the team captain worry about the scores and try to at least shoot an average score. All that anyone can expect is to equal his average score.

Position when shooting in the wind is slightly different from the position used in calm weather. The body must be slightly braced, feet a little further apart to avoid the sway from the wind. One can become accustomed to this by practice.

Many shooters stand facing the target instead of at a forty-five degree angle and after viewing the stance of different experts it is safe to say that a comfortable position is all that is necessary for good shooting. But do not assume any freak position; it is time lost to start that way.

When the proper comfortable position is mastered the next thing to consider is how to aim and hold the arm. I believe I can illustrate the proper way to line up the sights with the target by showing the system used by Captain Edward Langrish of the Hartford (Connecticut) Police Department. The following illustrations will be found at the back of Section 11:

Illustration No. 1: The proper way to align the revolver sights with the target is to have the front sight just filling the rear sight as to height and an even distribution of light on each side of the sight; the top of the front sight just touching the bottom of the bull's-eye or with a white line, if preferred. The old shooting phrase, "Set the bull's-eye on top of the front sight," is very apt. (See page 87 A.)

Illustration No. 2: This is a low shot because the front sight did not fill the rear notch as to height. (See page 87 B.)

Illustration No. 3: A high shot to the left, and left because the revolver was canted or tipped to the left; high because the front sight was held above the level of the rear sight. (See page 87 C.)

Illustration No. 4: A high shot because the front sight was held above the level of the rear sight. (See page 87 D.)

I believe the greatest handicap to beginners is the fact that they exert too great an amount of energy in the process of learning to shoot. They work too hard and instead of quieting the muscles and nerves by obtaining control over them they proceed to work themselves into a state of mind not beneficial to good shooting.

All the legs can do is to keep the body from swaying by equally supporting the weight. All the arm and hand can do is to hold the revolver as steady as possible while the shot is being fired. The function of the eyes is to direct the sights properly for a center shot. When undue force is exerted by the legs, body, arm, or hand, a wild shot is the result. All parts of the body must work in unison; if one part fails to perform its task, then the entire operation is at fault, and the defect must be corrected in future trials. Not only beginners are affected in this way, but many of the old-timers if they haven't practiced for several months.

The constant recoil of the .38 caliber or larger will affect the beginner and also the shooters who do not practice at least twice each week. There is a limit to the amount of .38 or larger cartridges that any man can shoot at one time without developing a tremor in his hand and arm. The beginner will reach this stage with a .38 caliber revolver shooting .38 Special cartridges after about twenty-five shots. If shooting the .45 Colt cartridge or the .45 automatic cartridge, the same degree of tremor would be reached in about twelve to fifteen shots. The same man by constant practice can overcome this tremor and raise the amount of shots fired from the .38 caliber to three hundred per day, and still obtain a good score with the last ten shots. With the .45 caliber the two-hundred shot mark may be reached before the tremor is noticeable.

I have studied this tremor for years and noted the almost unbelievable amount of shooting that the body could stand and still obtain good results. This, of course, only comes after long years of practice. Two thousand aimed shots with the .38 caliber may be reached with good results and eight hundred shots with the .45 caliber revolver or automatic.

It takes several years of continual shooting to reach this figure and even then different persons will reach the limit far below the amount stated. Good results will not be obtained if the contestant continues to shoot after this tremor begins. The only cure is rest and extending the period of shoot'ng by practice.

MAJOR H. L. HARKER
Chief Range Officer
Camp Perry, Ohio

CAPT. MAX B. WENDLANDT
Shooting Instructor
Detroit Police Department

CAPT. J. H. YOUNG
Portland (Oregon) Police Department

CAPT. JOSEPH SONNENBERG
New Orleans (Louisiana) Police Department

MR. GEORGE MARSHALL
Portland (Oregon) Police Department

MR. HARRY C. ALMY
Delaware County National Bank
Muncie, Ind.

DR. H. R. BRUNTON
Malden, Mass.

MR. ADOLPH P. SCHUBER
Champion Revolver Shot
New York City Police Department

DR. JOHN L. BASTEY
Boston, Mass.

MAJOR JOSEPH J. MAREK
Champion Revolver Shot of Chicago Police Department

LIEUT. PAUL A. SHEPHERD
Range Officer, Camp Perry, Ohio

MR. C. M. CORBIN
Pasadena (California) Police Department

COL. NORMAN SCHWARZKOPF
Chief New Jersey State Police

DR. CLAUDE A. WARNER
Baltimore, Md.

CAPT. EDWARD J. LANGRISH
Shooting Instructor, Hartford (Conn.) Police Department
Inventor of Limbless Target

CAPT. JACOB LIENHARD
U. S. Marine Corps
Firing Position

LIEUT. LEWIS A. HOHN
U. S. Marine Corps
Firing Position

45 B

LIEUT. RAYMOND T. PRESNELL
U. S. Marine Corps
Firing Position

45 c

LIEUT. WILLIAM WHALING
U. S. Marine Corps
Firing Position

SECTION 4
TRIGGER SQUEEZE

I am a great believer in a checked trigger for all kinds of shooting, as it prevents a slippage of the finger on the trigger which is sometimes taken for a creep. I have interviewed and noted many shooters who tell me they prefer the plain trigger because they place the finger high on the trigger and allow it (the finger) to slide downward as they increase the pressure, the shot being fired as the finger reaches a position near the bottom of the trigger. I contend that this is all wrong for the amount of pressure exerted may not be exactly the same each time and that will mean either a higher or lower position of the finger on the trigger as the shot is fired. And the muscles used in this operation will tend to move or displace other muscles of the hand, also the third joint of finger.

This idea should go the same way as the instruction which used to read: "Squeeze the entire hand as if you were squeezing a lemon or a lady's hand." This is wrong, because when squeezing the entire hand every muscle in the hand and wrist is moved or tensed. When squeezing with trigger finger alone the set of muscles attached to that finger are the only ones tensed by the operation of squeezing the trigger.

Many times some one will come to me with the complaint that the trigger creeps. I try it and find no creep. Then the mystery of the creep is shown to me. The revolver is taken in the position of a long lost child, the hammer cocked, and then one finger placed on the trigger and a finger and thumb of the other hand placed behind the trigger and in front of the guard to ease the trigger slowly backward. But this is not the way to find a creep.

It should be found as the revolver is shot in regular shooting position. And even at times when a creep is found in this way it is because the trigger is pulled back and pressed sidewise instead of straight back.

The trigger squeeze is very important, for the best shot in the world would never have become even an ordinary shot if he had not developed the proper trigger squeeze.

When the sights swing in line with the target, and one is reasonably certain that if the shot was fired from this position it would hit the bull's-eye, he should carefully tighten the trigger finger which must work in conjunction with the eye. Do not squeeze any other part of the hand. Care should be taken to squeeze the trigger slowly, not jerk or twist it, for that would result in a wild shot. When one is carefully squeezing the trigger he sometimes finds the sights swinging away from the bull's-eye, but he should not release the pressure on the trigger, he should hold what he has gained and as the sights again swing in line with the bull's-eye he should increase the trigger squeeze. This may happen several times before the shot is finally fired. If (he has faithfully) added (pressure) to the trigger squeeze at the right instant a bullet through the bull's-eye will be the result.

If the shots are inclined to go to the left, with a right-handed shooter, or to the right, with a left-handed shooter, a slight increase in the thumb pressure on the side of the arm will correct this.

The reason why shooters can call their shots in the target is because they know the exact position of the sights in relation to the bull's-eye at the instant of explosion.

To aid the trigger squeeze we must take into consideration the trigger pull. With an extra heavy trigger pull the shooter is very liable to yank the trigger and pull the arm sidewise. Still, the trigger pull should be in proportion to the weight and caliber of the arm. A Camp Perry model may be easily used with a two and one-fourth pound pull, but this would not do at all with a New Service arm to be used as a hunting arm. In the ten and twenty second work three pounds is about the proper pull with the revolver, and just as good scores can be made with a three to three and one-half pound pull as with a two and one-half pound pull. Squeeze straight back keeping sights in line with the bull's-eye, and squeeze slowly and carefully, not changing the pressure of the rest of the hand.

In the ten and twenty second work a very light spring should be used after the parts are thoroughly worked in (about five hundred shots). This greatly assists the cocking of the hammer by the thumb and also aids the hand and arm in keeping the revolver in line with the bull's-eye when cocking. This is one of the time-savers.

The spring must not be light enough to cause misfires, for in some matches a misfire will cause you the loss of a shot, for the range officer will ask you to try the same cartridge again and if it goes you lose the shot. This is very unfair, because in nearly every case the cartridge will fire the second time the firing pin will explode the primer because the primer metal is weakened by the first blow and the top of the primer is nearer to the anvil. If the primer in a misfire shows the firing pin indentation it means that the shooter has done his part; the only way he could be blamed for the misfire would be to rest the side of his thumb against the hammer and therefore lessen the power of the hammer fall.

Dry shooting will greatly help in attaining the proper trigger squeeze, as you can then see whether the sights remain stationary or move away as the hammer falls. Do not be discouraged if the desired results are not accomplished in a few days, for it takes time to develop the proper trigger squeeze. However, when this has been accomplished it is one more of the essentials which go to make up an expert target shot.

I am not trying to make target shooting seem like a hopeless task, but trying to impress the beginner with the things which he must do to become an expert target shot.

All persons cannot place the finger on the trigger at the same point due to the different sizes of hands and short and long fingers. Just in front of the first crease across the finger at the joint is the proper place, but a short finger will press the trigger ahead of this point, and a long finger behind the crease. A checked trigger in the above cases is invaluable.

Many of our experts have advanced the theory that they do not know or do not want to know just when the hammer is released. I cannot agree with this as I want to know, and do know, when the hammer is released.

The grip of the revolver is largely responsible for a perfect trigger squeeze. If the grip is not perfect no amount of caution will release the trigger properly. The educated trigger finger will know just the amount of pressure required to fire the shot and if the arm has a three and one-half pound pull about three and one-quarter pounds will be taken up before the thought comes to the shooter that here is the time for extreme care for the hammer is about to be released. If he did not know at what instant the hammer was to be released it would be very unfortunate for him if he were a trick shooter, hunter, or even a target shooter.

I realize that I will hear arguments on this point and the question will be asked: Why does the shooter collect nines, eights, and sevens when he is holding well, if he knows just when the hammer is released? The answer is—that the slight variation in sights occurs after the hammer is released and before the bullet leaves the barrel. The back lash as trigger is released adds to this and a slight variance in the gripping of the arm may cause the above result.

The shooter will call an eight or nine as the shot is fired and no doubt his sights were perfect when he squeezed the trigger, but the effort exerted by the trigger finger caused the sights to drift out of line with the bull's-eye. This may be proved by holding the revolver in shooting position without squeezing the trigger, then trying the same procedure, except the trigger is squeezed and the shot is fired. You will find the arm may be held in correct line with the target for a longer period of time when the arm is held without squeezing the trigger. Therefore great care must be taken and extensive study required, to perform the operation of squeezing the trigger without forcing sights out of line with the bull's-eye.

I may be asked how the shooter can take all this care in ten and twenty second work. He must do everything in ten and twenty second work that he does in slow-fire shooting, but he learns to speed up the operation just as the trick shot must do all the things a target shooter does to attain accuracy, only he learns to do them in a shorter time. The shorter distance used in Aerial Shooting is of great assistance to speed and accuracy. Ten and twenty second work is usually on a larger target than that used for fine target shooting; for instance, the Camp Perry twenty-five yard target, which is the fifty-yard Standard American with nine and ten ring black

SECTION 5
FLINCHING

Other men have fired a revolver without collecting broken arms and dislocated shoulders and no one has such a thing to fear. The only thing which rivals flinching as a shooting jinx is carelessness. It is better to stop shooting than to fire one shot carelessly. One will have all the trouble he wishes for in getting good scores without becoming careless.

Many times a new shooter will make excellent scores for a few weeks and then he will have a slump and for a short time he will have trouble in making anything which approaches a decent score. The main reason for this slump is flinching and the best way to correct it is by dry shooting.

I remember a short time ago a gentleman came into the range with his revolver and offered to give it to me if I would accept it. I asked him why and he said it shot low and to the left. I asked him to shoot it and after some persuasion he consented to fire five shots at fifteen yards. He had stated that several of his friends, all good shots, had the same trouble with it that he had. Sure enough, his first shot was six inches to the left and eight inches low, but it told me what I wanted to know. He fired another shot which went within an inch of the first shot, then he said: "Are you satisfied now?" I told him to fire one more shot and we would both be satisfied. He fired the next shot or attempted to, as this time he snapped on an empty shell which I had placed in his revolver, but the fact that it was empty was not responsible for the downward curve of his wrist to the left. He looked at the revolver and then at me. "What kind of cigars do you smoke?" he asked. I told him I was more interested in where those last two bullets would go than I was in cigars just then, and showed him how to hold the arm and squeeze the trigger, and the next two shots went into the black. Before he left the range he would not even sell the revolver.

Flinching is many times indulged in by shooters long out of the beginners' class. In fact, nearly all shooters are liable to fall into the habit and unless it is overcome no enjoyment is in store for the man who is trying to make a good score. Flinching must be carefully guarded against as every shot is fired. How many scores we see on the fifty-yard range that has fours, fives, or sixes in it, and the man who fired the shots will tell you that he had a perfect hold as the shots were fired. The answer is usually a slight flinch as the hammer falls, and at fifty yards a slight flinch is all that is needed to collect a five or a six.

Many recommend the .22 caliber weapon to cure flinching and this is very good, for with the heavy .22 revolvers now on the market one is using the same arm that he uses in actual shooting. Many times the lone shooter or the one who shoots with one or two friends, who waits until it is his turn to shoot, will develop a bad case of flinching when shooting on the line with other men who do not wait. It is best to practice with others and develop the idea of tending strictly to your own shooting regardless of when or how your neighbors shoot. This can very easily be done and it will be a wonderful help to any shooter who cares to enter the matches held each year in all parts of the country. Sometimes you will hear one shooter tell another that he was all ready to shoot when he was shot off. If he was just ready to shoot, his revolver would have been pointing in the right direction and if he was tending to his own shooting the discharge of his neighbor's revolver would not have disturbed him.

Practice under the same condition that you expect to shoot under, if possible, such as wind, rain, light, and noise. This practice will enable you to meet all kinds of conditions and will help your scores.

Holding the thumb on top of the frame and in a position to rub against side of hammer as it falls will cause flinching because it will cause the thumb pressure to be released at the instant of explosion.

Flinching is more pronounced in the lighter models of arms shooting a powerful cartridge, but it can be easily overcome by proper grip and thumb pressure.

Another cause of flinching is too much backlash in the trigger, which causes an unnecessary change in position of trigger finger as shot is fired. This has been corrected in the past by placing an adjusting screw through guard behind the trigger, only allowing the movement necessary to lift the end of the trigger out of hammer notch. This is not necessary in the modern arms, as this movement is carefully worked out when the arm is manufactured.

The thumb placed against the latch or end of the cylinder, or, in fact, any part of the hand that receives a sharp blow and has the skin broken by any part of the revolver due to recoil, should be taken care of and the fault corrected at once, for continued firing will cause a very bad case of flinching and a condition that is not easily corrected.

While it has been stressed several times in this book that a perfect quieting control over the nerves and muscles is necessary, it may also be added that each shooter must become accustomed to the noise or blast of the explosion. It is fear or expectancy of this report that many times causes the shooter to flinch.

Delicate ear drums easily affected by vibration will add to the shooter's troubles in his advance toward good scores, especially if large caliber arms are used. I have tried several kinds of ear stoppers and have discarded the use of everything but cotton. I find that is cleaner to use and answers the purpose. Do not roll it in a small hard ball and press into the ear as far as possible, but roll it lightly about the size of a marble and press it gently into the ear. Use fresh cotton every time the range is visited.

SECTION 6

THE REVOLVER GRIP

Many and varied are the ways in which shooters grip a revolver. The following are some of the most popular grips for a target and quick-draw shooting.

In many clubs and police departments I have found men who, when shooting, squeeze or tighten the entire hand when pulling the trigger. I believe this is a disadvantage and tends to pull the sights out of line with the target. One should not take a death grip on the revolver; it will only cause the hand to tremble and a wild shot will be the result.

The position of the thumb above the latch is very important. In laying the thumb along the top of the frame above latch avoid pressing downward as the shot is fired. This may easily be done in trying to avoid pressing thumb against side of hammer. Allow two-thirds of thumb to rest against the side of the frame and balance of thumb on corner of frame and above. The part of the thumb above the frame will assist in blocking flip of arm after the shot is fired, and will bring the sights into line quickly. A variation of three to five inches will occur at twenty-five yards from different degrees of thumb pressure.

The frame should be pressed between thumb and opposite part of forefinger near third joint, as in the jaws of a pair of pliers, that is, an even pressure on both sides of the frame, and the entire arm grasped tightly enough to keep the sights in line while pulling the trigger. This position is good for both slow and timed fire, for in timed fire the thumb above latch is in the most convenient place to cock the hammer quickly, and is also in the proper place to overcome (by pressure) the tendency to pull to the left in rapid fire and slow fire work. Many shooters who have trouble with the hand slipping up on the grip as the shot is fired will benefit their scores by placing the thumb in this position.

Shooters with a hand like a "ham" (as Colonel Dooley would say) find that the little finger is dangling in space, therefore they lock it across the butt of the revolver. Sometimes this is a material help, especially in rapid fire work, as it holds the revolver against slipping down through the hand when the explosion occurs.

At Camp Perry in 1927 there was heard some high-class arguments on built-up pistol grips, consisting of filling in the top of the space between the trigger guard and the front strap of the revolver. Personally I like the grip of the Official Police revolver just as it comes from the factory and, while I am a past-master as far as fool notions about a hand gun are concerned, I have never tried to improve the grip on this arm. When the controversy was at its height Sergeant Young and his Portland Police and several others, entered in the matches, took off the attachments and I could not find where the scores suffered in the consequence, therefore I am still of the opinion that just as good scores can be made with the arms as issued.

I have heard the many virtues of this addition or, as the shooters call it, gadget, made from dental wax, plastic wood, steel, aluminum and brass, and fitted for each individual need. Like many other so-called helps to perfect scores it must be tried and accepted or rejected like the skeleton hammer, the extremely light pull, and the very narrow sights. If the scores are better than the average stick to them until something better is found. The sooner the shooter settles upon one thing and makes no changes the better the scores.

This was proved at Perry in 1928. Just before the matches the ruling was made that police departments could use the Officer's Model with adjustable sights or the arm with stationary sights. Many departments immediately changed from the Official Police to the Officer's Model and found to their surprise that the scores did not immediately jump eight or ten points and some did not shoot as well as before. This was not due to the fact that the Officer's Model was not as accurate as the Official Police, because it is; the reason was that the men had practiced and become thoroughly familiar with the Official Police both as to action (worn in by use) and height of sights above the frame.

If time for sufficient practice with a new revolver had been allowed I can assure you that the Officer's Model would not have suffered by comparison. In favor of the Officer's Model would be the fact that sights may be adjusted to correct for the slightest variation in any direction, which is not easy with solid sights. Also different width of sights may be tried on the Officer's Model until the desired combination is found. Mid-range and special loads may be used by correcting sights. With the Official Police, sights cannot be easily changed and no sight allowance can be made for mid-range or special loads, but the accuracy of the arms is equal, grip and balance are the same, if barrel length is equal.

Shooting a revolver five shots in ten seconds and five shots in twenty seconds opens up a new field of practice. The proper cocking of the arm (and many months can be consumed by this alone for every fraction of a second saved will benefit the score) is very essential. Several years ago the tendency was to throw the revolver sidewise to allow a better leverage for the thumb in cocking and this will give very good results; many of our best shots still use it. I believe, however, that a split second may be saved by holding the arm in line, drawing the palm of the hand and thumb where they join away from the back strap of the revolver, and cocking the hammer straight back holding the grip with the three lower fingers. The little finger may or may not be locked across the bottom of the grip. Then, by practice, the proper amount of pressure may be brought to bear on the arm so that the arm will be carried only a few inches out of line as the recoil occurs.

Care must be taken in the ten and twenty second work to start properly, place the first shot and keep track of the time. There is plenty of time but none to waste. Sometimes in the ten and twenty second work the shots will group to right or left while the arm shoots center for slow fire. The remedy for this is to hold over enough to center the shots, as the change of group is caused by a slight flinch or yank of the trigger or insufficient thumb pressure.

Another fine grip is with the thumb below the latch. This position is especially adapted to quick draw and double-action shooting and is also a perfect grip for target shooting.

A checked wood grip is best for all kinds of shooting for with a rough check no slippage in the hand should occur, but whatever grip you prefer will give you good results if you grip the arm the same way every time.

I have tried several of the foreign pistols for grip and balance and I am still in favor of the American revolver grip. I still believe that we make the best revolver, automatic pistols, and single shot pistols here in the United States, and set triggers, reclining couches for the thumb, wrist braces and other appliances of like nature have no place on a he-man's revolver or pistol.

The same belief must be entertained by the rest of the clan, as I seldom see a foreign pistol or revolver in competition. It is true that matches are won with the Tell and other pistols of foreign make, but it is usually in matches where one or two days are consumed to fire fifty shots. American shooters are keyed up to the fifty shots in one hour at fifty yards and it is torture to them to enter a match allowing twenty-four to forty-eight hours for fifty shots.

If any addition or subtraction from the present American grips will help the individual shooter with a hand above or below normal size, I do not blame him for using it. The object in target shooting is to finish with the best possible score. Revolver grips, as furnished, may seem strange to the beginner, but constant practice will accustom the hand to the grip and a comfortable grip or hold will be the result.

Before leaving this subject of the revolver grip, let us go more thoroughly into the matter. Many times I have been told that placing the little finger under the grip will change the position of the group on the target. It will if the shooter has a small hand, for crossing the little finger will tend to change the position of entire hand to a point lower down on the grip away from the center of bore.

If the shooter possesses a large hand, one that fills the grip to the extent that the little finger is taking up space to bottom of the grip, then that man could easily cross the little finger on bottom of grip without changing sights for correction of group unless he exerted undue pressure with the little finger.

The little finger across the butt is of great assistance in rapid-fire shooting if the size of the hand permits such a hold. It assists in checking the upward motion of the revolver and prevents it from slipping downward through the hand due to recoil. It assists through leverage in cocking the arm.

A revolver may be fired with the little finger under the grip or with the little finger on front strap, with thumb above latch or with thumb below latch, without changing sights or position of group if care is taken to distribute hand pressure evenly at all points.

Proper Target Grip or Hold

Place thumb above latch along top and side of frame. Do not allow thumb to rest against hammer. Thumb pressure against side of frame very important.

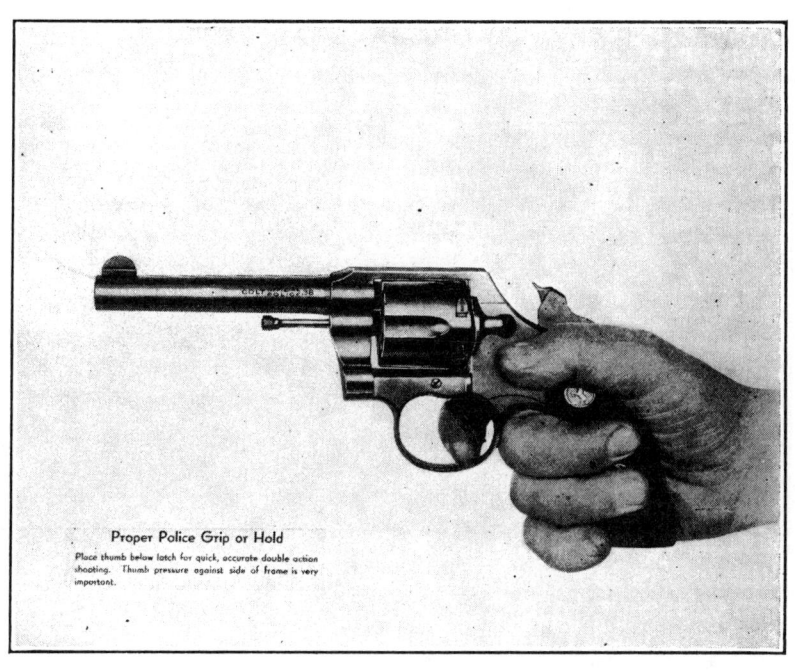

Proper Police Grip or Hold

Place thumb below latch for quick, accurate double action shooting. Thumb pressure against side of frame is very important.

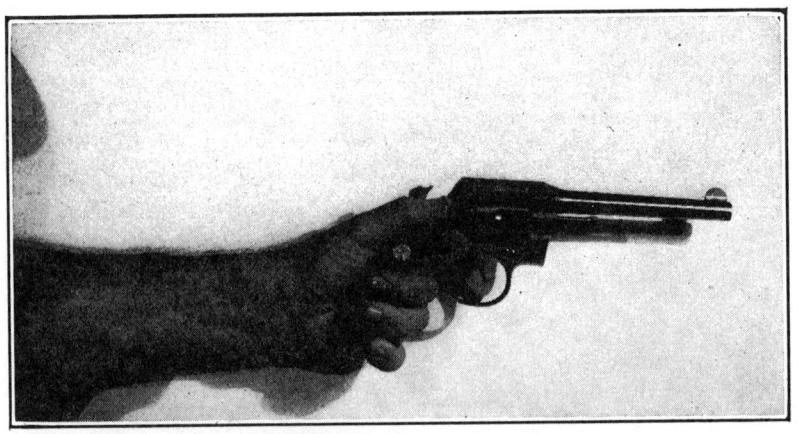

LITTLE FINGER UNDER GRIP

Cocking the Revolver for Rapid Fire
Hold revolver in line with the target, draw hammer straight back.

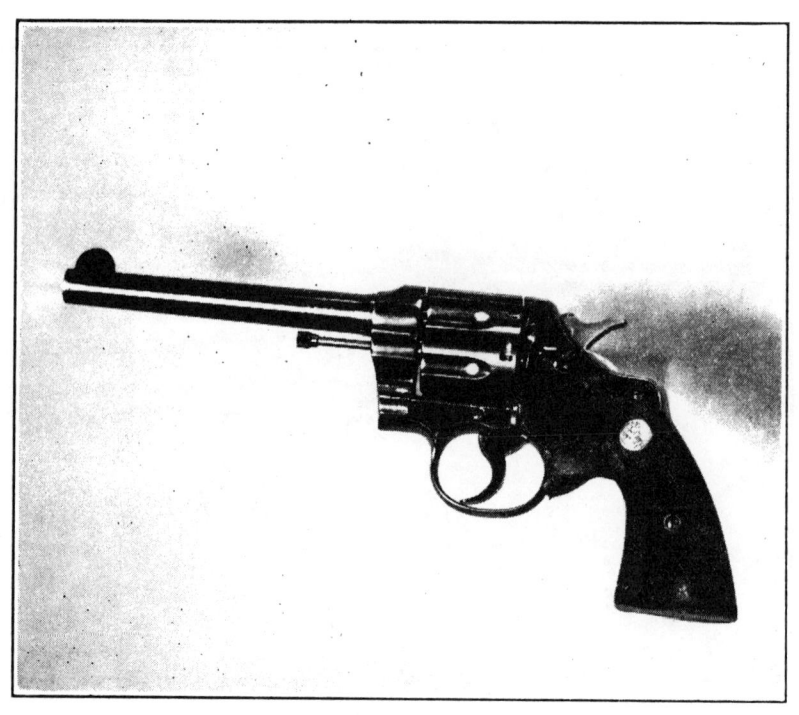

REVOLVER WITH GADGET OR ADDITION

SECTION 7
SHOOTING IN THE WIND

The indoor shooter who steps out to fire a few shots on a windy range for the first time is bound to get the surprise of his life, and not get the score he expected either. He must learn to shoot all over again even though aided by his indoor experience.

Only by practice can one in part overcome the effect of the wind. A steady wind can be leaned against, but there is the puffy wind which cannot be outguessed.

If the wind comes from directly behind or in front it does not affect the scores as does the cross wind. There is no set rule for shooting in the wind, the only way to master it is to shoot in the wind and rain at every opportunity. Practice in the wind will eliminate some of the wild shots, but not all.

In slow fire shooting we can wait for a lull but in rapid fire the stop watch and hard-boiled Range Officer waits for no man and so rapid fire should be practiced in the wind as often as possible. Many clubs are shooting on a sheltered range and to such clubs my advice would be to get out and shoot in the wind.

Try feet a little farther apart and muscles slightly tensed; hold slightly toward the wind on the target. If the wind is blowing from the right, hold toward five o'clock in a steady wind and these things may place one or two more in the ten ring.

Avoid all loose clothing, such as loose trousers legs, loose coat, or coat sleeves. Any part of a flapping garment will disturb the shooter and may cause a wild shot. A tight-fitting shirt or jacket is best for shooting in the wind, and remember that the wind plays no favorites; every one else is as much affected by it as you are. Use cotton in the ears, elastic bands on the coat sleeves and trousers legs and be happy. Practice with the same clothes on that you intend to use in the match; a tight-fitting cap is often better to use in the wind than a hat, because the hat brim will catch the wind and move the head from behind the sights. Place the hand and arm not used in shooting where it will not catch the wind,—for instance, the arm close to the body and the hand in the front trousers pocket.

It is necessary to practice in all conditions that may be encountered in match shooting. Save the scores and note the difference and improvement.

In the rain it is best not to use sight black, for it will not stay on and may collect bubbles on the sights; there is no glare, so sight black is not necessary. As soon as a match shot in the rain is over wipe and oil the revolver or pistol thoroughly.

A heavy revolver or pistol will give better results in the wind or rain than the lighter models.

SECTION 8
MATCH SHOOTING

Match shooting does not materially differ from other sports. If running one hundred yards practice for one hundred yards, if running one mile practice for one mile, if shooting fifty shots in one hour at fifty yards practice fifty shots in one hour at fifty yards.

If practicing for a match that calls for slow fire ten shots in ten minutes, ten shots each five in twenty seconds, and ten shots each five in ten seconds. One should shoot ten shots slow fire to accustom himself to light condition, appearance of sights, steady holding, etc. Then one string of ten shots each five in twenty seconds to gradually increase the speed, and twenty seconds to the experienced rapid fire shot is practically slow fire and should be within two points of the slow fire score. Then eight strings of ten shots each five in ten seconds. One hundred shots is enough for one day's practice and all such matches are won by the ten second score. The expert ten second man may be several points behind on slow fire and twenty seconds and still win on his ten second score.

The idea that he wants to know at all times how the match is progressing is strong in all target shooters, and this is one place where every man should tend strictly to his own business and let the team captain worry about little details, such as the scores being made by other members of the team or club. When doing team shooting try to outshoot the member of the opposing team that is on the line at the same time that you are and let your comrades do the same. Never go into a match with the fear that a poor score will be the result. All any contestant can hope for is to shoot his average score and remember if the first shot should be a six that several ninety-three and ninety-four scores have been made with this start.

Mark well what Sergeant Young tells you about harmony in a shooting team. The team cannot succeed without it. One grouch will spoil the prospects of the entire team as will some one who will not do exactly as he is told. The individual may profit by the mistakes of others. Worry has lost many a match; just make the best possible score and be happy. Shooting is a pastime or recreation and a wild shot is not a matter of life and death. If this should happen in one match try to avoid it in the next one.

Why do contestants who are making excellent scores on the home range take the trip to Perry and upon appearing on the firing line immediately get the idea of changing sight, trigger pulls, etc. They have made excellent scores at home and the sights that are right in Oklahoma are not far wrong at Perry, and the same thing goes for the trigger pull. A big shoot is no place to sight in a pet target arm if it can possibly be done at home. If an arm which has been doing dependable work for many months on one range is taken to another range and should shoot either right or left, look for light conditions; the trouble is seldom with the revolver. The shooter can check the time for changes in the arm by his score; if he is averaging over the ninety mark think over very carefully the matter of changing sights or pull. If not over eighty per cent is the average, then change everything if it will better the score.

The greatest handicap for contestants at Camp Perry is the fact that ammunition is furnished and many contestants feel that the more they shoot the better their chances are of winning the big matches. This is not true. The contestant who will content himself with his normal amount of practice will, when the day of the match arrives, make better scores then he who feels it is his duty to burn up all the ammunition in sight. The man who goes to Camp Perry or any other big shoot with the idea of winning matches should do all his serious practice work on his home range, and only shoot enough to keep in top form after arriving at the place where the shoot is to be held. Every contestant is either coming up or going back on the day of the shoot. We never stand still and on the day of the shoot we should be, by carefully timing our practice work, coming up; in shooting terms the man who is going stale is not in condition to win a match. Re-entry matches has been the downfall of many possible winners, —too much practice.

I believe I am well qualified to speak on this subject of too much practice. While a man may accustom himself by constant practice to shooting many hundred shots each day, my experience in the testing range has taught me that there is a limit to human endurance. Constant shooting day after day will eventually burn out or overtrain even a man with iron nerves. If a man, who has acquired, through years of practice, the ability to shoot with a degree of accuracy eight hundred to one thousand shots each day, cannot do his best work after such practice, how can a man who normally shoots fifty or seventy-five shots in practice each day or twice each week appear at the big shoot and fire four or five hundred shots without becoming overtrained.

One very serious handicap is the fact that many of the men who condition themselves on the home range must do so by shooting alone or with one or two club members. Added noise, change in conditions, and one hundred and one different things will tend to disturb him and consequently his scores will be several points lower at the range where the match is being held. But remember all the other competitors have the same conditions to overcome and their scores will not be what they were at home.

A good telescope in the hands of a team member or

coach will eliminate the bother of spotting every shot fired and will allow more time for study of conditions and corrections. It also lessens the eye strain and distortion of sight which comes from continued use of the telescope when spotting bullet holes in the target.

The world of sports loves a good loser. The man who can lose a match and shake hands with the winner and mean it is the man who is getting real pleasure out of his shooting hours. And there is always a next time to win. There is always a real thrill in coming back and beating the man who caused you to finish in second place the last meeting.

CAMP PERRY FIRING LINE

OLD TIMERS AT THE BIG CAMP
Camp Perry, Ohio

COL. JOHN J. DOOLEY
U. S. Cartridge Co., New York City

ROYAL CANADIAN MOUNTED POLICE

We were indeed fortunate in 1929 and 1930 at Camp Perry due to the fact that Commissioner Courtland Starnes, Commander of the Royal Northwest Mounted Police, allowed a revolver team representing the organization to be present. The members of this team were a credit to any organization and the general remarks of the contestants and visitors to the camp were, that the Royal Canadian Mounted team were wonderful fellows and that they hoped to see them at the camp in future years

We will look forward to resuming the pleasant relations with the team representing Canada in 1931 and future years.

SECTION 9
DON'TS FOR TARGET MEN

NEVER check up on the scores of others in a match until you have finished your own.

NEVER try to sight in a revolver or pistol in a match.

NEVER talk to your neighbor when he is shooting.

NEVER argue with the Range Officer or member of the opposing team.

NEVER try to take advantage of range conditions such as using some article for support.

NEVER keep the line waiting when it is your turn to shoot. Be ready.

NEVER take advantage of another contestant; be fair to him and you in turn will be treated fairly.

NEVER enter a protest unless you are sure you are right.

NEVER blame arms or ammunition for your failure to make a good score unless you have proof of your statement.

NEVER blame conditions at the range for your failure. The other contestants are shooting under the same conditions.

NEVER change revolver or pistol in a match. Use the same arm throughout unless it becomes useless through accident.

NEVER go on firing line with springs so weakened that the arm will misfire. You are only delaying the match and inviting the displeasure of the Range Officer.

NEVER go on the firing line with a dangerous trigger pull.

NEVER allow the arm to point in any direction except at the target when it is loaded.

NEVER allow the arm to point toward any object where a glancing bullet may be the result of an accidental discharge.

NEVER brag about your scores, let the scores show your proficiency.

In many instances things which are overlooked by the beginner are as an open book to the expert. A shot to the right or left will warn the expert of change in light, loose sights, etc., and no more shots are wasted. A slight change in position to overcome the force of the wind, an arm with an open rear sight to overcome conditions on a dark day or approaching darkness, and keeping the sights evenly covered with sight black or the black from one of P. J. O'Hare's acetylene lamps to repel the glare from the sun's rays, will aid in making good scores. Where no acetylene lamp or sight black is handy a candle can be used.

If the target revolver is carried in a canton flannel case instead of a holster the original factory finish will last for a long time. This is a holster of three thicknesses of heaviest canton flannel, with soft side in, and an extra thickness over front and rear sight, with a black cover for the sake of appearance, making a perfect protection for a gun.

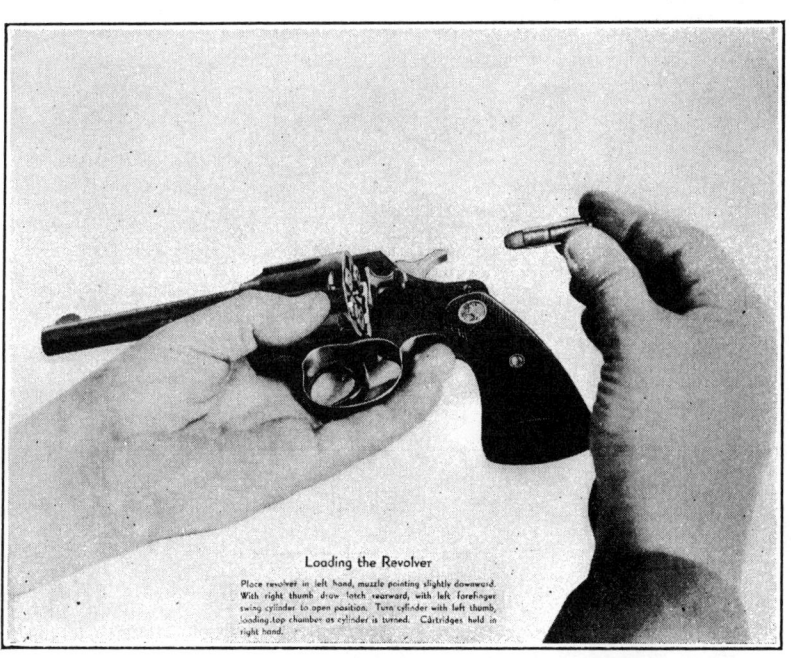

Loading the Revolver

Place revolver in left hand, muzzle pointing slightly downward. With right thumb draw latch rearward, with left forefinger swing cylinder to open position. Turn cylinder with left thumb, loading top chamber as cylinder is turned. Cartridges held in right hand.

Closing the Revolver
Holding revolver in loading position, close cylinder with left thumb, while latch is drawn rearward with right thumb.

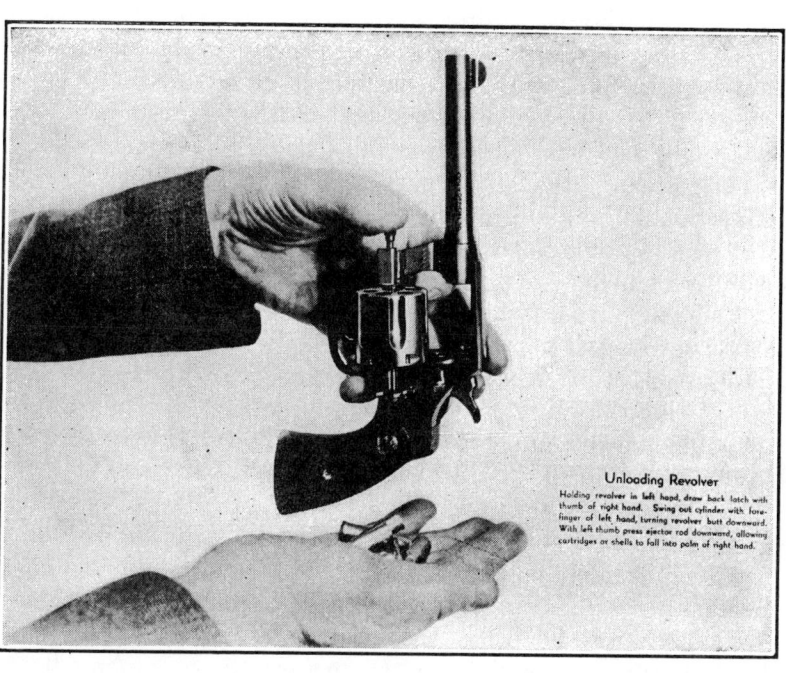

Unloading Revolver

Holding revolver in left hand, draw back latch with thumb of right hand. Swing out cylinder with forefinger of left hand, turning revolver butt downward. With left thumb press ejector rod downward, allowing cartridges or shells to fall into palm of right hand.

SECTION 10
DRY SHOOTING

Dry shooting, or, in other words, aiming and snapping the arm without ammunition, is very beneficial to the target shooter and is practiced by nearly every one who shoots. In some ways it is preferable to shooting the .22 caliber arm. It can be practiced in the house morning and night and one is then getting the hang and feel of his favorite arm. In shooting the .22 the light recoil may cover a slight flinch, but in dry shooting one sees exactly what he is doing. In quick-draw work dry shooting is a wonderful help.

I have seen thousands of cartridges wasted and thousands of discouraged shooters because they did not take the pains to discover what the trouble was and why they were not hitting the target. It is of no use to continue shooting in a blaze-away and trust-to-God fashion. If you don't know why you miss you never can correct the fault.

Knowing how to stand, how to line up the sights, the trigger squeeze, shooting in the wind, and light conditions are very important, but are you flinching? I know of no better way to correct flinching than by dry shooting. You learn all the other things mentioned, you learn to hold the revolver steady at the instant the hammer falls, and you learn not to fight the recoil. Many good revolvers are cussed because the damn thing will not group or place the shots in the ten ring. If the revolver could speak it might say: "If that damn hand would only be still and not try to yank my handle off when the hammer falls I could make a good target." Do not become careless when practicing dry shooting or all benefits which may be derived from it is lost. This is your time to study and find out where you are wrong.

One of the principal reasons why a new shooter cannot make a good score after he has a working idea of the position, etc., is that he cannot control the sway of his arm. It will take weeks and sometimes months to train the arm properly and dry shooting will do this, at the same time save money which would otherwise be thrown away.

It does not harm a good revolver to snap it without cartridges and it does help the prospective target shooter, especially in ten and twenty second work. A serious mistake in practicing dry shooting for ten and twenty second work is to hold the arm in shooting position and cock, aim, and snap five times without moving the arm. This is not the condition encountered in actual shooting. After the first snap, raise revolver sharply upward as near as possible like the recoil of the arm when a shot is fired, the idea being to accustom the arm to the upward motion of the revolver or pistol and also to accustom the eye to catch the sights quickly as the weapon is returned to firing position.

Captain Max Wendlandt, instructor of the Detroit Police Department, stands at the right side of the shooter and, as the hammer falls, he strikes the bottom of the revolver a sharp blow. This is a very fine substitute for the natural recoil of the arm.

The value of dry shooting is evident when our best instructors will recommend and teach it in their police schools.

I believe Captain Edward Langrish, originator of the Langrish Limbless Target and expert target shot, has advanced a very fine idea for ten and twenty second shooting by using an Eastman clock used in photography to help the beginner in timing his shots and getting inside the required time. Place the clock where it can be seen easily, toward the target and about six feet away from the raised pistol, which should be empty. When the hand reaches the starting point snap five times, of course, aiming properly at the target with an occasional glance at the clock. Without the recoil of the loaded revolver the ten second time should be between seven and eight seconds and for the twenty second between seventeen and eighteen seconds. The two or three seconds will be consumed in overcoming the recoil when arm is loaded. In a short time this clock practice will be unnecessary as the elapsed time will be known to the shooter within one second.

I remember the late Sergeant John Thomas, U.S.M.C., telling me that he snapped in for seven years before he came to Camp Perry and that year he won the N. R. A. Championship and the National Individual Match. He attributed his success to his snapping in practice. Sergeant J. H. Young, Captain of the Portland (Oregon) Police Team, one of the best revolver shots in the United States, is a great believer in dry shooting. The experience and judgment of such men should not be ignored by the beginner.

All dry shooting is not recommended; however, a few shots should be fired at every opportunity to check up on the progress. If bitten by the gun microbe this advice is unnecessary. Practice and plenty of it, both dry shooting and actual firing, are necessary if the top is to be reached, and the dry shooting, at times when no range is available, will assist in reaching the top.

Even experts after a few months' lay-off will find dry shooting the best way to come back, especially in fast work, and when changing from the indoor to outdoor range. If a slight tremor is noticed as the hammer falls this must be corrected, as it is usually due to a slight tightening of the grip or insufficient pressure between thumb and first finger on the revolver.

Use a target of proper size for aiming distance. In an ordinary room a black the size of a dime should be used for dry shooting; if on the range use the regular target. Do not use weights or other appliance on the arm, for then the hand and arm are not becoming accustomed to the revolver as it will be used in actual firing.

I believe in full charge loads or very accurate midrange loads at all times, as a slight variation in midrange loads may drop a properly aimed bullet out of the black, where a slight variation in the full charge loads would not lose over a point and the recoil is not disagreeable with full charge ammunition in the modern arms. Stationary sights require this, for all arms are tested with full charge ammunition.

Dry shooting is of great benefit in police work where both single and double action shooting are used. It is of especial benefit to the officer who has only fired a few shots. As the officer comes to the firing line he is asked about his experience with the revolver and if he explains that he has only fired a few shots and those some time ago, he is a fit subject for dry shooting, which will probably make him double the score he would make if allowed to use the cartridges when he first came to the firing line. The officer experienced in shooting, after he takes a course in dry shooting, will probably improve his scores only two or three points but this may be enough to put him over the top.

SECTION 11
EYES AND EYESIGHT

It is not necessary to have perfect eyesight to become a good shot. I have met many excellent shots whose eyes were far from perfect. It *is* necessary to see the sights clearly, but in many cases the bull's-eye appears to the shooter to be oval in shape and of a dull gray color. However, the shooter will soon learn what part of the oval object to hold on to get a center shot.

It is best to look directly at the target instead of looking out of the corner of the eye and in some cases the vision may be cleared by bending the head slightly downward. I have sometimes heard a shooter say: "Don't rub your eyes when shooting." I do not agree with this statement, for many times slightly rubbing the eyes will clear the vision.

The question is often brought up of a right-handed shooter using the left eye. This question can be answered in the affirmative, for the left eye may be used when shooting with the right hand, and the right eye when shooting with the left hand. The only difference is turning the head slightly to get the eye accustomed to this position behind the sights. Sometimes the eye on the same side as the arm used is not the best eye for target shooting. It is best to try out both and use the one giving best results.

The master eye may be determined by looking at some object with both eyes open and pointing the finger at the object, the edge of a door or window casing will answer the purpose. You are now seeing the finger pointed at the edge of door casing with both eyes open but you are directing the finger with the master eye. This may be proved by the following experiment: Close the left eye;

if the finger does not move out of line with casing the right eye is the master eye, and the one with which you were seeing the finger in line with the door casing. If the finger does move out of line with casing when the left eye is closed then the left eye is the master eye.

Do not strain the eyes before a match by looking toward a bright light. It is a good thing to arrive at the firing point a minute or two before the match starts to allow the eyes to become accustomed to the exact condition you will encounter. One valuable use for eyes on the firing point is to pick out the target one is supposed to shoot on. Many otherwise good target shots have discovered after the smoke cleared away that they had added to their neighbor's score by firing on the wrong target.

Shooting with both eyes open does not mean that both eyes are used in shooting. The master eye only is used. I am often asked if it is better to shoot with both eyes open. I shoot both ways and with right or left eye and in my own case I can see no difference. I have heard it argued both ways and can only say shoot whichever way you can make the best scores.

If the sights cannot be seen clearly with glasses, it is necessary to consult the oculist and he will shorten the vision to clear up the sights. Take the pet target arm along and try it. Take it to the window and try both sights and distance with corrected glasses. Amber-colored glasses are recommended for shooting when the sun is bright and also for shooting over snow. I use a pair of amber glasses that hook over the regular shooting glasses, which will save the expense of having the correct prescription ground into two pairs of glasses.

I believe that every one who shoots would be benefited by wearing glasses. On a bright day an amber glass will help even if a glass with no correction is used. Many who shoot without glasses would be benefited by using them and this may be proved by a visit to an oculist, taking the favorite revolver or pistol along and trying out the various glasses, holding the arm in shooting position. I am of the opinion that the sights will appear clearer and the target will lose that gray, oval appearance. I know several cases where I have corrected sights for well-known target shots that the correction was due to defective eyesight and a slight correction in glasses would aid materially and relieve the eye strain.

Men who are slightly far-sighted will, of course, have trouble in seeing the sights clearly and the sights must be seen clearly or unaccountable shots will be the result. I know the aversion of many people to wearing glasses for they feel that they are getting old, but glasses do not change the birthday and a few added points will mend the wounded feelings. The experiment is well worth trying.

If possible, when the test is made, patronize the optician who is a revolver shot himself. He will know your needs and be able to give an accurate diagnosis of the case. However, if the eyesight is perfect the examination will not be in vain and all glasses are a protection against wind and flying particles of dust. The eyes should be examined twice each year as well as the regular physical examination.

TABLE AND SKETCH OF SLIGHT ERRORS

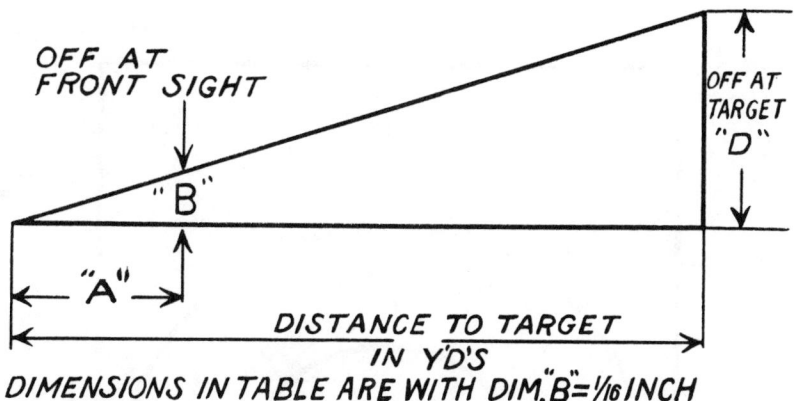

DIMENSIONS IN TABLE ARE WITH DIM. "B" = 1/16 INCH

DISTANCE BETWEEN SIGHTS DIM "A"	DIM. D AT 10 YD'S	DIM. D AT 13 YD'S	DIM. D AT 15 YD'S	DIM. D AT 50 YD'S
5.3 IN.	4.25	5.52	6.37	21.25
8" IN.	2.81	3.66	4.22	14.06

The accompanying diagram is to illustrate the error in accuracy which occurs when the shooter either pulls his revolver sidewise as he pulls the trigger or fires a shot when the sights are 1/16 inch out of line.

If the sights were 1/8 inch out of line, with a pocket revolver which is approximately 5.3 inches between sights, the error would be at 50 yards 42.50 inches.

If the same arm was used and the sights were 1/4 inch out of line, the error at 50 yards would be 85 inches or 7 feet and 1 inch.

    1/64" Divide figures under the distance by 4
    1/32" Divide figures under the distance by 2
    1/8" Multiply figures under the distance by 2
    3/16" Multiply figures under the distance by 3
    1/4" Multiply figures under the distance by 4

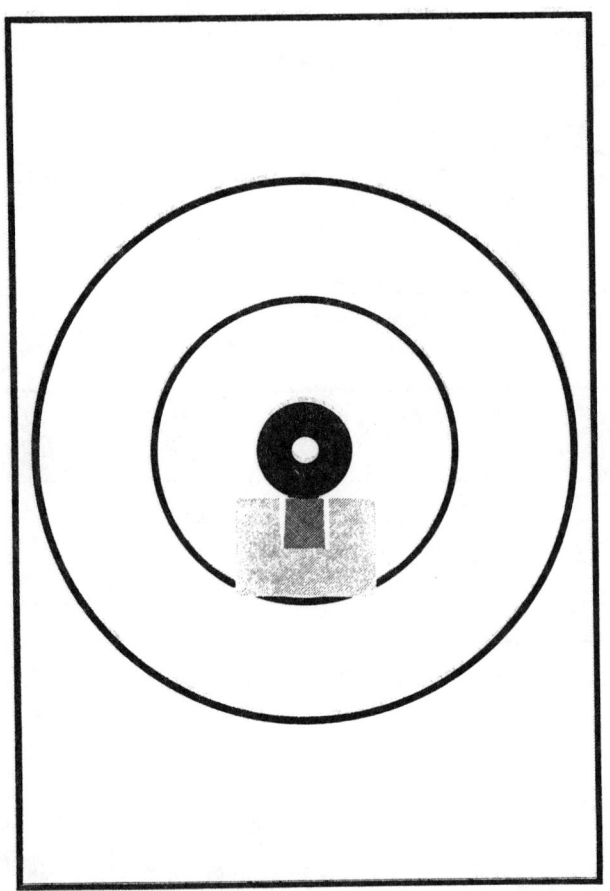

ILLUSTRATION No. 1

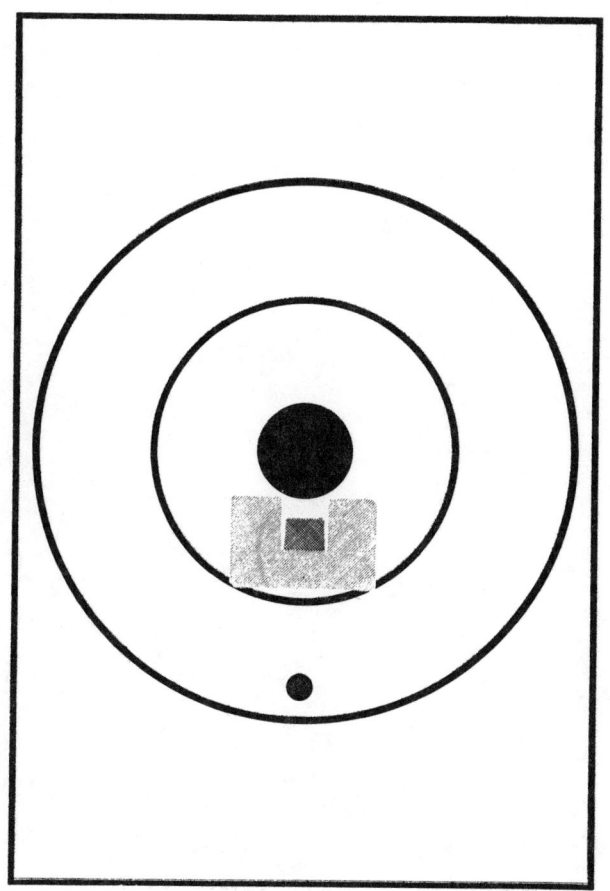

ILLUSTRATION No. 2

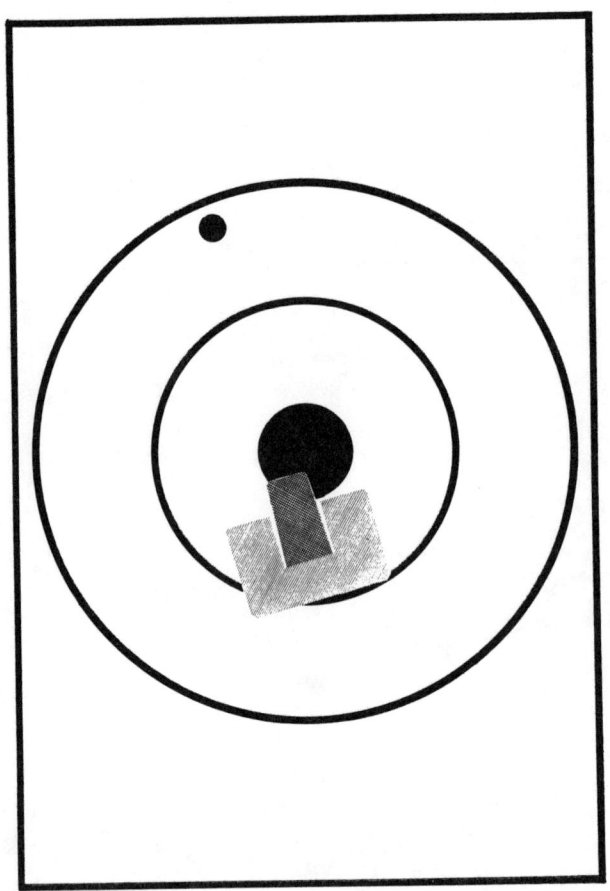

ILLUSTRATION No. 3

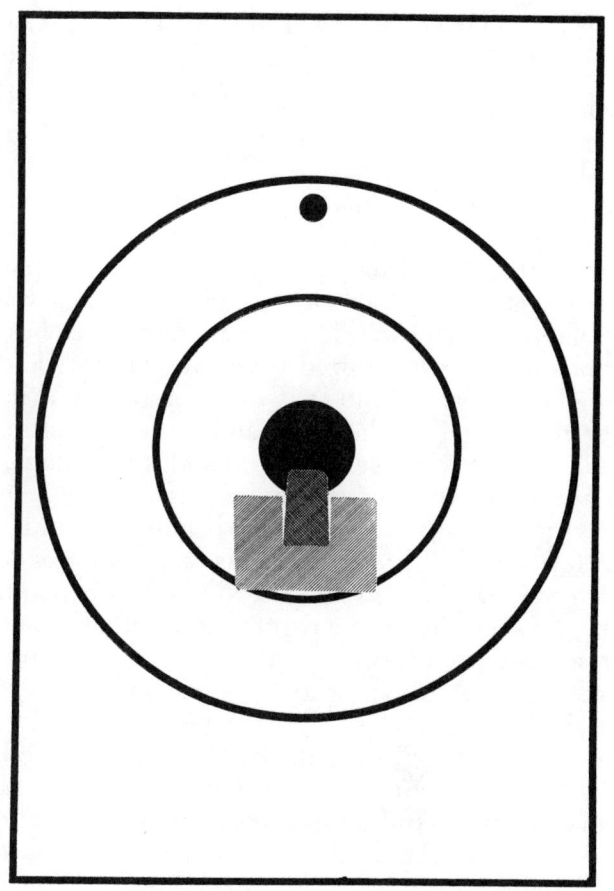

ILLUSTRATION No. 4

SECTION 12

LEFT-HANDED SHOOTING AND AVERAGE SCORES

Much pleasure may be derived by developing the left hand in target shooting. Often the left hand after a reasonable amount of practice will deliver as good scores as the right hand. I have spent many pleasant hours in shooting the right hand against the left, for in my earlier shooting days I had very few shooting companions, for shooting thirty-five or thirty-eight years ago was not as popular as it is now. In some of these matches after thousands of shots were fired there was very little difference in the scores. I find it is easy for the right-handed shooter to change to the left hand, as one position has been worked out to his satisfaction, and it is a simple matter to apply the knowledge acquired with either hand.

I am often asked what scores the beginner should expect after a few weeks of practice. This rests in a great measure with the man himself and the kind of a weapon he has chosen. If shooting on the regulation Standard American target at twenty or fifty yards, with a .22 automatic fired at twenty yards, he should reasonably expect to be in the sixty-seventy class. All scores mentioned in this section are quoted with the understanding that the beginner has at least spent three hours each week in practice, both dry shooting and actual firing, taking extreme care with every shot. With the .38 caliber and same condition he should be in the fifty-sixty class. This is not due to the difference in accuracy of the two weapons but to the difference in recoil and a longer time is required to acquaint oneself with the arm of heavier recoil.

A properly sighted arm will add many points to a fairly good score and I know of no better way than to draw a vertical line through the center of bull's-eye, extending to edges of target, then draw a horizontal line in the same manner. This divides the bull's-eye into four equal parts. Count the number of hits in each quarter of the target and if light conditions and holding are normal the number of hits in each quarter should be nearly equal. Counting twenty or twenty-five targets, if the majority of hits on this number of targets should be in the two o'clock quarter for instance, the sights need a slight correction.

Do not try to correct for windage and high and low shots at the same time. Correct for high or low shots first and, when this is accomplished, correct for windage. The reason for this is that all front sights do not stand exactly straight and the raising or lowering of front sight may slightly change the group to right or left, wherein the rear sight slides on a perfectly level surface and moving it to right or left will not change the group as to height.

The front sight standing to right or left is caused in many cases by dropping the arm and also by sight being bent to right or left by the owner to accommodate some peculiarity of holding or eyesight. It sometimes happens that a revolver or pistol may be handed to several men, who are asked whether the front sight tips to right or left; part of them will see it tipped one way, while the others will see it tipped in the other direction; therefore, each individual should have his sights adjusted in a manner that will allow the front sight to appear perfectly straight to his eyes. Dividing the target as before-mentioned will aid materially in correcting the sights on any revolver or pistol and will show the necessity of a slight correction that otherwise might not be noticed. Of course the tests must be made by a person capable of grouping his shots.

At the end of six months of faithful practice the pistol enthusiast should be averaging on the twenty or twenty-five yard target between eighty and eighty-five, and with the revolver between eighty and eighty-three. The scores between eighty-five and ninety-three will come in time but the man who can average between ninety and ninety-one inside of twelve months can indeed feel that he is progressing rapidly. He must not feel that he is not progressing if after continually shooting at twenty yards his first scores at fifty yards show a decided drop in average. If matches are to be entered at fifty yards, then the practice should be at this distance and the same applies to twenty-yard shooting. If both ranges are to be shot with the same arm without sight correction the arm should be sighted for fifty yards. The average scores with pistol and revolver should show a difference of approximately three points in favor of the pistol.

LEFT-HANDED FIRING POSITION

SECTION 13

HOLDING THE BREATH

No two persons hold the breath in the same manner when they are shooting. That is, the amount of air in the lungs required by one person to attain the steady hold may not be the same as that required by any other person. It depends upon the build and dimensions of the chest cavity.

Holding the breath is unconciously practiced in many walks of life. A lady threading a needle, mechanics when fitting delicate pieces of mechanism, doctors, dentists, surgeons and specialists in different lines of work at times hold the breath for the reason that they have found this practice gives them a steadiness otherwise unattainable. That is why it is necessary to shooters.

To hold the breath properly the shooter should experiment. First, hold the breath with the lungs about three-quarters full, with the arm extended and the hand closed as when holding a revolver. Lay a small level across the thumb and forefinger where the bubble can be seen easily, hold it as still as possible and note the tremor. Then try the same experiment with the lungs half full of air, then one-quarter full and so on until you have determined just how much air is required to give the best results.

The little level is important for another reason. It teaches the beginner to hold his revolver without canting. I have spent many hours in dry shooting holding a revolver to which was attached a small level such as the ones used by rifle shooters years ago. This was placed in front of the rear sight of my Officer's Model, which had a flat top on the frame.

The nerves and muscles of the lungs must be at rest and the breath must not be held too long. It is better to take the arm down, rest and start all over again than to try to fire a shot after the pressure on the lungs due to stale or foul air is noticeable, for a wild shot will be the result.

I have noted the time which elapsed in targeting one hundred revolvers, when the breath must be held for accurate work, as two hours. One hundred revolvers accurately targeted required nine and one-half hours labor and of course the shooter in this work unconciously holds his breath at the proper time.

Tight clothing over the chest will greatly interfere with the proper holding of the breath and if such are worn they should be loosened when shooting, but not to the extent that they will flap in the wind, but feel perfectly comfortable when the shooter determines the correct amount of air required for steady holding.

Practice the same way every time. Holding the breath is one of the many details to be mastered and it is very important. Do not slight one detail or it will interfere with all the rest.

Dry shooting and snapping practice will greatly aid the student in the art of holding the breath properly. Do not tense the muscles of the lungs to hold the breath. Do not release the breath just as the shot is fired; wait until after the recoil. Do not rush upstairs just before commencing to shoot. Rest fifteen minutes before going on the firing line to get the nerves under control and the breathing natural if you wish to get the best results.

The following is an explanation of fundamentals of breathing by Schuyler McCuller Martin, M.D., Troy, New York.

Holding the Breath

The subject of holding the breath represents an important factor in shooting. People from many walks of life have entered the field. The professional man easily grasps the subject because of his familiarity of bodily functions. The remaining classes,—the police officers, clerks, students and many of other walks in life, including the real novice,—are often in a quandary, searching for a true, easily appreciated explanation. To this great class the last paragraph may be sufficient. However, the expert who is ever desirous of knowing the why, is often interested in the technical side of the subject. Therefore both sides have been approached, hoping to meet the demands of all.

It is essential for the expert, as well as the beginner, to have knowledge concerning certain factors that enter into holding the breath. It is hoped the following paragraphs will serve such a purpose.

First: Let us bear in mind the anatomical parts involved in breathing; these in turn are numerous. The thorax (that boney structure of the chest frame) consists of a conical-shaped cavity, formed by the spine, ribs, and breast plate, inside of which lie the lungs, bronchial tubes, and heart. Above these are the trachea (the tube leading the air into the lungs and bronchial tubes); the larynx, or voice box; the pharynx, or back of throat. The glottis and its surrounding parts situated back of tongue act as a cover or protection to the parts below. The nasal passages. Separating the chest cavity from the abdominal cavity, we have that musculomembraneous sheet, the diaphragm, being attached to the spine, lower six ribs, and cartilage at lower end of breastplate. This structure is dome-shaped, with a central tendon attached to the pericardium, or sac, covering the heart. There are also chest, abdominal muscles, and throat muscles.

Second: Let us consider the mechanism of inspiration —an act by which the chest cavity is enlarged in its vertical and transverse diameters by a contraction of the diaphragm being pulled downward toward the abdominal cavity; secondly, by elevation of the ribs through the action of the muscles of breathing. The muscles involved are those attached to the ribs, whose function it is to elevate; those which rotate. The muscles beneath the shoulder blades. Chest muscles attached to the arm and shoulder, against which the rifle shot places his gun butt, and a muscle from the collar bone to tip of a bone located behind ear, known as the mastoid.

Third: We consider the mechanism of expiration—an act diminishing in size the chest or thorax and is performed by forcing the diaphragm upward, through the contraction of the numerous abdominal muscles; secondly, depressing the ribs through action of the internal rib muscles. A muscle attached to the breastplate and the ribs and muscles inside the chest wall. There are also muscles inside the throat that are brought into action.

Breathing as expressed in the preceding paragraphs is divided into inspiration (the act of drawing air into the lungs); expiration (the act of expelling or forcing air out of the lungs). For practical purposes it can be easily understood that there is a rest period between inspiration and expiration, which is called the inactive or normal position of the thorax or chest; at which time there is a minimum of effort or energy exerted and all parts at rest. This, therefore, is the ideal period for the shooter and with little practice can easily be accomplished.

The tense position requires a tremendous amount of energy and mental concentration to hold the various muscles, distracting the shooter's mind from the important features of his sport.

The Author, throughout his volume, in his instruction has advocated the correct position to assume in shooting being that attended by the least amount of effort, natural and relaxed. Likewise, holding the breath is best accomplished by assuming a natural position, completely relax and hold or stop breathing at a point between inspiration and expiration, which will be accompanied by little or no effort; this, in turn, will relieve him of trying to control his body muscles, permitting his full concentration on the acts of aiming, trigger squeeze, and firing.

SECTION 14

TESTING REVOLVERS AND PISTOLS FOR THE TRADE

It sounds like a simple thing to do. Some friend will order a revolver, for instance, an Official Police, with six-inch barrel, check wood stocks and checked trigger, to shoot center when held at six o'clock. They do not make any mention of distance or target to be used, which means that the revolver may be used at twelve, fifteen, twenty, twenty-five and fifty yards.

Fifteen yards is the usual testing distance, using a twenty-yard target. When holding at six o'clock on this target at fifteen yards and the bullets strike in the top half of the ten ring, the arm will shoot high at twenty and twenty-five and fifty yards. To avoid this the arm should be tested to strike just above the point of aim at fifteen yards.

The matter of holding, eyesight, and many other things enter into the perfect targeting of a revolver by one person for another. The method of holding or grip may be different; the thumb pressure due to long or short thumbs and muscular development may vary; the arm may be canted or tipped. The sights may be held with either wide or narrow white line below the bull's-eye, or, in shooter's terms, the bull's-eye may be set on top of sights, no white showing. The trigger squeeze that is perfect for one man may not suit another. The eyesight may be different, and sometimes different brands of ammunition may group in a different place on the target. All of these things enter into the perfect targeting of a revolver with solid sights.

Two shooters, even though they are practically equal in the above-mentioned details, may be shooting a light model such as the Police Positive Special, and the one who has mastered the art of shooting a light arm will shoot center and the one who has not will shoot to the left if he is a right-handed shooter. However, thumb pressure will correct this and possibly a slight change of grip.

Implicit directions for targeting are needed with an arm having stationary sights. They are: Favorite distance for target work; target used; aiming point, whether holding with a white line or touching the black; kind of ammunition used. Of course if the arm has adjustable sights, a change may be made in the sights to correct these troubles after the arm is received by the owner.

If the favorite target distance is fifty yards, then the revolver and pistol should be targeted at fifty yards. If the arm shoots correctly at fifty yards a little allowance can be made for twenty-five, twenty, fifteen and twelve yards. In the stationary-sighted arm the principal correction is for right and left shooting. Great pains are taken to make the arm shoot not more than one-quarter of an inch to right or left of the center of the bull's-eye. This is, of course, for fifteen-yard shooting. If the arm is corrected to shoot in that way at fifteen yards, it will shoot close enough to keep all shots in the ten ring on the different targets and ranges. Right and left shooting may be slightly corrected by turning the barrel in or out and by filing the rear notch on one side.

The right and left shooting disposed of, we have the high and low shots to worry about. As I have mentioned before shooters have different ideas about where to hold. Dr. John L. Bastey of Boston, Massachusetts, will hold center, therefore his front sight must be approximately twelve-thousandths higher than the man who holds at six o'clock. Lieutenant Jacob Saylor, Brooklyn Police Department, will shoot two inches low with a revolver properly sighted for me. Another of my friends with an arm properly sighted for me will collect a fine group of sevens at seven o'clock. To correct this I draw a line from the center of his group through the center of the bull's-eye and as far beyond the center of the bull's-eye as the distance from the center of the group to the center of the bull's-eye, then when I hold at six o'clock and hit the new center located by the line drawn through the bull's-eye he can hold at six o'clock and hit center.

It is very easy to correct an arm that is shooting low and it is well to leave room for a slight correction. If an arm is shooting low, and this cannot be determined with two or three shots, the arm should be shot until you are sure before making the change; file the top of the front sight a very little to make the arm shoot higher. Whenever I have occasion to file a sight for my own use I file it flat for when looking at front sight through rear notch the angle is upward, therefore you can only see the near edge of filed surface. Care must be taken when filing to leave right and left sides of the sight the same height or at least it must look so to the shooter. The top of the front sight must correspond in direction with the sides of the rear sight. The only thing not easily corrected is an arm shooting high, the only remedy is a high front sight.

Not only must revolvers and pistols be tested as to accuracy but they must function properly. The spring must be of proper strength to explode all primers both single and double action. The firing pin indentation must be near the center of the primers and, in fact, every working part must be thoroughly examined before the arm is finally passed.

It is possible that many arms are purchased by shooters throughout the country which shoot high or low, right or left, for him and perhaps it is his fault. I know hundreds of times I have been called upon to try out a revolver or pistol that the owner claimed was inaccurate, and found that the arm was shooting correctly for me. I find that my two partners for the last twelve years, Mr. Edward Kiely and Mr. James Molloy, shoot the same as I do and any arm tested by them I would feel needed no sighting in, before entering a match. This proves to me that many shooters' troubles are due to difference in holding and trigger squeeze.

No revolver or pistol will shoot as accurately when it is new as it will after five to eight hundred shots. This wearing in process is as true of a firearm as of an automobile or any other machine. A lighter spring may be used after an arm is thoroughly broken in. Proper care will lengthen the life of any firearm and proper care in target work will place many more bull's-eyes to your credit.

I have tried to convey to the readers of this section that the life of a small arms targeter and tester is not one continual round of pleasure. It must be remembered that many different models pass through the tester's hand and each model must be held slightly different according to weight, size, and shape. Seventy-five to one hundred small arms per day is all that any tester can pass as being properly targeted. Target arms and those used for police work are targeted offhand. Some smaller models are targeted from an arm rest. This method is used that the tester may rest his arms and be in better condition to shoot offhand the arms used for fine target work. The arm-rest shooting, if properly done, is a very accurate way to test the arms and many times is used to check up on the offhand shooting.

The different kinds of ammunition must also be checked up to see that all the makes are giving equal results as to accuracy and function. Many times it has come to my notice that one make of ammunition was the cause of many misfires or other troubles, and if the other makes function perfectly then ammunition and not the arm is at fault.

I have heard many gun-bugs (as Captain Hardy calls them) say they wished that they had a job with nothing else to do but shoot. After firing, as I am credited with doing, between two and three million shots, I am wondering if these same gun-bugs would still be willing to shoot from ten to twelve hundred aimed shots each day for years. I have found the best system was shooting with both right and left hand, about an equal number with each, and using right eye part of the time and then changing to the left. All kinds of ammunition should be used in the testing and every morning the tester should try one or two targets with his favorite arm to check up on his own shooting before beginning his day's work. If shooting glasses are worn they should be checked up several times each year to keep the eyes as near normal as possible. If the tester does not wear glasses the eyes should be checked up just the same to determine whether glasses are needed. The tester owes it to his public (as they say in Hollywood) to put his best efforts in this work and even then mistakes will happen.

All the above information will help to perfect and place in the hands of the shooter a perfect shooting arm. Of course, we cannot expect the impossible of the hand gun; the small, light models with short barrels could not be expected to do the accurate target work of the heavier target models with long barrels. Fifteen yards would be as far as the lighter, short-barrel arms would make a good target, that is, a two-inch group, but this does not mean that a target the size of a man could not be regularly hit at one hundred yards with the two-inch barrel.

It is best to procure a catalogue from the company manufacturing the arm you wish to purchase, or talk the matter over with your favorite salesman. Improvements are made on the arms from year to year and it is better to have the latest information.

Here is the proper information to send when ordering a firearm: model of arm, length of barrel, caliber, sights desired, trigger pull, checked or plain trigger, checked or plain front and back strap, targeted at what distance, targeted with what target, and what the normal aiming point is.

With this information the average shooter can be suited. If any peculiarity exists, it is best to send to the factory an arm that is properly sighted for the person ordering the new arm and, if possible, a target shot with it. This is a perfect check and the new arm can be furnished to group the same as the old one. Do not feel that all the bullets must pass through one hole when sending a target to the factory for testers miss the black as easily as men on the outside.

A few months ago a .22 Colt Automatic was returned to the factory and handed over to me with the claim that the group was not small enough at twenty yards. The group of ten shots measured one-half inch across and three-quarters inches long (at twenty yards) and on the target was written the following: "Gentlemen: This pistol should make a group no longer than it is wide, which is one-half inch, and I cannot make a better group than the one sent with this arm." My answer to this was: Neither can I.

Great care must be taken by the tester in passing revolvers and pistols, because at the present time thousands of excellent target men and women reside in the United States, and if one revolver or pistol should by chance pass through the target range not properly sighted it would be sure to fall into the hands of an expert, then trouble would be in store for the tester. When such an arm does fall into the hands of an expert he should not blame the manufacturer of the arm, for it is their belief that all arms are leaving the factory properly sighted. The tester alone is to blame if normal conditions exist. However, if at first we don't succeed we can try again, and all mistakes can be corrected if the arm is returned to the testing gallery for correction.

From twelve to twenty-four shots must be fired through each arm to properly test it and furnish a presentable target, for it is as easy for the tester to pull out the fifth shot as it is for the purchaser and the same language is used in both cases. All testers are able to express themselves very forcibly when this occurs.

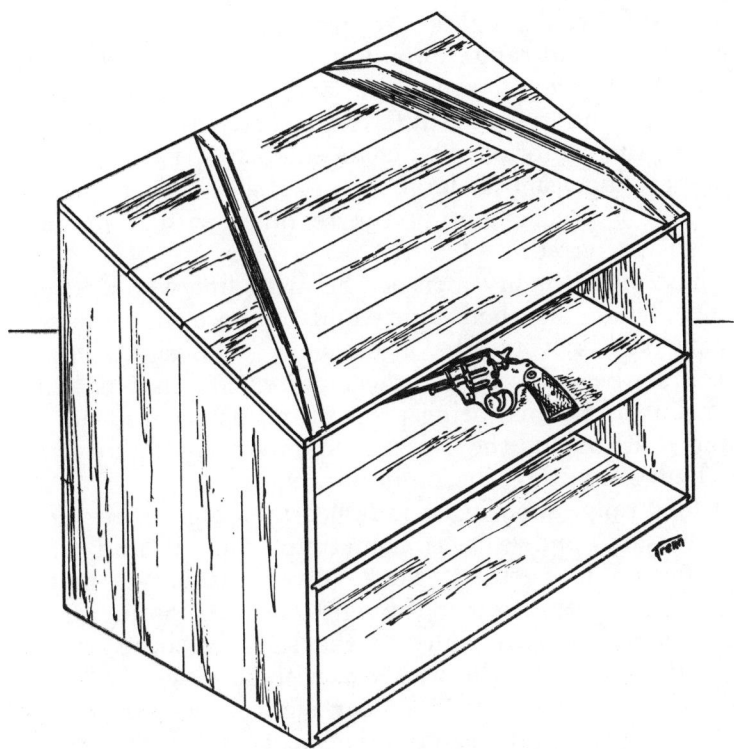

TESTING TABLE FOR ARM REST

SECTION 15
ADJUSTABLE AND STATIONARY SIGHTS

The question which bothers many shooters is whether to purchase a revolver with adjustable or stationary sights. And there is a great deal to be said in favor of both models.

The adjustable sights are preferable for those who wish to use mid-range ammunition or special loads and reload their own ammunition, and for those who wish to change and try out different sights. In a very few minutes the sights may be changed to 1/8, 1/10, or 1/12 inch partridge sights, large or small bead, and gold or ivory. For trick shooting the revolver with adjustable sights is preferred.

I have noted many men on the firing line who are continually changing their sights and to those men the stationary sights would be a blessing. The sights must, of course, be adjusted for the ammunition that is being used, but after once being properly adjusted need not be changed as long as the present sights are satisfactory and no change made in the ammunition.

If long range shooting is indulged in, a higher rear sight is necessary and this is sometimes true if mid-range ammunition is used. If the revolver is shooting to the left move the rear sight to the right; if it is shooting to the right move the rear sight to the left. In other words move the rear sight the way you wish to move the bullet hole in the paper. If the rear sight is adjustable for elevation and windage move the sight to right or left, high or low, as you wish to move the bullet hole on the paper. If the front sight is adjustable for elevation and the arm is shooting low, lower the front sight. If the shots are going high raise the front sight. Move the rear sight the way you wish to move the bullet hole in the paper and move the front sight in the opposite direction from the way you wish to move the bullet hole.

In many matches the adjustable sights are not allowed. The N. R. A. Individual and Team Championship matches at Camp Perry do not allow them. However, the stationary sights are now so well made that the adjustable sights have little, if any, advantage over them. The only change needed is possibly to open out the rear sight to admit more light in the stationary sights.

If an arm has been shooting in the ten ring and on the next trip to the range it should group to the left or right, do not blame the arm and do not blame yourself, until you are sure that the light conditions are not the cause of your trouble. There is no reason for changing sights on a properly sighted arm. It is better to hold to the right or left as the case may be, for with normal conditions (conditions under which the arm was properly sighted) the arm will again shoot center.

If a new arm with stationary sights is purchased which shoots low, it can easily be corrected by filing off the top of the front sight. If it is shooting slightly high this may be corrected by a lower six o'clock hold. If a close six o'clock hold carries the shots out of the nine ring at twelve o'clock, then it is best to return the arm to the factory for correction. Shooting slightly to the right or left may be corrected by filing the rear notch on the side toward which the bullet hole should be moved, but if shooting two or three inches to the right or left the arm should be corrected by the manufacturer.

Proper sights and proper sighting of the side arms are very important for without these the best revolver in the world is useless. We will, of course, always have the difference in eyes to contend with for very few hand gun students require the same sight adjustments.

At the 1927 Camp Perry matches one of my friends asked me to bring a six-inch barrel revolver to the firing line as he wished to purchase a new one. I brought one that I had targeted at the factory and for my eyes was shooting perfectly. My friend took it on the firing line and after three scores returned it to me with the report that it shot too high, all eights at twelve o'clock at twenty-five yards. The revolver lay in my tool box and another friend came along and asked if he could try it. He came back after the trial saying: "Fitz, that revolver shoots just two inches low and if you will file off the top of the front sight to correct this I will take it home." There was a difference of over four inches at twenty-five yards in the shooting of the two men and both were experts. Nothing except the death of a very dear friend will bring such a sad and sorrowful expression to a man's face as to purchase a new arm and find it does not group the shots in the ten ring. Still the arm may be shooting perfectly for the man who targeted it and for many others.

Another thing to take into consideration is whether you are shooting at the same size bull's-eye that the arm was targeted for. Arms targeted at fifteen yards on a twenty-yard target must shoot low at fifteen. The properly targeted six-inch barrel revolver shooting center at twenty yards will, at fifteen yards on the same target, shoot below the center in the bottom half of the black. The revolver sighted correctly for the twenty-yard target at twenty yards will, of course, shoot low at twenty-five yards on the Camp Perry Police target, but will be nearly correct at fifty yards on the Standard American target. Holding with a wide white line at six o'clock or even one inch should not affect the score except in cases where the contestant insists upon holding in the black; world's records have been made by experts who hold in the center of the black. The majority of shooters, however, hold at six o'clock or with a white line.

The one-tenth inch sights are now universally used either in stationary or movable form for fine target shooting. In choosing sights the length of barrel must be considered, as the one-tenth inch front sight on a seven and one-half inch barrel will not look any wider than the one-twelfth inch sight on a four-inch barrel.

Another peculiarity in rear sights is that a perfectly square notch will appear to tip in or narrow at the top and, of course, when the notch is cut with a wheel cutter this condition could not exist. To correct this each side must have a three-degree angle outward which makes the sight, when held in shooting position, appear perfectly square. If the front sight should be slightly tipped to right or left the rear notch should be changed to allow for an even distribution of light on each side of the rear sight, and the top of the front sight should be square with sides of the rear notch. If filing rear notch the end nearest the front sight must be filed wider than the rear end to keep a clear, sharp edge nearest the eye.

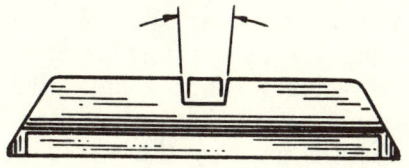

THREE DEGREE ANGLE REAR SIGHT

Many odd forms of sights are used, such as the square rear notch with a bead front sight; the bead front sight filed flat on top and a U rear sight; rear sight without a notch but with a one-thirty second inch piece of platinum or silver imbedded in the steel sight in a perpendicular position; and a bead sight may be used with the entire bead held on top of the white line. All these are very good and are eligible in matches where movable sights are allowed.

Smoking the sight with a miner's lamp or P. J. O'Hare's famous sight black will close up the rear notch and widen out the front slightly, but this will only be noticed in cases where very little light appears when gun is held in shooting position. It greatly aids the shooting accuracy in the bright sunlight. Paper matches and some of the wooden ones may be used to black the sights, but many of the imported matches will rust the sights. Some of the sights now furnished on revolvers and pistols are sand-blasted or roughened and this is an aid to fine shooting in a strong light.

In the days of the powder and ball arms and later in the days of the old Peace Maker the sights all seemed to run to the knife edge variety, and while we read of the wonderful shooting done with these arms I believe that some of the stories were slightly exaggerated. They did not have arms to compare with the ones we have today. The range of our modern revolvers is three times greater than the old powder and ball revolver and accuracy has increased in proportion. I am not going into the description of old and modern revolvers for these have been thoroughly described by Major Hatcher in his book, "Pistols and Revolvers"; but I have met many of the Western gun-toters of the old school and the West did develop the fastest men in the world with side arms because they found it necessary to be excellent shots if they wished to live to enjoy old age.

I find in revolver sights as in Lyman rifle sights that the eye will naturally center the sight, allowing the same amount of light on each side, and I am a great believer in plenty of light. I use the one-eighth rear sight with the one-tenth inch front sight, which combination in smoky ranges is far clearer than the close sight; even when shooting at shells and small objects it is just as accurate.

Years ago at Camp Perry I used to take along about three hundred wide (one-tenth and one-eighth) sights for the contestants and use them all. Then I commenced to open out the rear notch and found that this would answer the requirements of seventy-five per cent of the shooters. This refers to the .45 automatic, which is generally used there, and due to the shortness of this arm the regular front sight is fifty-eight thousandths of an inch. Plenty of light is preferred by many of the experts, especially in rapid fire.

While on the subject of sights I may mention that my observation in many years of testing revolvers has taught me that, though ninety per cent of the target men are satisfied with the way arms are sighted, the other ten per cent could only be satisfied on the first trial by sending to the tester one of their favorite arms, sighted properly for their eyes, then the sight could be corrected on the new arm.

It is best to send a target with the arm submitted showing group and point of aim. Arms shooting right or left, high or low, may be corrected in the same way. If arm is not submitted when another is purchased, the only way is to shoot the new arm as it is received, and return target and arm for correction. Very few corrections are made on the arms of expert shots.

I sometimes have a revolver handed to me as inaccurate, in other words, shooting all over the target. I look at the gun to be sure that I have not been handed one of those smooth bore shotgun pistols and then ask to see the target, for a glance at the bullet holes will place the trouble. If the bullet holes are perfect and the man is shooting standard ammunition the trouble is with him. The sights may be wrong, but the high grade revolver or pistol will group with correct ammunition and sights can easily be corrected.

I wonder how many of the shooters ever study the bullet holes made by their favorite arm. I remember several years ago two pistols were shown me,—one with one turn in sixteen inches, the other with one turn in fourteen inches. They were .22 caliber guns, using two hundred-yard ammunition. I left the room while both pistols were fired at fifty yards and on my return I could easily pick out the bullet holes made by each pistol. The holes made by the fourteen-inch twist were perfectly round and showed the perfect rotation of the bullet, and the bullet holes made by the arm with the sixteen-inch twist were ragged, not as clear cut, and showed a slight tippage. The correct twist for hand guns chambered for the present .22 caliber ammunition is fourteen inches.

If bullet holes are watched closely many interesting things may be noted. A new arm will not always make the perfect holes in the target that it will after fifty or one hundred shots. The bullet in flight may be compared to a top, a slight stagger as it leaves the muzzle, then after a few feet settling down to a steady flight and again the stagger as it reaches the end of its flight.

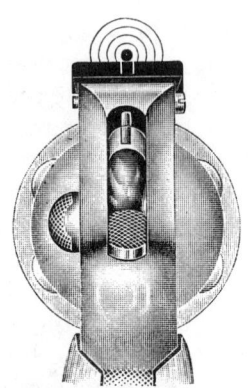

PROPER METHOD OF SIGHTING
FOR A 6 O'CLOCK HOLD

SECTION 16
GRIP MATERIAL AND CHECKING

I believe many of my readers will be interested in a discussion on the different materials used in the manufacture of revolver and pistol grips, also the checking of front and back straps, and the value of each in different branches of small arms shooting.

The rubber grips, for many years furnished as standard equipment on the hand gun, are now being replaced on many of the arms by the more popular checked wood grip. This is a great improvement and an aid to the shooter who wishes the last word in revolver or pistol grips. The rubber grips through use become smooth and slippery and if the hands perspire it is almost impossible to hold a revolver or pistol with worn rubber grips. If the arm is dropped a rubber grip will usually break and will sometimes break from the jar of a fired shot. I have also seen many rubber grips on the larger arms warped in a manner to allow dust and lint to enter the action.

The sport model grips made of pearl, both plain and engraved, are beautiful if the arm is to be placed in a collection or used for stage work. However, they are cold and slippery even when engraved and this type of grip is very brittle. It will not stand the rough usage to which some arms are submitted. Pearl cannot be checked properly and if checked at all must be cleaned or brushed frequently as dirt will accumulate in checking, destroying the luster of the pearl.

Aluminum has been tried and, while it may be checked, it is little used for it discolors the hands and clothing. Bakelite has also been tried and this may be made in plain or variegated colors; it will also stand checking, the only trouble being its tendency to warp, allowing dirt to enter the action. Fiber has also been tried, but the same trouble was found as with the bakelite.

Ivory has been extensively used in the manufacture of grips, especially for presentation pieces. It may be procured in many beautiful designs,—carved steers' heads, American eagles, gold inlaid work, the American flag, and many others, which become more attractive as they yellow with age. Walrus, hippo, elephant, and many other kinds of ivory are used, but they cannot be properly checked, and will sometimes crack from use or if made into grips before it is aged.

Sometimes ivory stocks are fashioned to form a groove or depression for each finger and the thumb, which tends to prevent slippage. Many plain wood grips are fashioned in the same manner with a thumb rest on the side, as on the Tell pistol, and the bottom of the grips fashioned to form a rest for the little finger and bottom of the hand. This type of grip is made for either left or right hand but will not interchange.

Grips are also made from buck horns, deer horns, moose and elk horns. If the natural or outside roughness of these horns is preserved they are attractive and have the natural checking or roughness to prevent slipping, which makes them very satisfactory.

The latest metal that may be used on fancy arms is Durigold. It looks like yellow gold and is a little heavier than aluminum. It may be checked and has a very rich appearance. The price is not high enough to prohibit it for this use.

Grips are, of course, fashioned from other materials besides those mentioned, but for actual service, whether for target, hunting, trick shooting, or police work, the roughly checked wood grip stands alone as the all-around perfect grip. If the checking is too rough on a pair of stocks a piece of sandpaper will quickly change it to the desired roughness.

The back and front strap on a revolver or pistol, by this I mean the metal frame at front and back of grip, may be finely or coarsely checked. This is a distinct advantage if any kind of a grip is used, except a coarse checked wood grip, and even with them it is an advantage, because with both grips and straps checked the arm can be lightly gripped without the arm changing position as each shot is fired. The properly or roughly checked grips, that is, all that comes in contact with the hand, will eliminate the need of many specially constructed grips now being used and the checked front and back strap will aid in this.

Plastic wood may be used to change the present form of grips. It may be used to build up behind the trigger guard the much-talked-of gadget, or it may be used on any part of the grips or straps. It is not a thing of beauty when the grips are so changed, but it will make any addition which the shooter requires. Some of these changes are all in the back of a shooter's head, but if he thinks they help, they do help. Plastic wood properly used will not fall off and has a roughness almost equal to checking. The little finger under the bottom of the grip tends to prevent slippage and depressions may be cut or filed in grip to keep the finger in the same position at all times.

Sometimes weights are added to the bottom of the grips screwed to the frame and in other cases the inside of the frame is filed away to lighten the weight of the entire grip. Both of these will change the balance of the entire arm.

My old friend, Max Wendlandt, of the Detroit Police Department, uses a revolver to instruct those who would crush the grip, equipped with steel brads one-eighth inch long covering nearly the entire surface of the grips on right and left side. I think that this is the finest instrument for this purpose that I have ever seen. I call it "The Silent Persuader." It would be of great help if the same idea could be carried out on the outside of the thumb to instruct in the application of proper thumb pressure.

SECTION 17

THE AUTOMATIC PISTOL

While the revolver and single shot pistols are very popular with both police and target shooters the automatic pistols are a very close second, and if we may judge by Camp Perry enthusiasts the .45 Colt Government model and the .22 Colt automatic are the peers of all hand guns. You will see the .45 in matches against the finest of target revolvers and the .22 automatic winning against the single shot pistols. This is not an occasional happening, but a regular thing which eliminates all chance of accidental high scores.

In 1919 at Caldwell, New Jersey, the .45 automatic came into its own. In the earlier years of its existence the comments and criticisms were these: sights not being attached to the barrel, short distance between sights, slide loose on receiver, trigger pull not right, etc. These all retarded its popularity, but only for a short time. A few shots from a properly sighted .45 automatic will convince the most sceptical that it is a wonderful arm and very accurate, extremely so if fitted with the .45 Colt Match Barrel. These barrels were first used in 1919 and after months of experimenting at the Colt factory. I took forty of these match barrels to the National Shoot that year and the records made at this shoot convinced the most doubting that the .45 automatic equaled any of the large caliber side arms in existence.

As to the sights not being attached to the barrel, the scores made from year to year are all I need mention to disprove this claim, but I will further state that the barrel and slide comes back to the same position each time. The function of the gun is the same, provided the ammunition is of even pressure and the bullets of normal size. A slide which is slightly loose on the receiver does not mean that the arm is not accurate. It is more accurate than a slide which is too tight to work freely. It comes back to the same place in the same way every time. The trigger pull is very easily remedied; government requirements call for a six to seven and one-half pound pull, but at Camp Perry a pull of four pounds or over may be used. This means a change in every arm used and I believe that a four and one-half pound pull will suit nearly all the shooters. It is very easy to make this change if the parts have not been put through the third degree by some enterprising soul. My advice to shooters is this: Unless you know the duty performed by each part and why it is there, do not try to adjust the arm yourself; send it to the factory.

The sear should never be worked on, the hammer only should be changed, and the angle of the notch on this should never be changed. I do not believe in a stone and use only a fine file for the work, allowing the parts to smooth themselves as they slide over each other. An automatic is different from the revolver in regard to pull. The revolver hammer is drawn back by hand with very little jar, while the automatic hammer is carried backward at the same speed as the slide and must also resist the jar of the slide as it reaches its forward position.

A great many times I adjust a trigger pull and some time afterward the same arm is brought to me with the complaint that the pull did not stand up and that the hammer follows or falls to a half-cocked position. Usually this is caused by cocking and snapping the empty pistol and sometimes by putting the thumb of the other hand behind the hammer as the trigger is pulled. If this sport is indulged in for a short time the hammer will follow as the slide closes.

The correct way to try out the .45 automatic after the trigger pull has been corrected is to fire twenty-five or fifty shots through it. In this way the edge of the sear will fall into the bottom of the hammer notch and will make its own seat as the arm is fired. The sear must fall into the notch and not on the middle of a smooth surface or a creep will be the result. The weight of the pull must be the force required to pull the sear out of the notch and the sear must come clean without sliding on the top of the notch. In other words, the force required to start the sear must throw it over the top of the notch, therefore, when the hammer is drawn back slowly without the forward action and jar of the slide the sear is not properly seating itself in the notch. After a little use on the firing line the arm may be used for dry shooting with little if any damage to the pull and when a revolver or automatic pistol is working properly my advice is to shoot it and to try to improve yourself instead of the gun.

.45 COLT'S GOVERNMENT AUTOMATIC

One point in favor of the .45 automatic is that you may have an old, much abused arm that has been through the war, with a rusted barrel and other troubles, but clean it up, fit a match barrel, correct the pull, fit the modern sights which cannot be jarred loose by firing, and you have a fine target arm at a small expense for overhauling. It is not necessary to have the arm re-blued as this does not improve the shooting. The heart of the .45 automatic is the barrel. With a good barrel you can correct everything else on the pistol, but without a good barrel you will never be satisfied with your scores. I have never seen a .45 automatic that would not shoot if properly corrected.

That echo of war days "They jam" is due more to the carelessness of the owner than it is to any fault with the pistol. It is true that the care and time spent on the war-time pistols cannot be compared to the exacting methods employed on the present-day .45 automatics, but even the war-time product in the hands of a man who knew how to use it gave very little trouble. A rusty chamber would cause a jam then and it will today in the very latest pistol which has been allowed to become rusty. I remember an instance in 1920 when a pistol was shown to me by a veteran of the World War and he told me that he been over the top eight times and that he had never seen a .45 automatic that did not jam. I loaned him mine to try and after seven shots he handed it back and told me the gun

.22 WOODSMAN AUTOMATIC

was like all the rest. I discovered the trouble was that the slide remained open after the last shot as it should do in all well-behaved .45 Government automatics. When I told him my deductions he told me that he had never heard of such a thing. Trouble is bound to develop where any man is handed a machine of any kind that he does not understand. Very little trouble is encountered from the .45 automatic if the owner has a working knowledge of the arm and keeps the barrel and chamber clean.

And now the .45 automatic's little brother, the .22 Colt automatic. Due to the fact that the bullet is seated in the barrel the .22 automatic is more accurate than any .22 caliber revolver. It is rifled for the two hundred yard ammunition, one twist in fourteen inches, a special chamber with the bullet resting on the lands in the barrel, which is the last word in .22 caliber accuracy.

Due to the shape and hang of the automatic pistols, to get the best work out of them stick to them and do very little work with the revolvers. This same rule applies to revolvers when working to perfect yourself with them. Both are very different and require careful study. I have seen expert revolver men pick up the .45 automatic on the day of the big match or a few days before and try to accustom themselves to it but that seldom works out satisfactorily.

This section is not written with the hope of turning some man who loves revolvers toward automatics. But

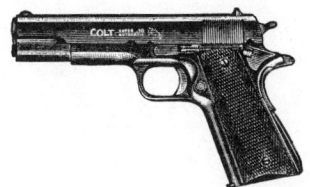

.38 SUPER COLT'S AUTOMATIC

in case he should enter a match in which either the .22 or .45 automatic pistol is also shot and he comes out second best, he should not feel that he has been beaten by an inferior arm in the hands of a far better shot; he has been beaten by a slightly better man with an arm that is just as accurate as his favorite revolver.

While on the subject of automatic pistols we must not forget the recent addition to the automatic family, the .38 Super Colt. This model is worthy of the consideration of every one interested in small arms shooting. It equals the .45 automatic as to accuracy at twenty-five or fifty yards and surpasses it in accuracy at the longer ranges. I believe that many who are annoyed by the heavy recoil of the .45 automatic will be pleasantly surprised with lighter recoil of the .38 Super Colt. At the same time it delivers a heavier blow than the larger caliber arm and at a greater distance. Due to the sturdy construction of this arm and modern .38 automatic ammunition, this pistol is in a class by itself for hunting or target shooting and answers every requirement.

SECTION 18
SHOOTING HISTORY

A boy of ten years of age strolled into his father's office and for want of something better to do proceeded to look over the big desk in the corner. After several compartments had been overhauled with neither gold or jewels as a reward, a pasteboard box was opened for inspection and inside it lay a beautiful ivory-handled, silver-plated, and engraved revolver, .22 caliber. Even at this age the youngster knew what it was for and how to shoot it (not hitting anything, of course). The box of cigars which was first thought of as a possible way to spend the rest of the day was pushed aside for the new find. What to do? First, to slip the treasure into the pocket (they put real pockets into the trousers of ten-year-old boys in those days), then another hunt for cartridges. Finally a box of .22 caliber short cartridges was found and the shooting equipment was complete.

Looking as innocent as possible the youngster strolled out of the store to hunt up a tin can, which was not hard to find, and then to get about four miles away from any houses. The can was placed on a low stump at a distance of fifteen feet and the youngster was ready for business. After several minutes spent in inspecting the revolver it was pointed as accurately as possible at the can.

As the gun was fired another boy jumped out of the bushes at one side of the stump, and the bullet had gone through his big toe instead of the can. While no monument was erected, that shot created more trouble for a certain young man than the first shot in the Civil War. On arriving home the culprit was disarmed and sent to bed.

The next morning when he asked what had become of the revolver a large tub of water was pointed to as the resting place of his newly acquired friend. When no one was looking the youngster got the bright idea of getting possession of the revolver and as an old-fashioned auger lay in sight the use of this seemed the easiest way. So a hole was bored near the bottom of said tub, but the revolver was not found. If shooting a boy in the big toe caused a disturbance, boring a hole in that brand new tub caused a riot. Several months were spent in the search for the revolver, and after a while he found it. For the next few months all the boy's spending money went for ammunition and then he told the owner of the gun how well he could shoot.

The demonstration that he gave of his shooting ability impressed no one, but he had learned to be careful and was allowed to keep the gun.

After months of labor the boy decided that the gun was at fault and he saved his pennies until enough wealth was accumulated to purchase a single shot pistol and then the fun began. He found that even with this pistol only a few holes could be found on the target a foot square with hand-painted bull's-eye three inches in diameter shot at twenty yards. The youngster then conceived the idea of getting closer to the target and walked up to five yards; at this distance things began to happen and by close study of the pistol the bullet holes were nearly all in the bull's-eye. Fifteen feet is a short distance, but it taught the youngster what he wanted to know and gradually increasing the distance one yard at a time, spending time enough at each range to eliminate wild shots, the fifteen-yard mark was reached. Several weeks were spent shooting at this range, all the time trying to extend the distance, but even one or two yards caused a decided drop in the scores. It was then decided that the pistol was too light, it was a Single Shot with six-inch barrel; so two heavier pistols with ten-inch barrels were purchased. From this time on all pistols or revolvers were bought in pairs and shot with right and left hand. With the new pistol and much perseverance twenty yards was reached and the scores ranged from sixty-five to seventy-five on the twenty-yard target.

For several years this pistol occupied every spare moment of the youngster's time and then came the rifle age. All the popular rifles then on the market from 1891 to 1910 were tried in all calibers and finally discarded for the revolver and pistol. Even the bicycle then coming into popular favor only held the interest of the young man for a few seasons, and that only for the reason that the money won in races bought perfectly good revolvers and pistols.

Both rifles and bicycle were laid aside for the hand gun and about this time the young man became interested in police instruction. Several dashes of cold water were applied to this, because at this time the use of a revolver by police departments was not as necessary as it is today.

The real pleasure of shooting was not attained by the young man until quick draw and rapid-fire work was added to the regular target practice. Reloading was the next step and at one time fifteen reloading sets for different cartridges adorned the workbench.

Then, looking for more worlds to conquer, the arms were taken apart and the mechanism studied. As the young man was mechanically inclined he would take a part out of the pistol or revolver and make a part by hand to replace it. This was a very fascinating addition to the already overcrowded pastime and from this practice came the idea of correcting trigger pulls and other ailments to which a hand gun is susceptible.

For lack of contestants the young man would shoot with right and left hand. A pair of revolvers of each model were used for this purpose and marked right or left, all the scores being kept. A few medals and prizes were added to the collection, but it must be here stated that revolver and pistol matches were not so plentiful as they are today.

The work of adjusting trigger pulls and sights, and general repair work, due to the young man's natural love for mechanics, will probably follow him to his grave. About 1897, in connection with a study of mechanism and inner workings of firearms, came, through an accident, the study of bullets fired from the same and different firearms. While on the range one day a bullet was picked up that had been fired from the .45 Single Action Colt revolver. The lines which showed plainly on the surface was enough to arouse the young man's curiosity and after a hunt and much digging several other bullets were found. A microscope was purchased and the bullets examined and placed in two groups as having different markings. The pair of .45 Single Actions was then shot and the bullets caught in cotton waste and compared with the two lots previously found. The bullets matched perfectly and he could tell from any bullet found on the range which one of the revolvers it came from.

After this discovery many weeks and months were spent in the study of land and groove marks and also in the study of primer identification and shells. Thousands of experiments were performed, rifles, revolvers, and automatic pistols were shot, and bullets, shells, and primers compared. The effect of bullets on wood, glass, stone, metal, flesh and skin of animals, direction of bullets, powder stains, the distance at which black and smokeless powder will be discernable on an object, the effect of a contact shot, the comparisons of bullets of different manufacture, and many other valuable results were studied. This work was not easy for no books were obtainable and the study of this subject was practically unknown. Other microscopes were obtained and the subject was studied until it was an absolute fact that bullets, which retained a certain per cent of the land and groove marks or identification marks, could positively be identified as coming from a certain revolver or pistol if that arm could be found.

At least one hundred and fifty thousand experiments have been performed by this confirmed gun crank and years of experience in this work has made the comparison, which then took hours or days to complete, only a matter of minutes.

At this time in the story the man mentioned feels a great deal like the Frenchman who was carrying a bear back to camp. To quote his words: "I take those barr an' start for camp; I start cross a stream on log; By Gar! 'bout halfway cross I think I fall, I hear a splash, I look 'round and it's me." And so the foregoing history tells you of my early shooting days.

From the old home I went to Boston and spent many pleasant years with the Iver-Johnson Sporting Goods Company in the revolver department. I was also shooting master of the Boston Rifle and Revolver Club. Twelve and one-half years after leaving Boston I again visited the club, and it was a pleasure to meet twenty-eight of the old members gathered again who had belonged to the club when I went away, and to see that the club was still going strong. As I mentioned in the club section, many lifelong friends are made on the shooting range and in my case this has proved to be true,—not only in Boston, but on the ranges all over the United States.

My love for the hand guns and their construction led me from Boston to the Colt's Patent Fire Arms Manufacturing Company in Hartford, Connecticut, and in the testing room or shooting gallery of that company I spent nearly thirteen years. This work in connection with expert testimony, my connection as instructor with the police departments in the United States and Canada, and unlimited experiments with firearms have made these years pass like that many pleasant hours.

The ladies also enjoy target shooting, and some of my most enjoyable hours on the range have been spent with my wife and niece, who enjoy punching holes in the target as well as I do. The variety of arms which are favorites with them are all the models and calibers that I use, from .22 to .45 caliber, including the automatic pistols.

MISS MILDRED HARKER, BALTIMORE, MD.
An Expert with Rifle, Revolver and Pistol

MRS. J. H. FITZGERALD
Firing Position

MISS GUSSIE L. KENYON
Firing Position

MISS ARLAYNE BROWN, ST. LOUIS, MO.
An Expert with Rifle, Revolver and Pistol

SECTION 19
THE REVOLVER CLUB

A revolver club is usually started by two or three men who are shooting enthusiasts and who wish to get their friends interested in the sport. They realize, of course, if they start a small club it means larger quarters and better equipment. It means competition and a larger circle of friends.

A very prosperous club may be started with twenty-five members and if one of the twenty-five owns a large cellar or garret it helps to lower the range expenses. If necessary fifty members can be induced to belong to the club and this is enough to cover the expenses of a good revolver range, the cost of dues being governed by the expense of procuring a suitable range.

If twenty-five members are planned for, then at least three targets should be available. If fifty members are planned for, six targets should be installed. This would mean a room about twelve feet wide and seventy-five feet long for three targets, and about twenty-two feet wide and seventy-five feet long for six targets. If rifle shooting is to be part of the club with a twenty-five yard range, then at least eighty-five feet will be needed to allow for backstop firing point, prone benches, etc.

A lounging room really is necessary in every range, otherwise the conversation and noise will interfere with the shooters. If the lounging room is to be behind the firing point, then the range will need to be more than seventy-five feet long, or, if it is to be on the side, then that much space must be added to the width of the range.

With a suitable range location in sight, the first step is to call a meeting of every one in the locality who would possibly be interested in pistol and revolver shooting. It is easy to secure the use of a hall, lodge room or possibly the armory for the first meeting. Then, through the founders of the club or some one imported for the occasion, sell to those present the idea of a pistol and revolver club for get-together shooting. Banks, sporting goods stores, and, in fact, every company or organization that has money or property to protect, should become interested in the proposition, and by all means the police should be invited to join the club. Interest local newspapers in the work. They can, and will, gladly help and will reach people who otherwise might never become interested.

While the audience is in a receptive mood it is well to collect the names of those who wish to become members. Many of them who have no intention of shooting, will join to help the cause along and often become enthusiastic members.

The case should be stated clearly: the range site in view, the expense of installing fixtures, rent, the number of targets planned for, the number of members planned for, dues based on that number, and the fact that the club will be incorporated. It is best to have two range sites and two lists of range equipment ready, then submit both, allowing the prospective members to vote on them. It is better to start a club on a small scale than never to start at all.

The range income is derived from dues, sale of targets, income from matches and sale of lead and shells. If lockers are purchased or built they will net a substantial revenue. Novelty matches will also meet with approval and bring in revenue.

One popular source of revenue would be club medals. They are: Marksman, Sharpshooter, and Expert. For example: ten scores of seventy-five or better may be exchanged for a Marksman's Medal. Ten scores of eighty-five or better may be exchanged for a Sharpshooter's Medal, and ten scores of ninety-two or better for Expert Medal. Targets should be witnessed by an officer of the club and the medals may be made of bronze for Marksman, bronze and silver for Sharpshooter, and silver for Expert. A gold medal may be given for ten scores of ninety-five or better. These medals may be purchased at a price that will, at ten cents per target, give the club a fair profit.

It will be necessary to elect officers for the club. A president, vice-president, secretary, treasurer, and shooting master are the usual ones. It is well to have a board of directors of which the officers are members.

When the club has reached the stage of incorporation a set of by-laws should be adopted and a club name decided upon. The N. R. A. By-Laws may be adopted or changed to suit the requirements of the club.

I may here cite what I consider the record in forming a club. I arrived in Muncie, Indiana, on a night that police and citizens were to form a revolver club. The city officials were deeply interested, especially the chief of police. The prime factor in this project was Mr. Harry C. Almy, vice-president and treasurer of the Delaware County National Bank. In less than twenty-four hours a club was started with one hundred and forty-five members enrolled. They now have indoor and outdoor ranges and the club is still growing. Mr. Almy is one of the best informed men on target and protective shooting in the country and if his ideas were followed we would have flourishing clubs in every city and town.

As in all other clubs and gatherings it rests with the officials of the club whether it will be a success or not. A pleasant word, a little encouragement here and there, will always help make new members and visitors feel at home. In one club of which I was a member for some years, the officers voted to appoint a reception committee to entertain visitors and new members. I made a motion that every member of the club be appointed on that committee, and I think the scheme was a success.

Fancy equipment in the club will not make the members better shots. Inexpensive equipment and plenty of practice will give better results.

Saint Louis Indoor Police Range

The new indoor range used by Saint Louis Police Department is one of the finest in the United States. In addition to the eight firing points it has two moving targets. They are placed in position at the firing point and as wheel is turned they travel along the left-hand wall to the target line; they may then be moved across the target line at any speed desired (about twenty-four feet) and to a horizontal position against right wall of the range. This is excellent practice for the police or any one who wishes to hit moving objects as targets. The carriers hold two targets and may be moved in either direction at will.

The twenty-yard target used is divided by fine lines into twelve sections, each line extending from center of target to the position of the figures on the face of a clock, and are so numbered. This is an aid to the contestants, as they can then see clearly whether the arm is grouping to right or left, high or low. It is true that one can do this on any target, but it is brought more clearly to the shooter's attention if the lines are used.

The design, material, and workmanship of this range are a credit to any city as are also the classrooms and offices. An up-to-date loading department is also installed and this modern equipment, in connection with last word in police training by Lieutenant Nick Bausch and his assistants, will perfect policemen in the performance of their duty in a few weeks and impart information to them that would take them years of actual police duty to acquire.

FIRING POINT, ST. LOUIS INDOOR RANGE
Capt. Nick Bosch at the Table

ST. LOUIS INDOOR POLICE RANGE
Arrangement of Targets at Backstop

SECTION 20

RANGES AND TARGETS

Many successful revolver clubs have started in some one's cellar. Cellars are usually twelve or thirteen yards long and targets may be procured for the twelve-yard distance. The twelve-yard Standard American target may be used for slow-fire shooting and for those who wish to practice for the twenty or fifty yard ranges. For those who wish to practice for rapid-fire shooting the twelve and one-half yard Colt's police target may be used for slow, rapid, and timed fire.

The first requirement for all indoor ranges is a suitable backstop, side wall, and other protectors. Captain Arthur D. Caswell, Anoka, Minnesota, will explain this protection in his article, "The Indoor Revolver Gallery," in the back of this section. Captain Caswell furnishes the best equipment obtainable for revolver and rifle ranges and is an expert in the installation of safe ranges.

If the indoor range can be so planned as to have the floor timbers run across the line of fire it will eliminate steel plate overhead except the first ten feet at the firing point. If the firearms are carefully handled one of the Caswell Portable Galleries can be used, with no other protection.

The favorite arms for cellar ranges are: The .22 single shot pistol, .22 automatic pistol, .22 official police, and .22 officer's model. Due to noise and annoyance to the neighbors the .22 caliber arms are universally used in cellar ranges. Many enjoyable evenings may be spent in a range of this kind and at the present time so many sportsmen are fitting their basements into a den that I believe they would find a little range placed in one corner a very welcome and enjoyable addition.

Mr. J. Allen Van Wie of Troy, New York, showed me a round bullet catcher twelve inches in diameter and after seeing him perform with it at a distance of thirteen yards I was satisfied that he had taken all necessary precautions against wild shots. I would not recommend this size of backstop for all dens, but I have seen many that were perfectly safe for the average revolver enthusiast. I have visited many cellar ranges and have yet to be told that the range was taken down because no one cared to use it.

If the indoor range is to be used by police officers, guards, and bank clerks, they will demand practical experience in rapid fire work and here the Langrish Limbless target and Colt Silhouette target can be used. As a money-getter for a club the Fitz Luck target is a wonder. Turkeys, chickens, or other merchandise may be shot for with a big profit and every one has an even chance to win no matter what his shooting experience has been. The .22 Luck target is more popular than the .38 target as it can be used for high and low count to win. The target for .38 caliber or larger arms should be shot at twenty yards if low and high scores are to be counted for a good shot may pick the low numbers at the edge of target at fifteen yards or less. The .22 target may be used at any distance between ten and twenty-five yards.

We have also the matter of telescopes. It is desirable in every range for the shooter to see where his shots are going and thereby make corrections. A small stand may be purchased to hold the scope in line with the target or the stand may be attached to the wall. A twenty or twenty-five power scope is recommended for this work. A telescope is very necessary at all distances over twelve yards as the shooter should check up on every shot fired at slow fire, first naming the shot to himself and then checking with the scope. Great care must be taken not to look through the scope for a longer period than is necessary, for the eyes will become distorted and blurred, which will make the sights and bull's-eye indistinct. Three to five seconds will do very little harm, but three to five minutes will be very liable to cause the above result.

In some ranges the very serious trouble is ventilation. After a few shots the smoke will so fill the range that neither sights nor target may be seen clearly. In many cases windows covered by baffle plate may be opened to clear the range and when windows are not available a blower may be installed connecting with the outside or with a chimney. If a ventilator is to be installed it should be placed, if possible, about eight feet ahead of the firing line. This, however, is seldom necessary for I have visited several large ranges where a great deal of shooting was indulged in and the only ventilation was windows, doors, or a connection with a chimney.

Range rules and *Safety* rules displayed in the range will assist both new and old members. I am forever preaching safety and this is due to the many accidents I have seen on different ranges and the careless handling of firearms which might have resulted in an accident. For instance, twenty-five years ago at Walnut Hill Range about twenty-five members stood around talking when one of the men raised his pistol, which he was holding, and said: "See that knot in the board; if this pistol was loaded I would hit it plumb center." He aimed and pulled the trigger and did just what he said he would do, but he did not know when he aimed at the knot that the pistol was loaded. Another near accident was at the Boston Rifle and Revolver Club range. I was teaching a lady to shoot and one of my instructions was to lay down the revolver on the shelf every time she left the firing point or when I was changing targets. She asked me to change targets and I stepped up to the firing point. I could not see the revolver and looked in her direction.

The revolver was aimed at my hip and cocked, not intentionally, but just through carelessness. I jumped backward just in time. The bullet went through coat and vest, flattened on my belt buckle and out through the coat and vest on the other side. At another time I was sitting at the range desk when one of the men at the firing point turned to tell me that he had a misfire. As he turned with the gun in his hand the explosion occurred and the bullet put two holes in a new hat I was wearing. In addition to these close shaves I have had one bullet hole in each leg, part of a little finger shot away and one shot through my face; therefore, I shall continue to talk on safety.

I have suggested that the police be urged to join the revolver club as this arrangement creates a friendship between citizens and police that is lasting and very beneficial to both parties. In this manner the police have a fair idea as to the citizens who should be eligible for a permit to carry arms, and the citizens have a clearer idea of the many trials and tribulations of the policeman.

Outdoor Ranges

In connection with the indoor ranges every club should have an outdoor range. This need not be an elaborate affair for some piece of ground can be found with a natural backstop adaptable to the needs of a revolver club. As fifty yards is the greatest distance that a revolver or pistol is used, unless small bore and long distance rifle shooting are to be used on the same range, a suitable place can be found which may be reached from any small city or town. Of course the larger the town the more miles to be covered, unless some military range can be used.

The natural backstop should be at least thirty to fifty feet high and even at this height care must be taken that stray shots do not get over the top as the revolver and pistols at this angle would carry from twelve to sixteen hundred yards. With a natural backstop the only thing necessary is two uprights and cross pieces at proper distance to hold the targets at shoulder height. If possible a table or bench should be in front of the shooters at both twenty-five and fifty yards to eliminate accidents and to lay the outfit upon. Some of the most enjoyable days of my shooting career have been spent on just such a range.

It is best for those who desire to enter in matches on other ranges to choose a range that is not sheltered, as it is those who are accustomed to shooting in the wind and to the light changes who will give the best account of themselves when they go to other ranges.

If a range can be found with pleasant surroundings the entire family would enjoy it as much as the confirmed gun-bug. The lunch basket, the range, the family,—what could be finer?

For the little club which wants a more elaborate and up-to-date range, pits may be dug and target frames erected, which means that the pit must be either lined with heavy planks or, better still, made from cement at least two feet thick and banked with earth and cement so that no bullet can possibly penetrate to the pit. On ranges where there is no range master stationed, it is well to equip pits with heavy waterproof covers if possible. Make pits roomy enough for extra targets, target frames, pasters, paste, spotters, etc., setting target frames at rear of pit; in this way the markers can see where the shots strike without pulling down the targets.

A range house is a welcome addition to any range, preferably with a porch and a few chairs and tables. A stove and dishes may be added, as hot coffee and lunches will be very acceptable to the members and such lunches may be paid for out of the entry fees. Heavy shutters and a heavy door, with a still heavier lock, should be added in some localities as a shooting house is always the special mark of the small boys. Thus we find we have a complete range with practically no outlay of money.

The Toledo (Ohio) Police Range, which is, I believe, the peer of all outdoor revolver ranges, was made possible through the untiring efforts of Lieutenant Charles Hennessy, Inspector Delehanty, and officials of the Toledo Police Department. It is one of the finest revolver ranges that I have ever visited. As will be noted in the photographs the natural backstop was missing and a heavy cement wall was used instead. I take great pleasure in showing views of this range as I feel that it will stimulate interest in other clubs and police departments throughout the country. This range was planned and built entirely by members of the department.

While in nearly all cases a safe range may be found within a reasonable distance, the occasion may arise to install a range where artificial safety devices are to be used: At firing line, a partition or wall seven feet high with stalls three feet wide for each shooter, the partition or wall to be filled with fine sand fifteen inches thick; a window through this and steel plate in the form of a tube small enough at the end next to the target to deflect all bullets that would not hit some part of the target or backstop, but it is rarely necessary to take this trouble. It is advisable to have one firing line for all distances whether shooting at twenty-five or fifty yards and two target frames or pits for each distance; this is to avoid accidents and for the benefit of the spectators.

Telescopes and stands are necessary and also a few folding chairs. Many ranges pleasantly situated call for a week-end camping party which the family can enjoy.

A site must be chosen that is suitable for both fifty and twenty-five yard ranges, for the man who wishes to make good scores at all the ranges must practice at all ranges and with the different arms required for the various matches. The man who only shoots twenty and twenty-five yards will be lost the first time he enters a fifty-yard match without practice, for his score will not be satisfactory. If all distances are to be shot with one revolver, it is recommended that it be accurately targeted for fifty yards and it will then, with a slight change in holding, be correct for the other ranges.

Fitz Range Rules for Safe Target Practice

1. NEVER handle, point, or look over the sights of any firearms handed to you without first opening the arm to be sure it is NOT loaded. You are being tried and your standing with other shooters depends on this one action.
2. NEVER take an automatic pistol or revolver out of your pocket or holster until you are at the firing line. If you wish to unload your revolver or pistol before it is your turn to shoot, step up to the firing line, unload, and show the arm to the instructor swinging cylinder out. If an automatic pistol is used, draw slide back, fasten it, and remove magazine.
3. NEVER glance into your pistol or revolver hurriedly and decide it is NOT LOADED. LOOK ONCE to see that it is NOT LOADED—LOOK AGAIN to be sure you haven't made a mistake.
4. NEVER load or cock a pistol or revolver in any range unless you are at the FIRING POINT and FACING the target.
5. NEVER lower a pistol or revolver so that it will point toward any part of the body. This is liable to happen when you are resting and between shots. When resting, lay the pistol or revolver on the table or bench if one is in front of you; if not, rest it in the other hand ALWAYS pointing toward the target.

6. NEVER turn around and talk to persons behind you when at the firing point without first laying your pistol or revolver on the table.
7. NEVER leave the firing point with your AUTOMATIC until you have drawn the slide back and fastened it, leaving pistol OPEN. Remove the magazine from your pistol.
8. NEVER leave the firing point with a revolver without swinging the cylinder out or removing same from pistol.
9. NEVER point the pistol or revolver upward or backward over the shoulder; by so doing you are making all parts of the range unsafe.
10. NEVER, in case of misfire, open the pistol or revolver for at least twenty seconds and keep it pointed toward the target.
11. NEVER try fancy shooting or quick-draw work in the presence of your friends until you have first tried it in private and know what you can do.
12. NEVER point a pistol or revolver at any one or anything you do not want to shoot.
13. NEVER fire a shot until you know your sights are in line with the target. You are only wasting your time and ammunition if you do not take pains with every shot.
14. NEVER talk to a shooter when he is at the firing point; wait until he has finished and steps away.

The Indoor Revolver Gallery
By Captain Arthur D. Caswell

There are many things to consider in the construction of even the most simple type of indoor revolver gallery; perhaps the most important item to be considered is its safety. The revolver, due to its short barrel and great power, must be handled with extreme care at all times. We cannot expect the novice to be able to manipulate the revolver as safely as the well-schooled expert, but he must be taught at some time and we cannot expect him to confine his practice entirely to an empty revolver. It is our duty, therefore, to see that he is fully instructed in the use, care, and manipulation of the revolver, and it is further our duty to see that our indoor galleries are so constructed as to insure the maximum amount of practical safety. In addition, it is always wise to have an experienced range officer on duty at the gallery at all times to see that safety regulations are strictly adhered to.

One of the first things to consider is the adaptability of the room which has been chosen for the indoor revolver gallery. Are the side walls, ceilings, and floors of the proper material to stop or deflect a bullet? If not, we must make them so. Usually the cheapest method of making the gallery bullet-proof is by the installation of steel plates, if the building is of wood construction. If the gallery is to be planned in conjunction with an entirely new structure it is advisable to see that all walls, floors, and ceilings are made up of concrete or, in case of the walls, only brick may be used. In no case should tile be used, as it will not stop even the .22 caliber long rifle bullet. For side wall and ceiling protection a light steel plate from $\frac{1}{8}$ inch to $\frac{3}{16}$ inch is normally used. Plates of this thickness will not withstand continual firing of the heavy caliber cartridges and for the main bullet stops it is customary to use not less than $\frac{1}{4}$ inch steel plates and in many cases it is preferable to use either the $\frac{5}{16}$ inch or $\frac{3}{8}$ inch thickness. For heavy caliber firing these should be set at an angle of 45° with the floor, while if only the .22 caliber cartridge is to be used the angle could be 60°.

In many cases we find that the only room available for the revolver gallery is a very narrow one, which we find is bad for heavy caliber firing for reason of the accompanying sharp report of the revolver. We can eliminate the objectionable report of the revolver if we can afford to install sheets of sound-proofing celotex or other material which will absorb the sound. Usually this is a very expensive item and oftentimes the lack of sufficient funds places this material beyond the reach of the average club. To offset this disadvantage the shooters may use for the main part .22 caliber revolvers or reduced charges in their service revolvers.

Where we find concrete or steel columns close to the firing points which would deflect a stray bullet back toward the shooter, it is a good idea to place a steel plate in front of the column or beam in such a manner as to deflect the bullet fragments toward the butts. In any case where it would be impractical to use the steel plate, oftentimes it is more simple to cover same with a 2-inch plank. These items should be considered because beginners are likely to do many things which will endanger other shooters as well as themselves, and a little careful thought may oftentimes save a serious or, at the least, an unpleasant accident.

The space alloted for the shooter's firing position should not be less than three feet and to enable a coach sufficient room we need at least three and one-half feet. Even four feet is none too much space for the shooter's position, and where this space is available it would be wise to use it. We find many types of firing points in different parts of the country. In some sections the open type is used, which is usually safe enough if skilled shooters only are to use the gallery. For police galleries where we are likely to have many new men firing at one time the closed or protected type of firing point is the most popular. Usually the closed type firing point or booth is made up of steel plates on either side covered with wood to further prevent bullet fragments from accidental shots from injuring the shooters within the booth or within the adjoining one. The steel plate used for this purpose is usually two to two and one-half feet wide by seven feet high and $\frac{3}{16}$ inch thick. The wood covering may be ordinary dressed and matched lumber or even a good grade of flooring depending on the amount of money which is to be spent for this part of the gallery.

The present standard revolver galleries in use today are the 10, 12, 12½, 15, 20, 25 and 50 yard ranges. The 50-yard gallery is usually out of the question, as the cost of a gallery of this length is not warranted from the practical standpoint. The 25-yard gallery is fast becoming a popular range for police and military shooters. The entire army qualification may be fired indoors in a revolver gallery of this length, and the police departments are able to start the new men out at the 12½-yard or mid-range with the preliminary firing, later changing to the 25-yard range, which is normally considered sufficient for any practical police firing. The 25-yard range enables the police officers to train at home for the police matches held at the National Matches each year, using the identical target and range. The 25-yard gallery has the advantage of being correct for the 75-foot rifle firing and, if the carrier is of the proper type rifle and revolver, firing may be conducted conveniently in the same gallery. The 20-yard range is the one adopted by the United States Revolver Association and all of their indoor matches must be fired at this distance. The target adapted to this range is of such size and proportions as to render high scores possible only by the expert and the firing is usually of a different type than that normally approved by police and military men.

In some galleries the mid-range firing is conducted at a point in front of the long range firing line and either a movable bench is carried forward or else secondary booths are installed and the carriers are operated by reaching overhead and pulling the puller cord instead of the hand wheel. If this arrangement is used strict discipline is necessary at all times to insure that no one handles a firearm of any nature in rear of the shooters. Again it is questionable whether this arrangement insures sufficient safety when many new men are to be instructed. In no case should any one ever be allowed to snap a firearm in rear of the firing point of any gallery or range, as many serious accidents have resulted from this practice.

Usually the first part of the gallery to be installed should be the bullet stop as all measurements are more or less vague until it is actually in place. There are many ways of supporting the steel plates of the main bullet stop and possibly the simplest method, where the room is not too wide, is by the use of an angle iron supported at each side wall. The plates may then be laid on top, lapped and bolted, provided the span between the bottom support and the angle iron at the top is not too great. If this span is too great or additional stiffness is desired steel tee irons may be placed from the floor to the angle iron, then the plates are laid on the tee irons and bolted securely to same. The bolts should be $5/16$ inch and spaced at about eighteen-inch centers. The use of an angle iron at the top further prevents bullet fragments from chipping the ceiling if properly placed.

In many cases club members will prefer to use wood beams instead of steel members for reason that they are more easily procured and perhaps more easily installed due to the usual lack of steel working tools. In any case it is desirable to use plenty of bolts and supports, as the more stiffness the plates have the longer life they will have as steel deflecting plates. Remember that for heavy caliber revolver firing the plates should not be less than $1/4$ inch thick and preferably $5/16$ inch or $3/8$ inch thick and set at an angle of 45° with the floor. At each side for at least a distance of fifteen inches down from the deflecting plates a light plate should be installed of about $\frac{3}{16}$ inch steel to prevent wear of the side walls by the fragments of bullets.

Oftentimes the steel plates may be supported from the rear wall by rods connected to the top of the steel plates and either securely fastened into the rear wall or inserted entirely through the wall and anchored to metal or wood braces on the backside of the wall. In very narrow galleries the plates have been supported by pieces of ½-inch pipe securely inserted in the side walls and continuing from the bottom to the top of the plates at intervals of about eighteen inches. The pipes project into the gallery only a couple of inches, which is sufficient to support the plates. When this method is used the plate is usually about $\frac{3}{8}$ inch thick to give the proper rigidity.

The height of the bullet stops usually varies considerably but it is advisable to have them start at the floor and continue to a height of at least seven feet and if funds are available it is nice to have the plates continue to the ceiling. In many galleries we find that the bullet stop is completely covered with wood or beaver-board. Usually the use of wood is not necessary and is rather expensive to keep in proper condition, so we find that beaver-board will prevent the fragments of bullets from being thrown forward, at the same time giving a background which may easily be painted to suit desires and it is also cheaply and easily replaced.

At the base of the bullet stop it is imperative that we have a good bed of clean screened sand to catch the bullet fragments, preventing them from being thrown back at the shooters. This bed of sand should be at least a foot deep and can be even deeper to advantage. In some galleries we find that special bullet-catcher chambers are in use, but the cost of these plates bent to catch the fragments is so great that it renders same prohibitive. The simplest method to safely catch the fragments is by the use of sand and it is doubtful whether the cost of the bullet-catcher chambers are warranted for large, permanent galleries.

For the modern gallery we have come to a point where we consider the target carrier an absolute necessity for safety and efficiency. It is one of the best guards against accidents and furnishes a convenient means of further speeding up the fire, thereby enabling a greater number of shooters to fire a given number of shots in a limited time. When we consider a target carrier system we should consider one which is easily operated, simple, and of extremely durable construction. The use of a carrier which does not work freely oftentimes upsets the shooter to such a degree that it impairs his scores. It should be simple, otherwise there is a possibility of its becoming easily placed out of order either by improper operation or by superfluous parts. It should be durable especially when the heavy caliber revolver is used, otherwise a poorly directed shot may easily place the carrier out of order.

The carrier should also eliminate any objectionable vibration when the target is in the firing position and should not be affected by the movement of other carriers or it will prevent the other shooters from bringing in their targets from time to time for inspection of replacement. The carrier should also be adaptable to any type of indoor target and should be so designed as to be practicable for all positions of rifle and pistol shooting without the use of a shooting table. An indoor gallery should not be limited to the sole use of either the rifle or revolver but should be adaptable to the use of both types of arms.

Oftentimes considerable trouble is experienced in properly stretching the trolley wire for the target carrier track. In the past the tension of the wire was applied by the use of eye-bolts. This method, while practicable under some conditions, usually was not entirely satisfactory for reason that the wire could not be stretched sufficiently taut. Really the most satisfactory method of stretching the trolley wire is by the use of the telephone man's "Come-along" or a device consisting of two slack-off blocks, two tackle blocks, and about twenty feet of $\frac{3}{8}$-inch rope. Usually the "Come-along" will have to be borrowed from the local telephone company, as it is not carried as stock in the average electric shop or hardware store.

When the "Come-along" is used to stretch wire the eye-bolts are only taken up sufficiently to insure that they will properly stand the tension exerted by the wire. This will later permit a means of tightening the wire after the gallery has been in use some time. It is apparent that the uprights and carrier supports should be installed in a most rigid manner to prevent unnecessary movement, which results in making the trolley wire slack.

We find that the target illumination is another stumbling block and is a problem in itself. Some shooters feel that they must have an extremely intense light, while others can shoot under a very mild light condition. It is normally well not to have the target illumination too intense as it causes target glare and also a strain on the shooter's eyesight, which results in headaches and poor scores, especially if many shots are to be fired. It is practically impossible to please the desires of every shooter and we must therefore work along compromising lines.

In some sections of the country the large enclosed type of flood-lighting fixture, using either the 500 or 1000 watt lamp, has proven satisfactory. With this fixture it is imperative that the lens be of the stippled or diffusing type as the clear glass lens gives a very unsatisfactory type of target illumination. Target illumination should ample, yet it should be mild in quality, as a sharp light is very tiresome to the eyes.

Recently the window type of floodlight has been used with satisfactory results. This is an inexpensive type of fixture using a 200 or 300 watt lamp. The fixture is of the open type and does not use a glass lens. It is also equipped with a strap iron bracket which is adjustable, making it very simple to install by the novice.

In conjunction with the target illumination we find that the painting of the bullet-stop and near-by background has considerable bearing on the uniformity and the quality of the light. In rifle galleries and in some revolver galleries it has been found that a soft, white background adds considerably to the proper target illumination. Usually a little yellow is mixed with the white paint and it is further imperative the paint used be a flat paint; a gloss paint will in practically every case give a most unsatisfactory result. In police galleries we often find that a flat black paint is favored for reason that it assists the shooter to concentrate on the contrasting white target, which means that he will be able to deliver quick fire with greater speed. Oftentimes, however, a white target against a black background will present a glaring object to aim at due to the great contrast.

Every revolver gallery should have a bench or shelf just in front of the firing point so that the shooter may place his cartridges in a convenient location and may also rest his revolver on it when resting between the firing. It is also desirable to have a container at each position in order that the empty cartridge cases may be placed therein immediately after firing each string. This will help to keep the gallery clean and neat, which further attracts the right class of shooters.

In general the gallery should be as convenient and attractive as possible and so arranged as to present a comfortable and orderly appearance at all times. There should be no obscure corners for the accumulation of dirt; in fact, every possible effort should be made to see that the gallery is spotlessly clean. An untidy gallery is a sad reflection on the range officer and the organization to which the gallery belongs. Clean, orderly galleries inspire the right kind of efficiency and discipline, which is a good start towards a wide-awake organization.

If possible arrangements should be made for a cleaning bench and shelves for target and ammunition storage. If possible it is also a nice thing to have a room for reading and lounging purposes. This room should be handy to the gallery, but not so arranged as to interefere with the men firing. In this room cards showing the range rules, grip and sighting charts, and other data pertaining to the development of marksmanship, should be displayed on the walls in such a manner as to enable the men waiting for their turn to fire to refresh their memories on these important items. Oftentimes high score targets are displayed to further encourage the right sort of shooting.

After the gallery is an actual reality every effort should be made to keep it in the best possible condition. Do not permit any careless firing or improper handling of firearms and last, but not the least, make full use of your gallery. Keep it in use as much as possible and remember that it is a means of permitting revolver practice under the most favorable conditions, day or night, rain or shine.

THE NEW TARGET PASTER

TARGET PASTERS

With styles continually changing in other necessities why not change the 1850 model target pasters? Advantage claimed for Fitz model paster is curved side, which corresponds to curve of 25 or 50 yard target, preserving the original curve of bull's-eye for clearer vision.

—AUTHOR.

BACKSTOP AND LIEUT. CHARLES HENNESSEY
Instructor Toledo Outdoor Police Department

SIDE VIEW—TOLEDO OUTDOOR POLICE RANGE

CLUB HOUSE. TOLEDO OUTDOOR POLICE RANGE

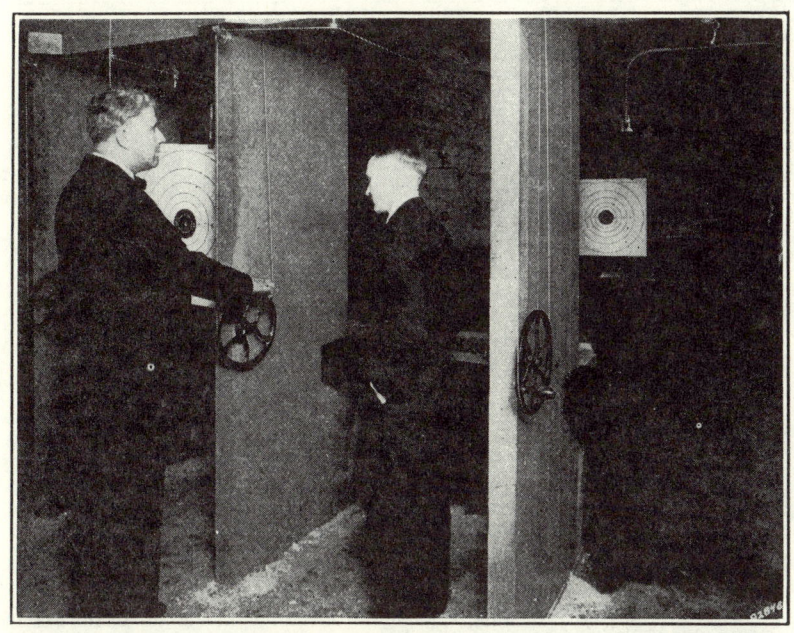

OPERATING TARGET CARRIER

Chief of Police Harry C. Lindholm (Minneapolis) operating the target carrier. Captain Arthur D. Caswell, the inventor, at the right. Note empty cartridge containers placed on wall of each booth.

A Caswell Installation

A CLOSE-UP AT THE BUTTS

Showing the target carriers locked into position eliminating vibration. Note that all pulley wheels are ball-bearing and that the target-holder extensions may be changed easily, adapting the carrier to any standard indoor target.

A Caswell Installation

FIRING POINT AT BOSTON INDOOR POLICE RANGE
Left to right: Desmond, Seibolt, Capt. Louis E. Lutz, Kavanaugh, Vail

A Caswell Installation

SECTION 21

QUESTION DEPARTMENT

BARRELS AND CYLINDERS

Q. Is it necessary to have the inside of the barrel measure to a thousandth of an inch of the dimensions set down by certain manufacturers and gun cranks?

A. It is not, as target pistols and revolvers in nearly all cases use lead bullets and a thousandth or two would make no noticeable difference in the groups as the bullets would still be large enough to seal the barrel against the escape of gas around the bullet.

Q. Is a taper barrel that is one-thousandth smaller at the muzzle than at the breech more accurate than a cylinder or straight bore?

A. Yes; a slight taper in the barrel is of great assistance to fine shooting, as in this manner the bullet is tight at all points from breech to muzzle in its passage through the barrel.

Q. Does a deformed or damaged muzzle cause inaccuracy?

A. Yes; it will sometimes cause the bullets to keyhole and group in a different place and enlarge the original size of the group.

Q. How about chamfer at breech of barrel?

A. I have experimented with thousands of barrels to determine this point and find that a normal chamfer does not affect the accuracy. Starting with no chamfer at all and gradually increasing one-thousandth at a time until one-eighth inch was reached, I found one-sixteenth inch chamfer the most satisfactory of all and a slight variation one way or the other from this measurement made no difference in accuracy.

Q. Does imperfect alignment of cylinder and barrel affect accuracy?

A. Yes; if cylinder and barrel are not in line the arm is inaccurate, the bullets will be thrown out of balance, sometimes a part of the bullet will be shaved off and may cause a keyhole in the target.

Q. Why is a slight chamfer at breech of barrel an advantage?

A. As the bullet leaves the shell it is floating in what is called a gas envelope without the guidance of lands and grooves and is only corrected and started on its true flight when it reaches the barrel. The slight chamfer eliminates any shaving of lead due to chamber being slightly larger than top of lands and tends to press the lead into the bullet instead of shaving it off.

Q. Does clearance between cylinder and barrel affect the accuracy?

A. Yes; if it is in excess of the normal distance, three to five thousandths, the clearance must be greater in the .22 caliber revolvers than in the larger calibers due to Lesmok powder, which will bank up on end of cylinder and barrel causing the arm to jam if it is not wiped off after every forty or fifty shots. There is no advantage in a distance under three-thousandths between cylinder and barrel because, due to collection of powder residue on end of cylinder and barrel, one-half of that distance will be closed.

Q. Should the cylinder be held tight by the mechanism at instant of explosion?

A. Yes; it should be held tight and absolutely in line with the barrel.

Q. Should high velocity ammunition be used in revolvers?

A. No; the rifling or twist is not made to handle it and it is not as accurate as the regular load.

Q. Why do revolver manufacturers not guarantee their arms with high velocity ammunition?
A. Because high velocity may mean anything. Revolvers will stand charges well in excess of the regular loads but they will not stand pressures only fit for rifles. Revolvers will stand pressures up to twenty thousand pounds but will not stand pressures of thirty thousand pounds or more. It would not be practical if they did, and due to the excessive recoil would not be pleasant to shoot, and longer range ammunition for revolver than that now on the market would be useless due to short distance between sights.
Q. What is the cause of a ring or swelled barrel?
A. The arms were fired with an obstruction in the barrel.
Q. Is it a help to the accuracy if lands should finish at muzzle at just six and twelve o'clock, or top and bottom?
A. No; the position of lands and grooves at muzzle make no difference in accuracy.
Q. If by an excessive load a cylinder and frame should be blown up would the shooter be injured?
A. No; not one chance in ten thousand of his being injured.
Q. Which is the most accurate, a barrel with right or left twist?
A. The direction of twist would make no difference in the accuracy.
Q. What is the reason for a revolver spitting small particles of lead and powder between cylinder and barrel, sometimes striking the shooter next in line?
A. The reason is not enough chamfer in the rear of barrel to catch the flying particles of powder and particles of lead if the edge of barrel should overlap the bore of

cylinder due to cylinder and barrel not being in line. The tendency of powder gases and particles of burning powder is to spread and the end of barrel must be slightly larger than end of cylinder to catch these flying particles.

Q. Will a slightly rusted or pitted barrel shoot accurately?

A. Yes; a barrel may be slightly rusted or pitted and still shoot accurately if it is not rusted at the muzzle.

Q. Is it necessary that lands and grooves should be exactly .0035 deep for extreme accuracy?

A. No; a slight variation would not affect the accuracy.

Q. What is the correct head space between head of shell and recoil plate and frame?

A. Just enough to clear with all makes of ammunition.

Q. Why are some shells loose in the chambers of a revolver?

A. Because there is a variation in the size of shells made by the different ammunition companies and the chambers of the revolver must be made large enough to hold them all.

Q. Does this slight looseness affect the accuracy?

A. No; it does not. As the explosion occurs the shell, being lighter than the bullet, starts backward until it seats against the recoil plate, expanding to the full size of the chamber as it moves and sealing backward flow of gas; then the bullet starts forward, guided by forward end of cylinder; as pressure decreases the shell will return to nearly normal size and can be easily extracted if elasticity still remains in the shell.

Q. Would it increase the accuracy of the pistol or revolver to polish inside of barrel until all marks and scratches disappear?

A. No; I have tried this many times, first shooting the barrel in the original state and again after polishing, and the best groups were made by the barrel in the original state.

Q. What is the shooting life of a barrel?
A. With metal case bullets in the .45 automatic the barrel is very accurate for five thousand shots, and with lead bullets the barrel is very accurate for one hundred thousand shots if properly cared for and muzzle undamaged.

Q. Will any barrel become wrung or swelled in one part if the arm is not fired with an obstruction, such as another bullet (due to weak cartridge) or some obstacle which nearly fills the barrel cavity?
A. No.

Sights

Q. What are the sights on a revolver or pistol used for?
A. The sights on a revolver or pistol are used as a guide by which the arm may be properly pointed or aimed at a certain point.

Q. Are revolvers and pistol sights corrected to place the bullets at the point aimed at?
A. No; the sights are usually corrected to hold at six o'clock on the bottom of the black in target shooting. The bullet to strike center or one to four inches above line of sight as the size of the black and distance may determine. A few shooters hold center and in these cases the sights are corrected to place the bullet at the point where sights line up on the target.

Q. If arm is shooting to the left, how may sights be changed to correct?
A. Move rear sight to the right or front sight to the left.

Q. If arm is shooting to the right, how may sights be changed to correct?
A. Move rear sight to left or front sight to right.

Q. If arm is shooting low, how may sights be changed to correct?
A. A higher rear sight or a lower front sight.
Q. If arm is shooting high, how may sights be changed to correct?
A. A higher front sight or a lower rear sight.
Q. Why are sights of different heights on the several models of revolvers?
A. The weight of the arm, the cartridge used, length of barrel, etc., all help to determine the height of sight. The lighter arms using the same cartridge as the heavier arms will require a higher front sight or a lower rear. The .32/20, .38/40 and .44/40 will require a lower front sight due to the slow burning powder used. Each model requires a different height of sight and this can only be determined by actual shooting; when this height is decided upon, the arms are so manufactured. One hundred arms of any one model should be shot and an average taken from the heights obtained after sights have been corrected.
Q. What is the correct amount of light to be seen at each side of front sight when the arm is in shooting position?
A. This must be determined by the shooter, as some men require more light around the front sight than others.
Q. Can all men shoot accurately an arm which has been properly sighted by an expert?
A. No; what a happy little world this would be if they could. Eyesight, method of holding, grip, trigger squeeze, and whether arm is tipped to right or left all enter into this grouping of shots in a different place.
Q. Will the bright sun in different parts of the horizon affect the grouping of shots in the bull's-eye?

A. Yes; the group will always drift toward the bright side. If shooting from north to south and sun should be in the east the shots would group toward nine o'clock. If sun should be in the west the group would be toward three o'clock. If sun is directly behind the shooter and shining brightly on target and sights the clearer vision will usually call for a group high in the bull's-eye. If on a dull, cloudy day when sights and target are not so clear it is customary to use a wider white line below the bull's-eye and a lower group will be the result. If the sun is shining in the shooter's face with the target dark, the group will be low in the bull's-eye.

Frame

The function of the frame of a revolver is to hold each piece of mechanism in place, to form a handle or grip by which the arm may be held when shooting, and to hold the barrel in line with cylinder assisted by the crane upon which the cylinder is mounted. Also to hold the rear sight. The most satisfactory frame is formed from a drop-forging hardened to the proper degree to withstand a pressure far in excess of that developed by the ammunition used in the different arms and also to withstand any amount of abuse. Target shooters, of course, do not drop or abuse their revolvers, but with the police this is different; anything may happen to a police revolver and this must be taken into consideration when the frame is made. The proper alignment of holes for hammer and trigger pins and all points which assist in holding the parts or mechanism of the revolver must be correct. The trigger guard is also part of the frame whose function is to protect the trigger, act as a guide for the finger, and to prevent accidents. How this may be used to advantage in police work may be found under the head of "Disarming a Criminal."

Q. What is the life of a good revolver?
A. A good revolver properly used will last a lifetime with very little repairs or overhauling. I have one that has been fired nearly two hundred thousand shots and it is still hitting on all six and has never been overhauled. However, to obtain the latest improvements in sights, frame, etc., and new appearance as to blueing, it is advisable to purchase new arms every eight to ten years.
Q. Will a revolver held in a vise shoot accurately?
A. No.
Q. Will a revolver held in a machine rest group the shots where the sights indicate or line up?
A. No; the shots will group from a good machine rest but I have never seen one that would group the shots in the bull's-eye with sights pointed as in off-hand shooting.
Q. Can an arm rest be used in the proper sighting of a revolver or pistol?
A. Yes; if properly made and both arms used, holding the revolver as in two-hand shooting and no part of the hands touching the rest. An inclined shelf that arms may rest on comfortably from standing or sitting position with a brace outside each arm to rest the arms against along the entire length of the forearm and about three inches high, a padded rest for side of head to get the eye behind the sights in the same position every time, will assist in rest shooting. Do the same thing the same way every time; care must be taken that rest shooting is not indulged in to the extent of injuring the off-hand scores.

CARTRIDGES

Q. What is the most accurate center-fire revolver cartridge?

A.. The .38 Colt Special and S. & W. Special cartridges. The Colt Special cartridge will cut a slightly larger hole in the target due to the flat nose of the bullet.

Q. What is the most powerful revolver cartridge?

A. The .45 Colt cartridge, forty grains, black powder; velocity, nine hundred ten feet per second; striking force, four hundred sixty pounds.

Q. What is the most accurate revolver cartridge of larger caliber?

A. The .45 Colt cartridge and .44 Special cartridge.

Q. Why?

A. The .44/40 and .38/40 cartridge are rifle cartridges and usually loaded with slow-burning rifle powder, which will not all burn in a revolver barrel. Particles of unburned powder may be found at a distance of eight to twelve feet from the muzzle.

Q. What is the length of revolver barrel considered most accurate for target shooting?

A. The six-inch barrel is considered most accurate for all distances. Many use the seven and one-half inch, but the six-inch is the favorite. The five-inch while very accurate will never be used in matches when six-inch barrels are allowed. The four-inch barrel in the heavier models is very accurate. In police matches many wonderful scores have been turned in with the four-inch barrel.

Q. Is the .32/20 an accurate cartridge?

A. What was said of the .38/40 and .44/40 cartridges is also true of the .32/20 as to powder; it is not as accurate as the .32 Police Positive or the .32 S. & W. cartridges.

Q. Why do empty shells sometimes fall under the ratchet or extractor when ejecting them from a revolver?

A. Because the front of revolver is tipped downward instead of upward when the ejector rod is pushed in to extract the shells.

Q. Why will a cartridge hang fire, sometimes exploding several seconds after hammer falls?

A. This is due to deep-seated primer, too small a hole between primer socket and powder chamber, firing pin too short, defective primer and powder oil soaked, and obstruction in firing pin hole that will slightly slow up the hammer fall, also excessive thumb pressure against side of hammer.

Q. Is hand-loaded ammunition as accurate as factory ammunition and as safe to use?

A. Yes; if the proper care is taken. Remember you are playing with powders that one added grain will increase the chamber pressures from two to three thousand pounds.

Q. What is the cause of a keyhole?

A. Wrong ammunition, as trying to shoot .22 Long Rifle cartridges in a W. R. F. revolver, a .44 S. & W. Special in a .45 Colt, a .38/40 in a .44/40 revolver, a cylinder which does not line with the barrel, a defective muzzle, a deformed bullet, a light powder charge, and a wrung barrel.

General.

Q. Would very loose chambers in the revolver cylinder affect the accuracy?

A. A certain looseness or tolerance must be allowed to accommodate the different makes of ammunition. A very loose chamber would affect the accuracy.

Q. When revolver is fully loaded and great pressure must be exerted to draw hammer to rearward position, where would be the first place to look for trouble?

A. Look at firing pin hole in recoil plate for burr, which may be filed off to correct trouble. See that latch is in proper position. If that does not correct the trouble, look for loose bullet in shell which may jump forward and bear on barrel.

Q. Does it harm a revolver to snap it when empty?
A. No; it will never harm a good revolver.
Q. Why is the hammer nose or firing pin loose in a revolver?
A. Because in that way guided by the hole in the recoil plate the blow is more direct. With a rigid firing pin the blow is downward, as in some of the older models.
Q. Is a checked front and back strap an advantage in holding the revolver?
A. Yes; the checked front and back strap is an advantage as the arm does not have to be grasped so firmly to prevent slipping. While checked wood grips are of great help the checked back and front straps are an advantage.
Q. If trigger is not released when hammer falls or after every shot, will cylinder turn?
A. No!
Q. Why does the muzzle of a revolver or pistol flip or move upward at the instant of explosion?
A. Because the handle or grip is below the center of the bore.
Q. What is the cause of a wrung or bulged barrel?
A. This is caused by an obstruction in the barrel. A piece of tobacco, candy or even a wad of paper may cause this, but in a large per cent of the cases it is caused by the absence of powder or a weak charge with just power enough to drive the bullet part way through the barrel; firing another bullet

after the first will cause a ring or bulge in the barrel and destroys the accuracy. The foregoing is not the fault of the revolver as many shooters think; even a very tight bullet may be fired without damage to the revolver. Careless reloading is many times the cause of this condition.

Q. Will a new arm always group as well as after use?
A. No; a new barrel will group well but will improve with use.

On the Range

Q. If target bull's-eye should stand several feet above the eye height or line of vision, what would be the effect with a correctly sighted revolver or pistol?
A. The group would be low. A height of six to eight feet above eye height would cause the group to drop from one to two inches depending whether the distance the shots were fired from was twenty-five or fifty yards.

Q. At what distance, twenty-five or fifty yards, will the group be lowest on the target when target is six to eight feet above eye height?
A. At twenty-five yards.

Q. If the target bull's-eye should be six to eight feet below the eye level what would be the effect as to place the normally sighted revolver or pistol would group?
A. The group would be high or about the same distance above the center of the bull's-eye as it was below center when shooting at a raised target.

Q. Would rough or uneven ground at firing point help or handicap the shooter?
A. Rough, uneven ground is a handicap to the shooter. He should try to place the feet in as near a normal position as possible.

Q. Would rough, uneven ground between target and shooter assist or handicap the scores?
A. This condition would slightly handicap the shooter. Better scores can be made on a level range.

Q. Do clean, new, carefully pasted targets improve the scores?
A. Yes; clean targets allow a clearer vision.

Q. Is a white, shiny target the best for shooting?
A. No; a dull white or light straw color target will give the best results.

Q. Will a shadow across the target and bull's-eye affect the score?
A. Yes; the best shooting can be done on a target evenly lighted.

Q. Can best results be obtained when shooter is standing under a tree in the shade?
A. No; this was clearly demonstrated at the National Shoot in 1919. One firing position was under a tree and the scores made from this point were lower than at any other point on the range.

Q. Can good scores be made when standing under a roof or awning for shade?
A. Yes; unlike the tree, with its moving shadows of leaves and branches, the shade from roof or awning is solid and does not distort the vision of the hand and sights.

Q. Do white pasters overlapping the black or black pasters overlapping the white lower the scores?
A. Yes; the bull's-eye will appear out of round. The original line of the bull's-eye should be clear to the shooter and to the man who pastes the target, otherwise a close shot may be scored one point lower or higher than its value.

Q. Should the targets be perpendicular?

A. Yes; if targets are tipped to right or left it may cause the shooter to tilt his revolver in the same direction. Some men line up the revolver as to canting by the target they are shooting at.

Q. Will a loose target or one swaying in the wind affect the scores?

A. Yes; the target should be stationary. The arm will do all the swaying necessary.

Q. Should a shooter practice rapid fire from raised pistol position or from position of extended arm?

A. From raised pistol position, otherwise when shooting on a range where this rule is enforced his scores will show a decided decrease.

Q. Should the shooter place the foot, leg, knee or body against any object which may be at firing point (bench or table)?

A. No!

Q. Should a shooter load with six cartridges when the score or half score calls for five?

A. No; the shooter should load with five cartridges in any match which calls for five or ten shots as a score. It is dangerous to have a loaded cartridge in the revolver or pistol after the score is finished.

Q. Should any windbreak, whether object or person, be used by a contestant in any match?

A. No!

Q. Should wrist straps or arm braces be used?

A. A wrist strap may be used if muscles are strained or sore, otherwise no braces or straps should be used.

SECTION 22
MISFIRES

A misfire is not always the fault of the revolver or the cartridges. In many cases it is caused by the cartridges remaining in the chambers so long that the oil finds its way to the powder between the bullet and the shell. This is called an oil-soaked cartridge. Oil or water may work in through the primer socket and destroy the fulminite in the primer.

A good rule for protection is to change the ammunition every four weeks. If ammunition is not available in quantities to allow this, at least change the first two cartridges to be fired. One is then assured of the first two shots and the ammunition should never be more than three months old. If care is taken to allow only a thin film of oil to remain in the cylinder the cartridges will be dependable when three months old.

Misfires which we cannot guard against are the ones caused from defective primers. I have found many without the anvil, and no powder in the shell. I have found a great many shells without an opening from the primer socket to the powder chamber and these are very dangerous if the arm is opened before the primer cools. I have several times received a cut on my face by swinging the cylinder out too soon. It is dangerous to open and examine any revolver immediatly after a misfire. At least twenty seconds should elapse before the arm is examined. A misfire might result from a deep set primer which the firing pin will not reach, and this fault may be easily discovered if the shells are examined.

Another very frequent error is made by persons not accustomed to the use of firearms. When they are firing double action the trigger must be released after each shot to allow the parts to fall back in place ready for the next shot. I have seen many such cases where the shooter claimed that the arm was defective. If single action is used the trigger must be released after each shot, otherwise the cylinder will not turn and the hammer will fall on the exploded shell. This is a very common occurrence, but the recoil will usually take care of this trouble if the arm is not held too tightly.

Another source of misfires is from the revolver used for target shooting single action with the spring lightened to aid in cocking of the hammer. Due to the longer hammer fall when fired single action no misfires will occur, but before this arm is used for quick protective work it should be thoroughly tried double action to make sure that no misfires will occur.

Misfires may also be caused by using a heavy oil in the mechanism. I once discovered a revolver with the mechanism lubricated with LePage's glue mistaken for gun grease. Neither heavy oil or gun grease should ever be used; on rare occasions a drop of sperm oil will aid the working parts. If the arm is dropped in the water or mud it should be taken apart and thoroughly cleaned and each part wiped over with an oily rag; before replacing side plate, oil the working points, such as trigger, hammer pin, safety, etc., with a toothpick.

In target shooting when the thumb is placed high on the frame be sure that the pressure is not exerted against the side of the hammer to the extent of slowing up the action and thus causing a misfire.

Oil the firing pin and note whether a pierced primer or moisture has caused it to rust, for if it has rusted or corroded it may not fit the firing pin hole and such rust or corrosion may form a cushion on the end of the firing pin and cause a misfire. The firing pin hole through a pierced primer or moisture may be coated with rust and cause the same result.

SECTION 23

THE TWO-INCH REVOLVER BARREL

So much controversy has been started over the appearance on the market of a practical revolver for protective and police use that I am anxious to air my own views on the subject.

I think I am a pioneer as a believer and toter of the two-inch barrel arms. Thirty-two years ago I sawed off my first pair of long barrels and fitted sights to what was left. I was surprised with the accuracy obtained and have since that time used many two and two and one-half inch barrels for pocket and holster use.

Some of the advantages of the two-inch barrel are: in a scuffle the barrel is so short that the man holding the revolver has far more leverage than the man who is trying to take it away from him, which is not true of the four or six inch barrels. A man less powerful than the user of the gun could grasp the barrel and could twist the revolver out of his opponent's hand. As an arm to carry in an automobile the barrel is so short that the revolver may be swung either right or left across the steering wheel without striking it. Then the shooter who carries cartridges in the revolver until they become oil-soaked has an advantage with the two-inch barrel, for usually a bullet from defective ammunition will stop from two and one-quarter to three and one-quarter inches from the cylinder and this, of course, would fall out of the two-inch barrel, leaving a clear barrel for the next shot. I do not recommend using old ammunition, but sometimes even with new ammunition a defective shell is encountered and then the two-inch barrel will help. I have never had a bullet stop in a two-inch barrel revolver.

It is an undisputed fact that the short barrel is faster on the draw than the long barrel. And as for accuracy— the cry of manufacturers and others who do not make or use this two-inch model carrying the powerful .38 Special cartridge is that it is not accurate. I know it is accurate enough for any work that a police officer will ever be called upon to perform and I have hundreds of times fired six shots at a Colt's Silhouette target at one hundred yards placing all six bullets in a vital spot. At two hundred yards I have hit the silhouette three times out of six shots. At twenty-five yards a good shot can group his shots in an eight-inch center or in a four-inch center at fifteen yards, and inside of that distance at close range, six to twelve feet, it is the king of all protective weapons.

I believe that the two-inch barrel revolver will be one of the most popular models ever brought out for police and protective use and I feel that I have been very instrumental in bringing this about. I know that many of my friends and readers will look at the figures quoted as to accuracy and say: "I have made better scores than that with my two-inch," and I know that this is true. I saw Captain Tom Pettit, Chief of the Identification Bureau of Des Moines, Iowa, cut the groups which I mentioned fifty per cent.

In shooting an arm of this weight and short sight radius care should be taken on long shots to properly line up the sights and to exert an even pressure on each side of the frame. This holds true for all light-weight revolvers. A few shots fired carefully will convince you that a two-inch barrel is worthy of your consideration as a protective weapon.

Several times the possessor of a two-inch barrel has told me that he couldn't hit anything with it. I found this to be true not only with the two-inch but with the four and six inch barrel revolvers fired by the same man. I do not claim that a man who has never been taught how to shoot a revolver can make good scores with a revolver having a two-inch barrel, but I do claim that a fair shot will be agreeably surprised with its accuracy and it is a very comfortable revolver to carry either in the pocket or holster.

DETECTIVE SPECIAL .38 CALIBER REVOLVER

SECTION 24
OBSTRUCTIONS IN THE BARREL

Many shooters have wondered after firing a shot why the barrel has collected an egg-shaped swelling. The revolver has usually been blamed when really it has nothing at all to do with it. It is caused by some obstruction in the barrel when the shot was fired.

It may be caused from a bullet with an oil-soaked cartridge with only power enough to carry the bullet part way through the barrel; or it may be a piece of tobacco, candy or pocket lint, in fact, any small article carried in the pocket or fallen into the holster that has worked into the barrel. However, the bullet lodged in the barrel will account for ninety-five per cent of this trouble.

I remember a police department which I visited some time ago where the men showed me eight revolvers, each with a bullet lodged in the barrel, and they told me the arms were defective. I pushed the bullets out and with fresh ammunition fired several hundred cartridges in the eight revolvers without any trouble whatever. Bullets have been known to lodge in the barrel from fresh ammunition because the loading machine did not throw the proper charge. This is one of the reasons why the arms companies will not guarantee firearms when hand-loaded ammunition is used. They know that hand-loaded ammunition if properly loaded is not going to cause trouble, but if loaded carelessly is bound to wreck the finest of arms.

If a weak explosion is heard when the shot is fired, investigate to see if the bullet has left the barrel before firing another shot. See that the barrel is clear before firing the first shot.

I have found barrels with the entire six bullets lodged in the barrel and, of course, it was ruined. When a bullet or other obstruction is lodged in a barrel and another bullet is fired, the compressed air between the two bullets causes a swelling or ring in the barrel destroying the accuracy of the arm. If the first cartridge fired is so weakened that the bullet stops at rear end of barrel and another shot is fired, the second bullet would stop before it was clear of the cylinder; thus the powder and gases would form a blasting charge instead of an explosive charge and the revolver might be ruined. If the last bullet should enter the barrel before striking the second bullet, then the gas pressure would be relieved by the escape of gas between cylinder and barrel and only the barrel would be ruined.

Care should be taken to wipe thoroughly cartridges that have been dropped on the ground before placing them in a revolver or pistol, because particles of stone may imbed themselves in the grease or lead and scratch the barrel as they pass through.

An obstruction in the cylinder may be carried into the barrel by the bullet and cause the barrel to swell or be forced out of round, but this does not always destroy the accuracy of the barrel.

SECTION 25

CARE AND CLEANING

As soon as possible after firing the revolver it should be cleaned. We now have on the market ammunition which eliminates the cleaning, but we also have several million rounds of the old issue.

Use a good solvent and a felt or bristle brush. An old toothbrush is handy to brush off the rear end of the barrel, recoil plate, and front end of cylinder. Then push a brush through each chamber of the cylinder several times; clean the barrel in the same way with the brush thoroughly moistened with solvent. Wipe off all excess oil on the outside of the arm and only leave a thin film of oil in the cylinder and barrel; more than that is not necessary. Oil the firing pin slightly, as a pierced primer may have allowed the powder gasses to corrode it and if left in this condition it will rust. Do not oil the mechanism of the revolver unless it has been dropped in the water, or on some very rare occasion when the action shows signs of rust or is gummed up by an accumulation of oil and dust.

A revolver should be oiled and cleaned every week whether it is shot or not. Perspiration from the body may cause rust. A little care of his revolver will pay the shooter big returns if he should need to use it in a hurry. We are all apt to neglect that part of our equipment which we seldom use; but it doesn't pay in the care of a revolver, for the perfect revolver and the trained hand form an alliance to protect life and home.

In my travels I have examined thousands of good revolvers which were no better than a club of the same weight simply because they had been neglected, allowed to rust and become gummed up to the extent that they could not be fired even if the cartridges were fresh, which they were not. The arms were useless. A little pitting in the barrel or pitting on the outside does not render a revolver useless, but being carried in the pocket day after day, year after year, with no care will spoil the best revolver ever made.

I spoke of felt brushes in this section and I believe that some years ago I brought out some samples of the best brush ever invented for revolver and pistol cleaning. It consists of a twisted wire handle closely fitted with coarse hard wool and extending the entire length of the rod. With a brush of this kind the muzzle of the arm cannot be harmed and it will, when saturated with a good solvent, clean the arm from ten to twenty times before the brush becomes dry.

I use an aluminum fishing case cut to fourteen inches and a brush for each caliber carried. There is also room in the case for a brass rod threaded with a brass brush, but I find that if a film of solvent is left in the arm when it is fired that I seldom have use for the brass brush.

Care must be taken if a brass or steel rod is used to protect the muzzle. More so with the revolver and pistol than with the rifle, for with the rifle in a cleaning rack both hands can be used to guide the rod, but in the case of the revolver or pistol the arm is usually held in one hand, the rod in the other.

One of the worst enemies of the hand gun is the holster lined with felt or broadcloth. This will, when carried close to the body, collect moisture and when the arm is left in it for any length of time will rust the arm, and very likely when it is drawn will carry with it parts of the lining firmly rusted to the steel. If a revolver carried close to the body is lightly wiped over with an oily rag every night in warm weather it will usually protect it against rust.

It is not necessary to spend an hour in cleaning a revolver or pistol. With the brush such as I have described and a good solvent one minute will clean a revolver or pistol and it can safely be put away until it is needed. If a revolver is exposed into damp weather or at the seashore it should be wiped thoroughly and cleaned as soon as possible. If carried in a holster on a hunting trip exposed to rain and snow it is well to wipe over with a cloth moistened with solvent before starting and to clean it thoroughly on return whether it is shot or not.

If arms are carried back and forth to the range a cloth pocket made from three thicknesses of canton flannel and covered with a thin black cloth made with a snap at open end to keep the arm from slipping out is a fine carrier. It is thick enough to protect the clothing from oil and the arm from ordinary knocks and scratches. Arms carried in a case like this will look like new for years and there is no danger of a case like the one described collecting moisture.

If an arm is used for target shooting only, a little excess solvent will do no harm. If it is carried in a pocket or holster, loaded, a slight film of oil is more satisfactory.

Sights that have been blacked should be thoroughly cleaned and oiled before the revolver is put away. Care should always be taken to keep the grip screw tight, otherwise dirt and lint will find its way into the action.

SECTION 26
BEING YOUR OWN REPAIRMAN

For many years I have followed the adventures of the amateur gunsmith and have observed the results of his labors. In some cases I have been agreeably surprised at the results and in other cases I have also been surprised and astonished at the number of things Colonel Colt forgot to do when he built his revolver and pistol. If sears, hammers, and other more or less necessary parts of the revolver and automatics had the growing qualities of tomatoes I believe a profitable crop could be gathered around the firing line at Camp Perry and other ranges I have visited. Therefore I am just a little in favor of the factory-corrected shooting irons.

One little improvement which was brought to my attention some years ago at the big shoot was a new method of fixing the trigger pull. Several .45 automatics were handed to me for adjustment and I found one side of the hammer notch gone by way of the file. I inquired why this was done and the men informed me that the pistol had at first a seven-pound pull and by taking off half the notch they expected to get a three and one-half pound pull. The only trouble was that the thing doesn't work that way.

Improvement number two—the persons or person who invented the scheme of splitting the locking lugs in the slide with a chisel; well, that also passed away.

I believe the greatest enemy of a gun is an oilstone in the hands of a person who does not know how to use it properly. Then the ordinary oilstone is not as smooth as a number six Swiss file about half worn out neither can you get to the corners as well with a stone as with a file. Though you may stone the hammer notch and sear ever so smooth let one part slide over the other and you have a beautiful creep.

It must be remembered that the object of the notch is to create a trigger pull of a certain weight, but whatever the weight required, be it two and one-half, four, or six pounds, it must pull clean. That is, the weight required to start the trigger or sear out of the hammer notch must pull it clear over the top of the notch. In the .45 automatic the mistake is often made in dry shooting before the sear is seated by actual shooting after the pull is adjusted.

In a revolver a pull may be lightened by using a lighter spring. If a lighter spring is not available the original spring may be ground or filed. Care must be taken, however, to grind or file the leaves of the spring lengthwise and to file nearly the entire length of the top and bottom leaf. The points of hammer and trigger, which constitute a smooth, clean trigger pull, are as delicate as some points in a watch. A man must be an expert with a file to change these points and leave both surfaces in position to bear evenly at all points. Two or three thousandths in the wrong direction will ruin a very fine pull.

If a revolver is to be taken apart the first requirement is a screw-driver that fits the screws, placing the thumb of the hand holding the revolver in such a position as to guide the screw-driver into the screw slot without slipping, otherwise the head of the screw and the adjoining frame will become scratched and defaced.

Sometimes a burr on the firing pin hole in the revolver will bear against the head of the shells and in this way block the turning of the cylinder; this may be removed with a small file. Here is one of the first places to look if the action does not work smoothly. Another trouble which will cause a jammed action is a bullet jumping forward in the cartridge next to the one being fired. Care should be taken when a jam occurs not to use excessive force as this may damage the action. Side plate screws should be examined when the arm is cleaned as they sometimes work loose and if this happens the mechanism may slide out of place, causing a jam.

I have always claimed that it takes between five hundred and one thousand shots to break in a revolver before it will do its best work and the owner accustoms himself to hang, trigger pull and sights, but this does not mean that good work cannot be done before this breaking-in process. I have seen a great many of the profession appear on the firing line after a trip to Commercial Row and win the price of the arm the first day; however, I still claim they will make better scores with the arm after the above-named number of shots.

Remember, dropping any hand gun does not improve the shooting. Neither does it improve the shooting to take the revolver in one hand and when the cylinder is open throw or snap it back into place. If you wish to save scratches and other cylinder trouble hold the revolver by the handle or grip, grasp the cylinder with the thumb and forefinger of the other hand, thumb on left side of frame, forefinger on right side of frame in depression between chambers, and close with depression halfway between top and bottom strap and close until locked by latch.

Many things can happen to a revolver and so it can to any other piece of mechanism whether it costs twenty-five dollars or twenty-five thousand dollars. I do claim that many things that happen are sometimes the fault of the shooter. For instance, taking the arm apart when it is working properly, polishing and stoning parts and working points, putting undue strain on parts by holding cylinder when cocking the arm. I have noticed thousands of shooters testing a revolver for a creep by using both hands and placing the left thumb behind the trigger when pulling with the right. The proper way to test for a creep is to hold the arm out in a natural shooting position and then try to find the creep.

Shooters spend many hours designing new grips for their pets but if this time was spent in shooting perhaps another champion might be with us. Many times a shooter can change his sights if he is careful and works slowly, and thus improve his scores, but care must be taken that he does not change them in a way that will bar his arm in certain matches. He should also be careful not to damage the muzzle or change it in any way.

If an immovable front sight is to be moved to right or left it should be done by turning the barrel in the frame. This can be done by fitting two blocks, one on each side of the barrel, either of wood or soft brass cut out to the exact taper of the barrel, the blocks not quite meeting (about $\frac{1}{8}''$ apart) when the barrel and block are placed in vise, first removing the cylinder and crane from the revolver. Paper should be used between blocks and barrel to protect the bluing. Use a piece of hard wood one and one-quarter inches square and one foot long placed through cylinder space; hit a series of light blows on the end of the stick until the barrel is screwed in or out to the required distance. The barrel must not be moved back and forth many times or a loose barrel will be the result.

A jam is sometimes caused in an automatic pistol by the extractor not grasping the head of the shell firmly. To test for a possible jam at this point, remove hammer from the pistol to avoid accidents; take out magazine and place cartridge in the chamber; draw slide back slowly and just before the rim of the shell touches the ejector at left side allow the slide to go slowly forward and note whether the cartridge is held in place by the extractor. If the extractor has the proper tension or grip on the rim of the cartridge it will return to the barrel chamber as slide goes forward; if tension is insufficient the cartridge will drop at front end and sometimes drop down through the magazine cut or space. If this should happen, take out the extractor by removing firing pin stop and bending front end three-quarters of an inch from point slightly inward; replace the extractor and again try the chamber test. When it has the proper tension the cartridge will return to former position in the chamber. Some of the jams in the .45 automatic come from a wartime magazine because the sides or lips are spread apart and rear top corners are split. There is no cure for this except a new magazine of commercial quality.

We do not have the troubles that I will now mention with the new commercial arms, but with the war products and those through long use or neglect that have had new parts replaced for the old and that were not properly fitted. At this time may be mentioned that from these improperly fitted extractors comes the annoying shell that will come back when extracted and strike the shooter in the face or some part of his body. This is caused by the bottom corner of the extractor hook not being rounded or filed away to allow the shell, as it is pushed over by the ejector, to leave the recoil plate at an angle that will carry it through the porthole in slide at any angle that will cause the shell to go to the right of the person holding the pistol. A properly filed extractor hook will eliminate this trouble. I encounter every year at the camps automatic pistols that have slides from one pistol, a receiver from another, as well as other parts from different pistols, but if these are fitted properly they will work perfectly.

Misfires with some of the cartridges used at the big shoot are unavoidable as the primers are very hard and even with the heaviest of springs and perfect firing pins this will occur. If, through defective ammunition, a bullet should stop in the barrel be very careful in driving it out; protect the muzzle from contact with the rod, with cloth, paper, or other substance when driving the bullet out, and clean the barrel thoroughly, for particles of steel, brass, or grit may become detached from the rod and the next bullet may scratch the barrel.

The front sights now furnished on the commercial pistols will not jump out. I have cut over hundreds of the front-sight slots in the older pistols to take the new sight and they can hardly be pulled out with a vise. If one-eighth or one-tenth inch front sight is used, this new type of sight with heavy square base is the only one the shooter can depend upon.

As issued for government use the .45 automatic has a long hammer spur and it is not an uncommon sight at the different ranges to see the shooters with a piece of adhesive tape between thumb and first finger. This spur may be partly ground off on an emery wheel if it interferes with good scores by striking the flesh between thumb and finger.

The greatest improvement which can be made on a .45 automatic pistol is the fitting of a new match barrel. When fitting a barrel to some of the old automatics place the barrel in arm; draw slide rearward until it locks open; then insert little finger through port, draw it upward on runway to assure yourself that bottom edge of barrel does not extend out over the runway, for if it does it will cause a jam. Remove the protruding edge with a file, taking care not to change angle of runway in barrel and leave a runway smooth for bullet to slide over.

Such work as fitting new hands and bolts should be done by the factory or a first-class repairman, because if parts are not correctly fitted the revolver is out of time. Drawing the hammer rearward will show whether the bolt is falling correctly or not. It should fall near middle of bolt runway in cylinder, then slide forward to bolt cut in cylinder. If it falls too early it will fall before it reaches bolt-cut runway and mar the fine finish of the cylinder. If it falls too late it may cause a throw-by, in factory terms, or fall beyond the bolt cut. This timing is corrected by shape and size of bolt at the rearward end as it drops from spur on lever. Sometimes after fitting a new bolt the hammer cannot be cocked because the bolt will not lift out of bolt cut, which may be corrected by changing curve of lever.

While I could go on and on through the different repairs that may be required with revolvers and automatic pistols I will again state that the factory or a good repairman in your own town is by far the safest for your favorite arm. Tools less experience mean nothing, and experience less tools means the same thing.

Perhaps if I had not had handed to me thousands of fine revolvers that had been nearly ruined by homemade adjustments I would get a thrill out of this section and proceed with the entire bag of tricks necessary to place your revolver in new condition. I do not mean to discourage those who are capable of repairing their own arms, but to discourage those who are not, before they get into serious trouble.

Mention has been made of emergency repairs which I have made at different ranges. The repairs which I have made at different ranges were not emergency repairs but correct repairs, if proper parts and tools were available. If not, the owner was notified of the fact and advised to return arm to factory for proper adjustment.

FITZ INSPECTING PISTOLS AT CAMP PERRY

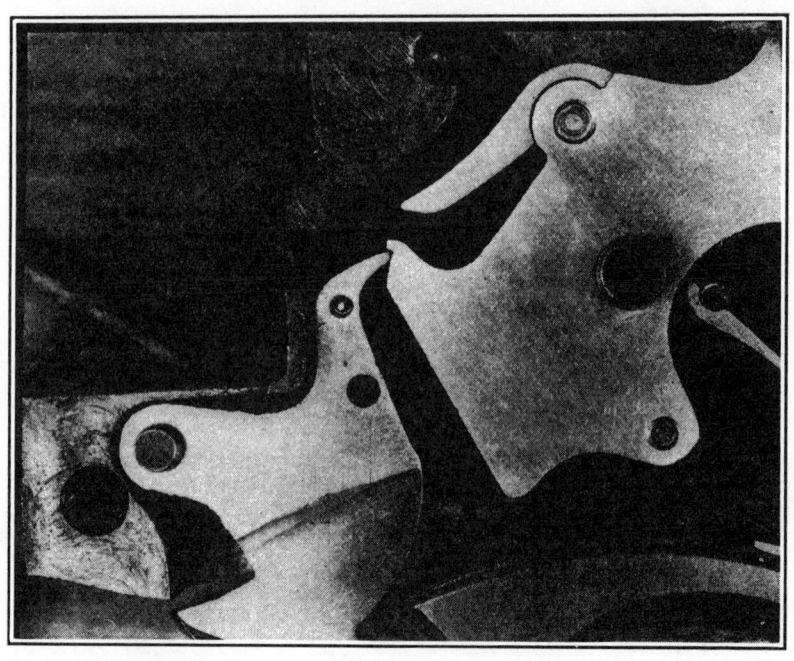

A PROPERLY CONSTRUCTED TRIGGER PULL ON COLT'S NEW
SERVICE REVOLVER

SECTION 27
PAST MASTERS AND PRESENT

Many stories have been written about the old gunmen of the West and many of the stories are of impossible feats performed with the hand gun. I do not believe that such stories were ever told or even thought of by the settlers of the West, but that they originated in the mind of some ambitious writer who did not have a working knowledge of firearms and their uses. Even in this day of jazz we hear of men being shot with an automatic revolver in calibers ranging from .28 to .58. We also hear of some desperate criminal who is at large with several revolvers in his possession who will kill any one who tries to arrest him, but when he is rounded up he is usually captured without a shot being fired.

I may cite a case which happened several years ago. A writer came to me and asked if I would go to the range with him, and through questions and a demonstration of trick shooting and quick-draw work give him material for a story. I consented and we journeyed to the range. I answered the questions which he asked and, after the exhibition, I asked him to show me the copy before it was published. Two days later I was given the story to read and what a story that was. One paragraph credited me with firing at two targets fifty yards away with a .45 automatic in each hand and placing several hundred bullets in each target that a teacup would cover. Another stated that I fired from the hip at the same distance, registering hits so fast that they could not be counted. It is needless to say that the story never was published in that form.

I believe that I know the possibilities of the hand gun and when statements such as the foregoing are made I do not blame the person about whom the story is written as much as I do the inexperienced writer who wishes to produce a sensational story. We may mention the case of Wild Bill Hickok. I do not believe he was ever responsible for the stories of the many impossible feats which he was supposed to have accomplished. We will never know the exact number of men that were killed by him, but we must admit that any man who has killed in single combat between fifty and one hundred men, who in their own mind, at least, were considered his superior in speed and accuracy, was not only an expert in the game of life and death with a revolver, but possessed pluck as well.

It is true that the men who settled the West were not target shots and the eastern standard seems to measure all men by their ability to hit a target. The old gun fighter would give a sorry exhibition at this kind of shooting, and sadder still would be the story of a target shooter meeting one of the quick-draw artists at a distance of six to ten feet. There is only one answer to this; the target man would be killed before he knew what it was all about. In target work men shoot for pleasure and in quick draw and protection work they shoot for keeps. For speed and accuracy at short range and the ability to protect themselves when their lives were in danger, the old Western gunmen were grand, and I know personally many of the present-day peace officers in the new West and South who are just as fast as any of the old school. In fact with the modern arms they are superior to any of the men of fifty years ago.

An old friend of mine, in relating a gun fight which he had with a colored man whom he was trying to arrest, said: "Well, Fitz, you know I never could hit one of those darn targets, but I hit this bird three times and that's the first three shots I ever fired that were all in the black." This same quick-draw shooting for our present-day peace officers is a life saver, and I shall never be convinced that, at short range, inside of fifteen feet, with the low hammers used on modern double-action revolvers, that an officer should shoot single action.

This theory is taught by our target shooters and not by experienced man hunters. I know many officers who have grown old in service who never could hit a target, but they have come through several gun fights always getting their men and they shoot double action.

Our present crime situation is little changed from that encountered by the peace officers of the old West. When guns are used the fastest man wins; single or double action, the loser is dead just the same. In the old days the East would have developed just as fast men with the hand gun as the West, if occasion required it, but it did not. Such men are developed by necessity. While eastern men were living in comparative safety, the western men were fighting their battle against heavy odds. The sturdy pioneers and their families, who journeyed to the promised land beyond the law, knew the value of the hand gun and relied upon it at all times. It was their constant companion.

Whether East or West, the man who takes the time to perfect himself in any branch of shooting will become an expert in that work. It does not follow that because he is an expert target shot he is expert in the use of the revolver in quick draw, hunting or trick shooting; he must practice each branch until he has mastered it. We cannot compare the quick-draw artist with the target expert; neither can we compare the rifle shot, who only shoots at a target, with the hunter who shoots at moving game.

I do not agree with many of the writers that Wild Bill, Billy the Kid, and others of the old West were born, not made. It was necessary for them in their calling to attain accuracy and speed with the hand gun and this they were able to do because they were naturally quick of motion and they took their practice seriously. They were brave men, as were also many of the men they killed, but a brave man who is slow of motion is no match in a gun fight for a man who is quick of motion and equally brave. A large per cent of the killings in the West were due to the desperado or bad man. Indians were not the only menace which the pioneers encountered in their efforts to establish homes for their families and themselves. The bad man appearing on the scene, coming from all parts of the world, lured by the prospect of an easy life and the absence of law and order, was a sufficient reason for the settlers to perfect themselves in the use of the hand gun.

Law and order is the salvation of any new settlement, but this usually comes from a condition of lawlessness which becomes unbearable to the home builder. Such was the condition in California when the Vigilantes were formed to enforce the law. The outraged citizens knew of no other course to pursue. Judges and public officials were corrupt and the end of justice could only be reached by the methods they employed. The same methods would be of great assistance today. We have in our modern cities too many murderers and gang leaders who, with permits to carry arms in their pockets, walk the streets in comparative safety as far as our laws are concerned, only fearing death from the hands of rival gangsters. Three cheers for the gang wars; they rid the country of men whom the law cannot seem to reach. When one gangster kills another we are fifty per cent a winner, and if, as it sometimes happens, the law should apprehend and execute the murderer then one hundred per cent efficiency is reached.

The old frontier men were working under a handicap in the powder and ball days, due to the weight of the weapons, time consumed in loading, etc. This condition continued until about the year 1870 when the Colt Single Action Army was brought out in the .45 caliber. This arm was at once the favorite and is to this day with many of the old-timers. This arm was adopted by the United States Government in 1873 in a .45 caliber; later on it was brought out in a .44/40 caliber and so on down through the small calibers.

The old Westerner still takes great pride in his ability to draw and shoot accurately at short range and well he might. There is no man feared by the criminal as much as the man who has the reputation of being a fast man with the hand gun. He is let severely alone by this element. He enters a dangerous locality with an air of superiority and sureness of purpose, which at once notifies the persons present that he is not a safe man to fool with. The greatest of all human persuaders, the eyes, the swing of shoulders, position of hand and revolver all show this to even the person unversed in gun lore. We owe our beautiful West to the quick-thinking, fast-shooting pioneers, the greatest body of men the world has ever known. May they rest in peace.

COLT'S PATTERSON REVOLVER, MODEL 1836

SECTION 28

SPECIAL ARMS FOR QUICK-DRAW WORK

Ever since the introduction of revolvers for defense purposes certain enthusiasts have demanded special arms to gain that fraction of a second so necessary in quick-draw work. Perhaps occasionally a revolver is spoiled in carrying out the ideas of the owner; if so, mark it experiment number one and recall the pleasure attained in the wrecking of a perfectly good revolver.

Many of the ideas carried out are very practical, for instance, the cut-away .38 and .45 models with the two-inch barrels. No claim is made to beauty in these arms but they will deliver the goods. I believe I am the pioneer butcher of revolvers for quick draw, for thirty-two years ago I tried out my first two-inch barrel and this was followed by the cut-away trigger guard, cut-off hammer spur, rounded butt, cut-off ejector rod, straightened trigger, etc. I choose the .38 Colt Police Positive Special in the small model, because it is the most powerful revolver of its weight and a very fine balanced arm. I choose the .45 New Service because it is the most powerful hand gun, and with a two-inch barrel and cut-away in the same manner as the light model it is the king of them all. Two of these arms can easily be carried in the trousers pockets or overcoat pockets.

Perhaps some one would like to ask why do we cut up a good revolver and here is the answer: The trigger guard is cut away to allow more finger room and for use when gloves are worn. The .45 really has plenty of finger room without cutting the guard, but I prefer my own cut away and it does decrease the weight and change the balance. The hammer spur is cut away to allow drawing from the pocket or from under the coat without snagging or catching in the cloth and eliminates the use of thumb over hammer when drawing. The ejector rod end and part of the ejector rod is cut away to prevent rod end from catching or wearing through cloth in pocket. The butt is rounded to allow the revolver to easily slide into firing position in the hand. The trigger is straightened as far as rear of guard will permit and cut off at the bottom to allow it to swing inside the guard to give a flatter surface for the finger to rest on. The front of guard is sloped inward so that finger will roll toward trigger if guard is struck by the finger in a hurried shot.

The top of the cut-away hammer may be lightly checked to assist in cocking for a long range shot. In this operation the trigger is started backward until cut-away hammer can be reached by the thumb, then hammer is brought to full cock as in the original model. This should be practiced with the revolver EMPTY until one is sure that it can be accomplished without the hammer slipping from under the thumb.

In rounding the bottom corners of the grip where front and back strap join the bottom plate allow rounded corners to extend one-half inch upward all around both wood and steel leaving the surface smooth. This may be changed slightly for different size hands.

In cutting away the trigger guard use a metal saw and first cut the front end of guard where it joins the frame. Then cut the bottom of guard one-eighth inch in front of the bottom of trigger WHEN THE HAMMER IS DOWN.

The hammer may be ground off on an emery wheel until it is of the required shape to prevent catching. It is best to remove the mechanism from frame when making the changes. A fine file and fine emery cloth will smooth the parts; if, however, the owner insists on a perfect job, of course, it would mean having the arm being reblued at the factory.

In regard to cutting-away process and other changes which gun cranks require, I do not blame any factory for refusing to accept such orders. If the shooters who lean toward freak arms were familiar with factory routine and the trouble encountered by a factory in producing freak arms they would hesitate before ordering. This does not mean that a factory may not be induced to make a two-inch barrel for a forty-five New Service and they may be induced to cut away the trigger guard and hammer or blue the arm after these changes. This, of course, is special work and the charges may seem excessive unless one knows the time and trouble caused by such work. Rounding the corners of the frame and grips would probably not be attempted by a factory, because such a process would ruin the original lines and also the checking on the grips.

I have been asked many times if cutting away the trigger guard is a safe procedure and if there is any danger in carrying a revolver cut in this manner. I may repeat the number of years that I have carried this combination and up to date I am still walking without a limp. *But* at this point I wish to state that I take no responsibility for any accident which may happen to my readers or their friends who try the different branches of shooting mentioned in this book. I am stating my experience in hand gun work and if the rules laid down in this book are followed we will all live to a ripe old age, or at least die of some other disease besides lead poisoning.

The main springs in arms changed as I have described should be lightened to the extent necessary for a fast, smooth action but they must not be lightened to a point that will cause a misfire either in single or double action. If any revolver will shoot double action without misfires it will never fail in single action shooting as far as the revolver is concerned for the hammer falls a greater distance from the full cock notch than from the double-action feature.

I suggest many hours of practice with the Fitz Special or cut-away model with the *revolver empty*, drawing and snapping before actual firing. When any revolver or automatic is carried in the pocket be very careful when placing the hands in that pocket and do not place the finger on the trigger when walking or running for a misstep or stumble would be very liable to fire a shot. The danger in a holster is not so pronounced for the trigger and guard are at least partly covered, but the natural inclination with many people is to put the hand in the pocket, especially if some foreign substance, such as a revolver, is carried occasionally. It calls attention to that particular pocket.

The arms pictured in this section are accurate and powerful enough to take on a hunting trip in the big woods or for protection in the more thickly populated districts. Of course the two .45 caliber two-inch New Service are the most powerful, but the .38 caliber might be taken on a hunting trip to use on small game and it makes a light arm to carry for protection.

When shooting these arms be sure the revolver is clear of the holster or pocket and pointing toward the target before completing the operation of firing the shot.

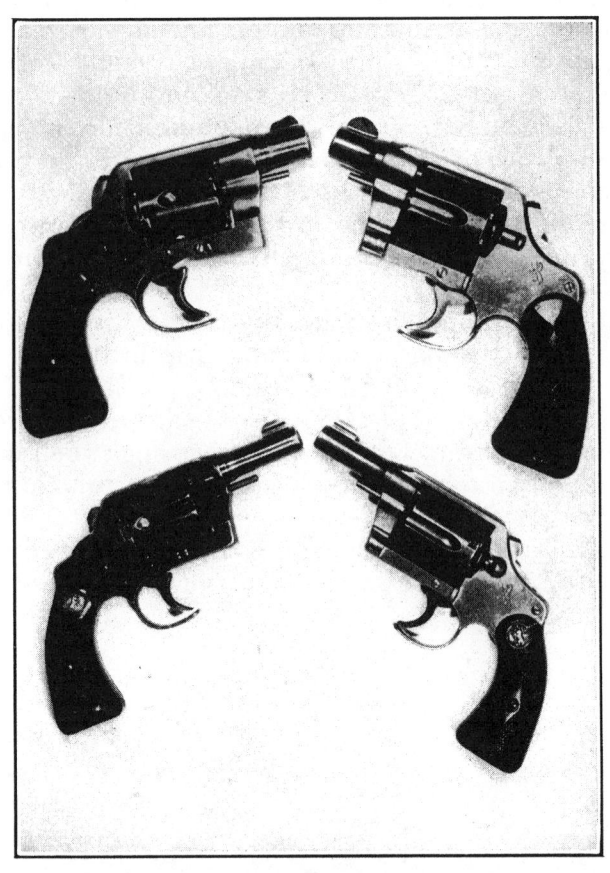

TWO NEW SERVICE 2-INCH BARREL REVOLVERS REMODELED (Upper)
TWO POLICE POSITIVE SPECIAL 2-INCH BARREL REVOLVERS REMODELED (Lower)

My favorites for many years—AUTHOR

SECTION 29

QUICK DRAW

Quick draw is a very fascinating sport and one in which many are interested. I rarely speak before a club or police department where I am not asked to show the quick draw. Let me caution the beginners: BE SURE that your revolver is empty before trying quick draw or any new tricks with a revolver. Do not load it until you have first mastered the stunt you wish to try with the revolver or pistol empty.

Quick-draw shooting is practical police shooting, the recognized system of protection used by proficient peace officers throughout the land, and it means just this: when occasion requires it, get your revolver quick and shoot quick and straight when you do get it. Know the position of your revolver and get it without taking your eyes from the object you are to shoot at. Shoot double action if it is at short range and quick draw is not necessary at long range.

The double-action revolvers are referred to because they are universally carried, due to the weight of the arm and time which must elapse before the beginner would familiarize himself with the manipulation of the old Peace Maker. Whether the revolver is carried on the outside or under the coat a little practice in getting it out will gain valuable time.

The first article to purchase is a revolver suited for your particular need, and a belt and holster should be purchased after the arm is decided upon. A New Service or arm of corresponding weight would call for a two, two and one-half, or three inch belt if revolver is to be comfortably carried. If a lighter arm of thirty-two to thirty-five ounces is carried then a belt of one and one-half to two inches may be worn. If the 22-ounce revolver is worn, then the one and one-half inch belt is sufficient. I may here describe my own belt, which is heavy because I carry two New Service revolvers on it. It was made for me by Captain A. H. Hardy, Beverly Hills, California. It is three inches wide and at the top on the inside is stitched a thin piece of tough, serviceable leather in which are cut buttonholes to match the trousers buttons. The bottom of each hole is finished with a punch to prevent tearing. If revolvers are to be carried in the trousers pockets more buttons and buttonholes may be added to support the extra weight. If the revolvers are carried in holsters this is not necessary. No belt loops or hooks are necessary, as the belt never changes position after once being attached. Another advantage of this belt is that a holster never changes position due to the buttons.

Now for a heavy, serviceable holster, for it is money thrown away to buy the light, flexible holsters which flood the market. I have encountered thousands of men carrying such holsters and they are what I term "suicide holsters," for the reason that they will buckle or snag nearly every time the arm is drawn. Another holster which is dangerous is the one that is too short for the revolver, with the barrel sometimes extending through the bottom from one to two inches. Open-end holsters are recommended because all dirt and lint will fall through, but they are not recommended when they are too short to cover the barrel and sight. Of course only open holsters are spoken of for quick-draw work because it is hard to associate safety straps, springs, and closed or flap holsters with quick draw.

Before the holster is procured the user must determine what kind of a draw he wishes to become accustomed to,— the cross-stomach draw, suspender draw, the side draw, the leg draw, the shoulder draw, the pocket draw, the hip pocket draw, or the sleeve draw.

The cross-stomach draw is an old favorite of mine and very fast if it is perfected. Some years ago in the West a sheriff, an old friend of mine, told me in no uncertain terms what he thought of the cross draw and asked me to draw and see what happened. His idea was to grasp the wrist of the gun hand and block the draw. The only reason that it wasn't a complete success was that I did not draw the way he thought I would. As I drew I placed the other hand and arm outside the one I drew the revolver with and as he caught the wrong wrist the muzzle was against his stomach.

The cross draw requires a holster that would not be right for any of the others. It should hang on the belt, butt pointing slightly outward one inch above the top of the belt and at an angle of thirty degrees, the butt tipping toward the hand with which the arm is to be drawn, then it does not have to be lifted out of the holster, but is drawn with a circular motion, with barrel nearly parallel as the revolver leaves the holster. Due to angle and crouch the holster in all cases should be fitted to the revolver with which it is to be used. This holster may be fitted after loop is fashioned to hold revolver at thirty-degree angle, by cutting away holster to allow the finger to fall on trigger as arm is grasped. By cutting away leather on belt loop and holster back, the hand will fall naturally on grip so that position of hand will not have to be changed after draw. (See two-inch holster in this section.)

Moisten the holster with water until it is thoroughly pliable, cover revolver with gun grease, including inside of barrel and cylinder; place the arm in holster and with fingers press leather around revolver until holster is shaped to the arm. Be sure leather is wet enough to retain this shape, but do not soak it in water. I use a paint brush and moisten it from the outside. When thoroughly fitted place in the sun and air for about six hours until the leather is partly dry, then remove the revolver and clean it thoroughly. Allow the holster to set for several days until thoroughly dry, then oil with a small brush and pure Neet's foot oil and you then have a holster that you can pass along to the next generation. A revolver will not drop out of a holster so prepared.

I am not stating that the cross draw is the fastest draw in the world, but we who live in cities cannot wear two revolvers low down on the legs and tied down; so about all that is left for us in civilian clothes is the *cross draw, shoulder holsters,* and *pocket draw.* The two, four, or six inch barrel may be used. I would recommend .38 or larger. The two-inch Detective Special is the fastest, due to the short barrel; the four-inch of the same model is very light (22 ounces) and universally carried. The Official Police, in four, five, and six inch barrels, is heavy and serviceable. Requirements and personal choice, also size of hand, will determine what arm to purchase.

Why I specified that the holster must be cut away in a manner that would allow a perfect grip of the revolver while it was still in the holster is that the hand, thumb, and fingers will take the position before the draw is started. This will enable each of them to fall in place on the revolver handle, saving time in drawing and also eliminating any change in hold after arm is drawn.

When preparing to start practice in quick draw cut the finger and thumb nails close or broken nails will be the result. Do not try for speed until thoroughly familiar with the position of the revolver and the position the hand must assume for a smooth, easy draw. Learn where the revolver is and be able to place your hand on it correctly without taking your eyes away from the object you want to hit. When you have acquired this first step you are ready to practice the draw.

It is best to learn each operation separately, that is, draw, aim, and snap. I have noted many persons practice the draw who could not seem to avoid tipping the revolver when it was drawn. Practice drawing until the revolver comes out straight up, sights level. In this work the muscles are held more rigid than in target shooting. Practice this first third of the draw until the revolver seems to jump into your hand smoothly and easily. If you speed up before you have learned the position of the trigger and guard you will have a battered nail and tip on your trigger finger.

We have progressed to the pointing stage and here the trick is to allow the barrel of the revolver to replace the finger in pointing. Nearly every one can point his finger accurately enough to be inside a six-inch circle at twelve feet and with a little practice the revolver barrel will take the place of the finger if it is correctly grasped in the hand. Up to six feet, or, in the case of the expert, eight feet, the arm need not be brought above waist level; as the distance increases beyond this point time and accuracy are gained by pushing the revolver outward and upward, pulling trigger at the same time, the hammer falling as arm and revolver reach the end of the thrust.

We have now reached the third stage or snapping. I stated before that it was best to take up each stage separately, or after perfecting the draw learn to point; after being able to draw and point, learn to squeeze the trigger, and then combine all three. Stand in front of a large mirror and learn what you are doing. Revolver empty or seven years bad luck, and the price of a mirror will be the result. In final practice do not make the mistake of drawing, pointing, and then putting the revolver back in the holster. Draw, point, and snap; go through the entire motion. The last stage, snapping, or trigger squeeze, is very important. I have heard many argue that a double-action revolver could be fired as quickly single action as double in this quick-draw work, but I have never found any one who could do it and I do not believe it can be done, so we will speak of double action up to fifteen feet.

In cross draw BE VERY CAREFUL TO KEEP ARM AND HAND NOT USED OUT OF LINE OF FIRE; rest arm against side of body and tense muscles to hold revolver against side sway, pulling trigger straight back. In this work I do not recommend holding thumb along top of frame above latch as in target shooting; lay it alongside of frame below latch and slightly bent or in position thumb will take when revolver is drawn, not forgetting to use *thumb pressure* to eliminate putting revolver to left. In rear of this section are pictures to further explain the cross-stomach draw.

The position of the crouch, of course, is changed with different individuals, but in my own case I have found this position very fast, between twenty-five and fifty one-hundredths of a second. In the crouch revolver is pointed with the body movement at the hips; this speeds up the draw as you are aiming with the body or assuming a position that will tilt the thirty degree holster to a level position, bottom on a line with top. The shot is fired just after the revolver leaves the holster on the line it is drawn.

The holster for cross draw may also be used when drawing a short barrel revolver, to fire a shot with the revolver upside down, using the other hand. In this draw the revolver is grasped in a manner that will bring the third finger on trigger and little finger along bottom of frame as a guide, the thumb and two first fingers grasping butt. As the bottom of butt is usually parallel with barrel at short range up to six feet aim or point with bottom of butt six inches above point you wish to hit with a bullet. This is only used for an emergency shot where opposite hand is engaged or out of commission.

With practice a revolver may be drawn and fired faster than the ordinary man can draw and fire with revolver in normal position. Use the Langrish or Colt Silhouette targets for quick-draw practice. The upside-down draw is faster than drawing by twisting the wrist to grasp butt which is in reversed position.

In the rear of this section may be seen my old friend, Dr. H. R. Brunton, wearing the best suspender holsters I have ever seen. They are very useful in carrying revolvers to and from the range and to see the doctor get a gun out of one of these holsters will convince the onlooker that the suspender holster is very practical. Even when they are not used to carry revolvers they are not uncomfortable. The holsters are attached at three points and in this holster light, tough leather may be used, taking care to have holsters extend below barrel. This draw is faster than the shoulder draw, due to lower position of revolver and tied-down holsters.

The leg or thigh draw, hand height: Revolvers worn in this position usually on cross belts at a height that will allow the half-closed hand to just sweep the butts and bottom of holsters tied down with rawhide thong around leg (this is better than a buckle and strap attached to chaps or trousers). Attach the holsters in a manner that will swing the butts slightly outward and muzzle slightly to the rear about ten degrees. The position of the draw is standing on balls of the feet which are twelve to fifteen inches apart; a slight bending of the knees and throwing stomach slightly forward add to the speed of this draw. As the guns are thrown forward the body is bent backward to aid in bringing revolvers to a level position. The hands are closed to a position that will enable the fingers and thumb to close quickly around butts as they strike. This is a very fast draw and preferred by the western gunmen of the old school and many are still being worn in the wide open spaces.

The side draw from belt is very good and much used, but it is slow if revolver is worn high on belt because the elbow must be bent at such a sharp angle to grasp the butt and at a sharper angle to draw the revolver, especially if five or six inch barrel is used. The holster on the belt cannot hang far below the belt unless it is tied down because it is liable to buckle. A holster with a stiff heavy back to prevent this is disagreeable to wear and by use will become flexible. I have noted thousands of revolvers carried in this position and ninety per cent of them so carried are slow in coming out, due to being carried too far back, ill-fitting holsters or wrong angle of holster on belt. Many police officers and others whose duty it is to *protect*, believe that all that is needed is to carry a revolver. *It is not. Carry it where you can get it.* The fastest angle of holster on belt for drawing from this position is—bottom of holster one inch to rear of center of holster top and worn just ahead of the hip joint. The speed is aided by throwing the shoulder upward and forward as the arm is drawn. Holsters should be cut away as before described and properly fitted. If the holster is worn too far back it can only be reached by one hand.

The shoulder holster used in the shoulder draw is a favorite with many, but it has its faults. First, it is disagreeable to wear unless the wearer is used to the old-fashioned suspenders. Secondly, it is too far for the hand to travel when the hands are hanging at side in a natural position. Two kinds of shoulder holsters are on the market,—the open-top, old-style holster and the spring holster or new model. The first, or open-top holster, is very awkward and hard to draw from because the revolver must be drawn upward, sometimes striking the arm or catching in shirt or coat lining and it may buckle if not tied down to belt. The latter, or spring-shoulder holster, is ideal if this position is satisfactory, and very fast because the revolver is not drawn but ripped out of the holster without being drawn, saving valuable time. The position of the body when drawing: side on which the revolver hangs should be toward object to be hit and shoulders thrown in direction away from target as arm is drawn and shot fired from breast height if at short range. Much may be said in favor of the shoulder holster, when riding in an automobile, train, or other conveyance, or in a sitting position, or under coats that are worn buttoned but are open at the top. It is not as good to wear on a hunting trip as a belt holster, due to rifle or shot gun striking it if worn on shoulder from which rifle or shot gun is fired.

The front pocket draw, while not universally used, is very good. The front pocket is a good place to carry a revolver, especially one of those mentioned in the section "Special Arms for Quick Draw." The pocket is lengthened so that butt of revolver will be one inch below pocket opening and opening should be one inch longer than regular. The extension in bottom front corner of the pocket should be V-shape and wide enough to hold revolver loosely. This extension may be made of canton flannel, soft side in and seam on inside for muzzle to rest upon. The side of the pocket may be fastened to the outside trousers seam to avoid snagging. Use the thumb over hammer when drawing regular model. We feel many times that a revolver would be a good companion on an automobile or camping trip, but in hot weather it is not easy to conceal especially if the coat is not worn all the time, but it may be carried in the front pocket as described above. It is comfortable to wear and after a few days will not worry the wearer.

While this draw from hands at side is not as fast as some of the others it can be improved with practice and at first appearance or feeling of danger the hand may be slipped into the pocket and owner may still look peaceful and innocent. In this position he need not fear any kind of a draw as he has his revolver in his hand. In this draw the hand and arm must do the work. The position of leg draw would assist but this is a surprise shot from an innocent position and the leg-draw position advertises the intentions too plainly to be misunderstood.

The hip pocket draw, while not as slow to the man who has practiced it, is condemned for many reasons. The hip pocket draw was at one time universally used and every one knows about that pocket as the logical place to carry a revolver. Any one can appraoach from the rear and get possession of the revolver before the owner could stop him. It is a place where, if the gun hand is held, the revolver cannot easily be reached with the other hand. Every revolver carried for protection should be carried to hang in a line or in front of arms hanging at the side. To slightly speed this hip pocket draw use leg draw position. Holsters are made that fit hip pocket and hold revolver upright, many of them with safety straps. If any of my readers should use such an outfit the only place they will find sympathy is in the dictionary.

The sleeve draw is performed with a small revolver and an elastic band, such as a piece of an inner tube, about three inches long. The revolver is worn butt down in position to be grasped by the other hand. It is disagreeable to wear for any length of time and hands must be brought together before the draw.

The swivel draw is performed by using a specially constructed swivel, part of which is attached to the belt and part to side of revolver, allowing butt to be grasped and muzzle brought in to line without detaching from belt, or it may be detached for a long shot. I see no advantage in this combination as it is not as fast as cross or leg draw and body must be turned, as angle of fire from one position is limited and distance must be short.

Another combination on the same order is the holster attached to belt by swivel of the same kind and holster cut away in a manner that will allow revolver to be fired while in the holster or may be drawn if desired. The holster, of course, has an open end. The same disadvantage is noticeable in this as in the gun and belt swivel,—the handle is not stationary and may swing as the arm is grasped.

Another surprise draw is the waist-band draw. In the absence of a holster the arm may be carried in the waist band or, in other words, next to the shirt inside the belt and trousers. This is very effective and I have never dropped a revolver carried in this position. It is usually carried as in cross draw as to position, and while not as fast as holster draw it is dangerous for the other man. Of course the arm will be more liable to rust from body perspiration.

Several years ago while traveling in the South I gave a demonstration to a certain police department. In the course of the quick-draw work I caught my shirt as the revolver was drawn, nearly spoiling the draw. A gentleman who was present came to me after the exhibition and asked me to go across the street with him to a clothing store. There he showed me a garter that, if attached to bottom of shirt and stocking, always kept the shirt down in place. I have used it ever since and have never since caught the shirt in quick-draw work.

Several surprise draws are used, as the leg and stocking draw. A small, thin holster is strapped around the leg on inside above the ankle, lower end in stocking, and a small revolver is used. The surprise may be aided by a long shoestring that may be untied by stepping on end with other foot, then, in stooping down to tie it, get the revolver and surprise is complete. The hat is another place to carry a small revolver or automatic pistol for the intentions would not be suspected. The back of the neck between the shoulders is another hideout for small firearms or knife and a place which should be searched if looking for weapons. A large necktie or open shirt may sometimes conceal a weapon as a shoulder holster may be worn under a shirt. The glove or mitten draw is sometimes used if trouble is anticipated at a given time and consists of a glove large enough to cover a small revolver and the hand. To get into action pull off the glove.

The overcoat cuff is sometimes utilized in carrying a small revolver. If cuff is large enough the revolver is carried muzzle toward hand and butt up on inside of wrist.

The outside pocket draw, if hand is in pocket, is very fast and dangerous for the hold-up gent, as a command of "Hands Up" means hand and gun up at the same time. The overcoat pocket is better adapted to this than the inside coat pocket due to size and weight of cloth. Shooting through the pocket may be accomplished if thumb is held up straight toward top of hammer as shot is fired. This will prevent the hammer catching in cloth.

Wearing a holster continually in the same way and place in connection with a few minutes each day spent in practice will accustom the wearer to the feel and balance of revolver and holster to the extent that when trouble comes the revolver will seem to leap into the hand. In fact many times in police work, when all appearances indicated trouble, I have found my revolver in my hand ready for business.

An incident of this nature happened to me some years ago in Boston, Massachusetts. I was going to my hotel about one-thirty in the morning after a visit to an old shooting pal of mine, and was walking along a street with several large trees on the edge of the sidewalk. When about twelve feet away from an extra large tree I detected a movement or enlargement of the tree shadow cast by a distant street light. The sensible thing to do in a case of this kind would be to cross the street, but I decided in case of a hold-up both parties might be surprised and kept walking. As I passed the tree I saw no one but sensed when about six feet beyond that some one had stepped from behind the tree and was following me. We had only proceeded a few feet when an automobile came along and picked a spot just behind me for a backfire and, before I realized that I had moved, my friend of the tree shadow found a .45 New Service muzzle trying to push the third button of his vest in the direction of his backbone. I saw that his hands were empty and stepped back. After he got his breath back he exclaimed that he only stepped behind the tree to light his pipe and I explained to him the etiquette of a dark street, trees, etc., and the folly of using a windbreak when lighting a pipe when the wind was not blowing and also that it is customary to light a match or use a lighter when starting a pipe, which flash I looked for when passing the tree. He explained that he stepped behind the tree before he realized that he had no matches and I offered him some, but he told me that he had other things on his mind at that moment and didn't care to smoke.

Be careful in your first gun fight so that the following epitaph may not apply:

> Here lies the body of Quick Draw Sam,
> Whose holster buckled in a jam,
> His gun was old, his hand was slow,
> 'Twas old Judge Colt that laid him low.

When two revolvers are carried, while they would in all probability be the same model and length of barrel, use one as the right-hand gun and the other as the left-hand gun. I do not believe in changing them. Such little things make no difference to the average gun-toter, but it does to the confirmed addict who weighs and studies every move connected with this work. We must choose the things that really count in this work and eliminate the things which are of no assistance. While I do not claim assistance from this, it has always been my hobby to buy all revolvers or pistols in pairs, using one with left hand and the other with right hand, never changing them.

In this work of quick draw, remember when you reach for a revolver something is started that must be finished with speed and accuracy, and it is better to never attempt to draw than to bungle it and lose your life. Do not attempt to draw for protection or to foil a hold-up man until you are possessed of four things,—sand, a good revolver of .38 caliber or larger, a good holster, and the ability to draw and shoot fast and straight. How many men carrying arms in the course of duty have these qualifications? Sand may be acquired through the knowledge of firearms and confidence in your proficiency with them.

In quick-draw work use an oval motion that does not necessitate stopping the hand and starting over again, many spectacular tricks may be performed with a revolver,—the spin, the double roll, reversible roll, etc.—but I think it is best to follow the straight and narrow path, quick draw by the shortest and fastest route.

We may here add a few more words on the subject of holsters. A thinner holster may be used for an automatic than for the revolver due to the front sight being low down close to frame and no cylinder to catch the leather. The automatic is not considered in the same class with the revolver in quick draw due to added operation of throwing safety off before arm is ready to fire. After the first shot the automatic has the edge on the revolver due to shape of grip and pointing qualities, but what will the automatic man be thinking after said revolver man gets in the first shot.

In closing this section I wish to add that I hope some of the gun-bugs take as much pleasure in reading this work as I have experienced in writing it. I realize that controversy may arise from my version of quick draw. I have been asked many times to write on this subject and this is the section referred to by Julian S. Hatcher in his book, "Pistols and Revolvers and Their Uses."

Remember in all quick-draw work keep the arm not being used out of danger.

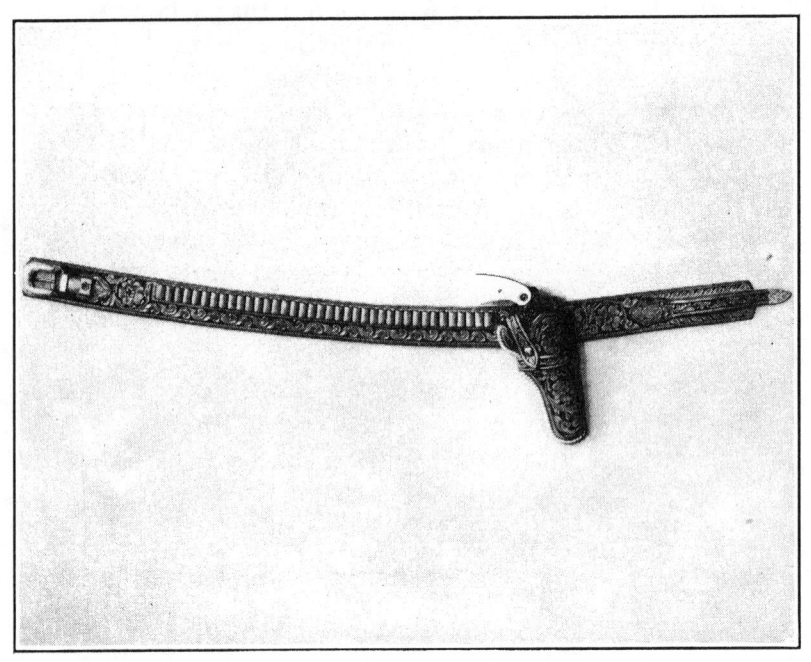

HARDY BELT AND HOLSTER

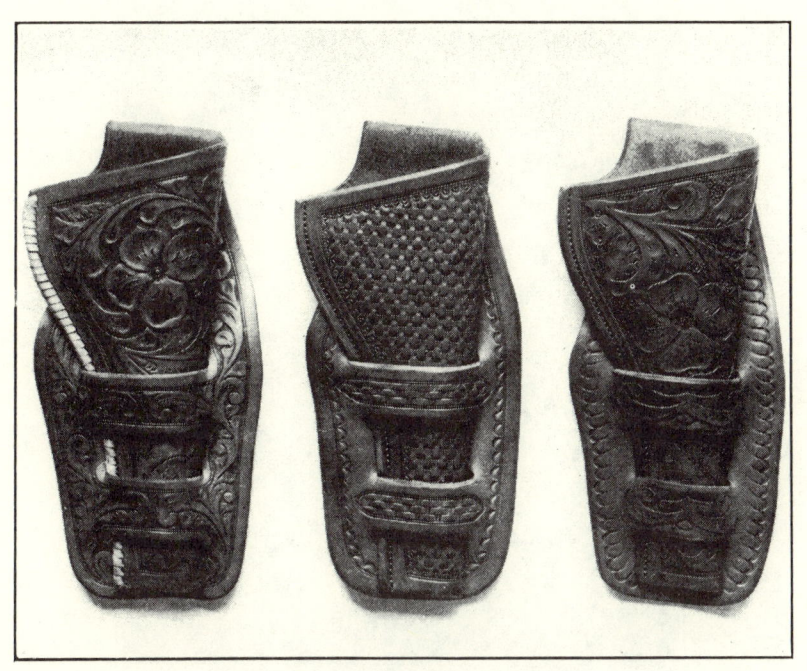

QUICK-DRAW BELT HOLSTERS
Made by A. H. Hardy

POSITION No. 1
CROSS DRAW—START

Note position of right arm which is out of danger. Note angle of holster.

POSITION No. 2
CROSS DRAW—FINISH
Note position of body, which aids in aiming the revolver and speeding up the draw.

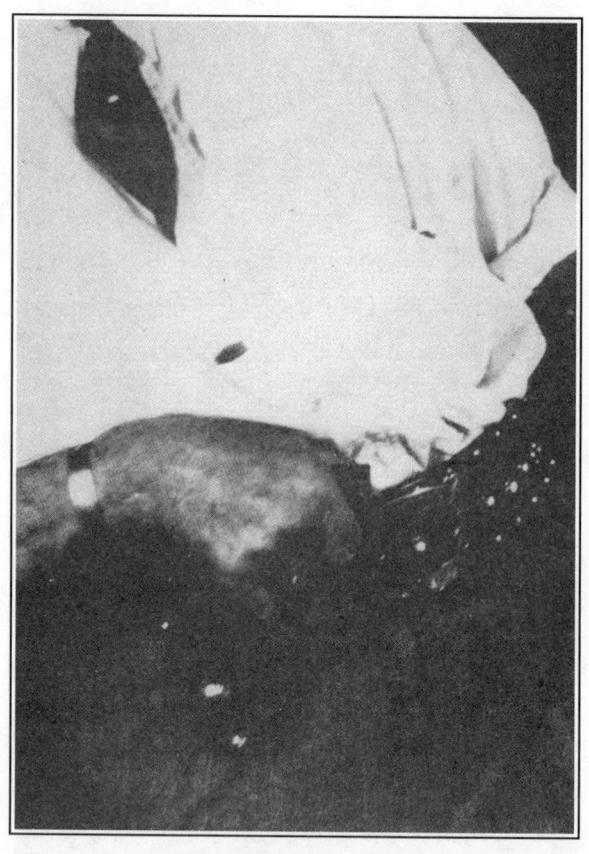

POSITION No. 1
CROSS DRAW UPSIDEDOWN, GRIP—START, WITH 2-INCH BARREL

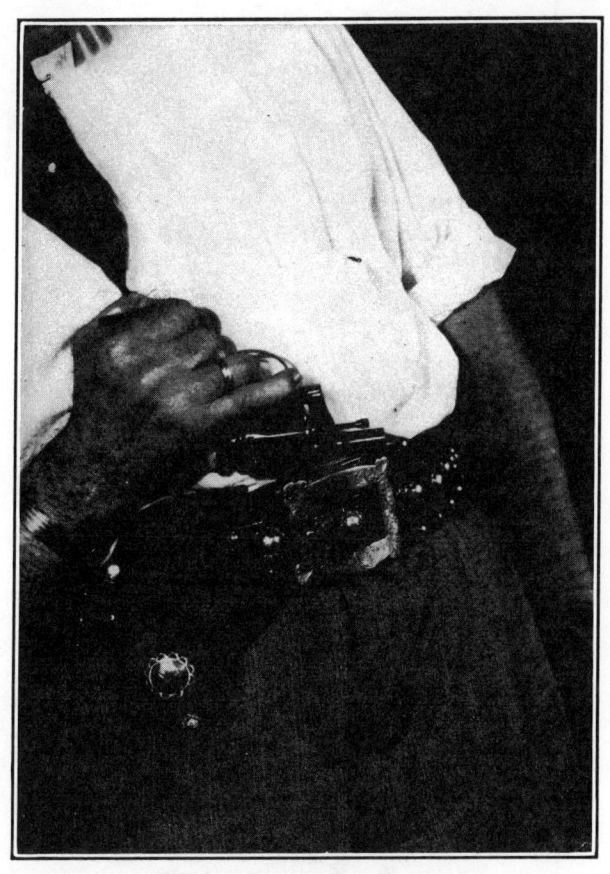

POSITION No. 2
CROSS DRAW UPSIDEDOWN—FINISH, WITH 2-INCH BARREL

DR. H. R. BRUNTON
Suspender Holster with .45 Automatic

THE FAMOUS TWO-GUN LEG DRAW

A very fast draw from cross belts and tied-down holsters. Note angle of holsters due to body position.

SIDE DRAW HIGH ON BELT
Note angle of elbow and arm

SECTION 30
TRICK AND FANCY SHOOTING

Trick shooting is a very enjoyable branch of revolver shooting and when a fair degree of accuracy is attained your friends will enjoy it also, but when visiting the range for the first time to try out the flying objects it is just as well to leave the friends at home.

In this kind of shooting the favorite revolver is the Officer's Model, six or seven and one-half inch barrel, with a medium-sized gold-bead front and U rear sight, such as is used by Captain Hardy, Mr. and Mrs. Topperwein, and others. The usual ammunition is mid-range sharp shoulder because of its light recoil and the clean-cut hole made by the sharp shoulder loads. We have had in the past a few who have resorted to shot cartridges but the nationally known fancy shot would not think of such a thing. His tricks are performed by skill only and not by any short cut.

The first thing to consider is a safe range where stray bullets will do no damage, and large targets, such as the much abused tomato can, should be used until they can be hit regularly. With an audience it is not so much the size of the object that counts but the hitting of it every time. As in other branches of shooting it is practice that makes perfect. When the old tomato can becomes easy to hit try smaller objects,—small cans, apples, blocks of wood, clay pigeons, glass balls, in fact anything of the required size. Avoid all fake shooting, such as small objects thrown at short range that may be broken by the powder blast. Practice real shooting.

I wish my old friend, Captain Hardy, were sitting here at my elbow while I am writing this section, for I know his suggestions would be of great value.

Fancy shooting is not all at flying objects. A very good start for an exhibition is made by laying on the back and breaking six candy wafers, crackers, or other small objects. The revolver will be reversed or upside down and twelve o'clock will be the aiming point instead of six o'clock as when the revolver is held in a normal position. The distance is twelve feet or more, governed by the size of the targets and ability to hit them. Stand in an upright position, lay the revolver in the palm of the right hand, sights to the right, and hold at nine o'clock to hit the objects; turn the hand over, sights to the left, and hold at three o'clock; do the same with the left hand.

Splitting a vertical card is a nice little trick and easily accomplished if the arm is properly sighted. The proper way to line a revolver up for this trick is to draw a line on a white paper and change sights until the arm is correctly centered to hit the line regularly at twelve feet; then try a horizontal line and correct the sights until you can regularly hit the cross where the lines meet. It is harder to hit the horizontal line than the vertical.

Hitting a swinging object is another pleasing shot. Some accomplish this at the end of the swing, but this is not as spectacular as hitting it when it passes the center. Try a small toy balloon hung by a string about five feet from the ground; cut the string with the first shot and hit the balloon before it reaches the ground. It falls slowly and there is plenty of time. Another trick is shooting two revolvers at two objects, both stationary or one stationary and one swinging.

I do not recommend shooting an object from the head of another or too close to the fingers. A revolver is not as accurate as a rifle for trick shooting, and a safe tolerance must be allowed. The Colt .22 caliber automatic pistol is very spectacular in fancy shooting due to its speed of fire, and the extreme accuracy of the arm makes it possible to hit wafers and other small objects in rapid succession.

Shooting at an empty eggshell held by an assistant, who puts on a rubber coat and cap, conveys the idea that the shell is full and this will always cause a laugh. One trick which should always be avoided is placing a cartridge head toward the shooter and exploding it by striking the primer with a bullet. I used this trick for years without trouble, until on one occasion the primer came back, cutting my cheek and embedding itself in the face of a man who stood behind me.

The trick of one man holding the revolver by the grip with a string passed through the trigger guard and resting on the trigger, passing one end of string over each shoulder to an assistant, the revolver is cocked and seemily the assistant, who stands back to back with the shooter, fires the gun. But the real explanation is, the assistant holds the arms rigid while his companion with sights lined up on the object he wants to hit presses against the string until the shot is fired. This is a legitimate trick and must be practiced to perfect it.

Shooting at two tin cans ten or twelve yards apart, the shooter standing between the cans aiming a revolver at each can, seems very difficult, but it can be done by using the surest hand as the anchor, first glancing at this sight, then at the other, going back to the first hand, and noting if the sights still line up with the target. If they do, go back to the other revolver and squeeze both triggers at the same time. Cutting the spots out of playing cards may be done regularly at short range, and with a target on each side of an axe blade splitting a bullet on the edge of the axe is not as hard as it looks.

The novice should stand at a distance that will give him ninety per cent hits and increase the distance as his accuracy improves. Many original tricks may be worked out by the student of this work and in a short time an excellent exhibition may be given.

The idea of some people that a man who can hit a small object in the air must be a wonderful target shot is not true. The expert on flying objects will have to learn all over again when he tries for good scores, and the target man will encounter the same trouble when flying objects are substituted for the bull's-eye. Then the man who is a ninety per cent shooter on flying objects will have his troubles when using the revolver on running game. Each man to his own particular line and if he wants to shoot them all, study them all.

I remember an incident which happened at Englewood (New Jersey) police range outdoors where I was giving an exhibition. A large oak tree grew on a bank about thirty-five yards away and fifty feet above the range level. This was in the autumn and the leaves were nearly all off the tree, and at just that instant a large oak leaf started from the top of the tree. I turned around and fired a shot at it as it was doing a perfect tailspin toward the ground. (This was the best shot I ever made and I couldn't do it again in a week.) As the leaf flew in two pieces, cut clear across, some one called out, "Shoot the big piece." I opened the revolver and threw three empty shells and three loaded ones in the bushes and imparted the information that my revolver was empty.

At another exhibition a fishhawk, flying so high that he looked about the size of a common house fly, attracted the attention of the audience. I was lying on my back breaking candy wafers at fifteen yards, so I fired a shot at him. Shortly afterward a fish about six inches long struck the ground a short distance from where I was lying and one of the audience ran and picked it up. In examining the fish he found where the large claws had pierced the side of the fish. He showed this to the astonished crowd and then called to me: "Say, Fitz, why didn't you hit that hawk?" I answered: "What, and pay a fine of ten dollars?" I do not think I came within twenty feet of the hawk, but the report startled him into dropping the fish and the claw marks appeared about the size of the .22 caliber bullet that was used.

Long range shooting, one, two and three hundred yards, is an addition to the exhibition, but is not as spectacular as the short range work where something is broken. Two targets swinging are, of course, broken where they cross, timing the shot by the speed of the targets. Shooting with a looking-glass is accurate and very simple after the idea of lining up the sights is mastered. Many hits may be made in this manner and it is a very steady position due to the locked arms. The revolver held upside down may be used in connection with the mirror as it may be when shooting a revolver lying on the right or left side.

The .22 target revolver has not been mentioned in connection with this work, but it is a very accurate gun and dependable, besides being cheap to shoot. It is capable of performing as well as either of the others mentioned, and as to durability I have never been able to wear one out. The new heavy model, .22 caliber arms, Officer's Model and Official Police, are wonders in trick shooting. These revolvers, or two revolvers, .38 and .22, and a .22 caliber automatic pistol, are enough for almost any kind of an exhibition, but if the urge for variety is felt add the .45 automatic Government Model to the collection and your audience will get a thrill out of the performance of the national arm and you will be agreeably surprised on your first trial.

Avoid shooting at bottles or glass of any kind, as the distance for sure hits is less than it is with a rifle, and some of the audience may be cut by the flying particles.

The more equipment carried the more exciting the performance if hits are registered regularly. All stands and target holders should be neat and businesslike and of the folding variety. If the exhibitions are to be given in a hall light charge ammunition should be used and an adequate folding backstop added.

A good folding backstop is about eighteen inches square, using one-eighth inch steel for the back, one-sixteenth inch for the sides and one-eighth inch for the bottom. By using hinges this will fold up to about six inches in thickness by eighteen inches square. Heavy cardboard or heavier board should be used for the front and the same general construction as the larger backstop mentioned in the subject of Ranges. If a backstop of this kind is not at hand fill a wooden box eighteen inches square and twelve inches deep with dry sand. If portable backstop mentioned above is used, see that the hinges or joints are so placed that all corners are tight to prevent lead spattering out to mar the woodwork or furniture and place the backstop or sand-box on a stand about four feet high.

Shooting with the front sight covered by a piece of pasteboard at a medium sized target will add another trick to the collection and a little practice will show you how, both eyes open. Many pages have been written in the story books about hitting a can thrown in the air at a rise of ten or twelve feet six times before it strikes the ground, not drawing the arm until after the can is thrown. This trick will take some study and if you do not succeed, do not be discouraged; go back to your old tricks.

A small can held shoulder high and released, drawing the revolver from holster, and hitting said can before it hits the ground is always good. A small can or clay pigeon placed on the toe of the shoe and kicked into the air, drawing from the holster and hitting it before it reaches the ground will get applause. Marbles, pennies, and empty shells hit regularly may close the exhibition to the satisfaction of all.

Some very good advice is to stay with one trick until it is perfected before going on to the next. Do not slight any of the tricks or become careless; the exhibition will suffer if this is done. Do not hurry the shots; take plenty of time and get results. Do not fire any shots that will endanger the life of any one and do not appear careless to the audience. An explanation of the different shots fired and a few remarks made at the right time will help in putting the tricks over.

HARDY AND FITZ
Gun-Bugs

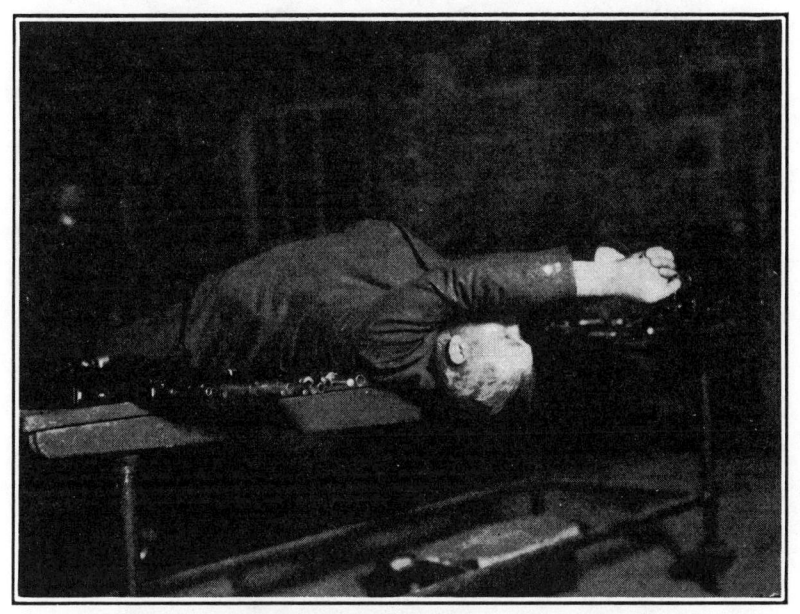
SHOOTING LYING ON BACK

SHOOTING WITH LOOKING GLASS

SECTION 31
HUNTING WITH THE HAND GUN

Revolvers and automatic pistols are very well adapted for hunting; the only trouble seems to be that we have remained in the same old rut. As soon as we think of a hunting trip our thoughts go to the high-power rifle as a companion. When styles change in hunting arms as they have in ladies' wearing apparel, I expect to see the two-inch barrel revolver the most popular of all hunting arms.

Many hunters in the West are now using the hand gun for hunting. My friend, Elmer Keith, can get his game at as long a range with his old Peace Maker as the average hunter can with his favorite rifle, and there are many others doing the same thing.

Some years ago I entered a match with a seven and one-half inch Officer's Model revolver in which were eleven other contestants armed with their hunting rifles. Now it is a known fact that very few hunters can group their shots in an eighteen-inch circle at two hundred yards. I am not saying this is true of sporting Springfields and other target arms that are used for hunting trips. I mean the ordinary hunting arms and the ordinary hunter behind the gun. However, my revolver was properly sighted for two hundred yard shooting, fitted with a small micrometer rear sight brazed to regular rear sight, and I was fortunate in getting thirty-four out of a possible fifty on the old army target with an eight-inch black and won the match. I am not speaking of this as a wonderful score, but a fair average of what a man can do with the hand gun. This score would, of course, be impossible on a windy day.

The ease with which a revolver may be carried, compared with the seven-pound rifle in the morning which is seventeen pounds in the afternoon, would lead any one to think that the little hand guns have some advantages. It is not so much the model of the arm carried on a hunting trip as the ability of the hunter to place a bullet in a vital spot. A miss is just as effective with a revolver as it is with the most powerful rifle.

For long shots with the revolver the prone position may be used, holding the revolver with both hands, or resting the revolver against a tree, or sitting back against a tree or stone supporting the revolver with both hands and knees. This is very accurate for long range shooting if time permits all this preparation, but I do not believe that any good revolver shot would accept such aid up to one hundred yards; the average distance in wooded country where game is shot is between twenty-five and fifty yards. The same tricks are used with a revolver as with a rifle in hunting or stalking game.

We may now speak of the different cartridges and their values as game stoppers. In the section on cartridges as man stoppers, no lengthy explanation was given, but if my readers feel blood-thirsty they may apply the values given in this section to that subject. Perhaps every one will not agree with me on the relative value given here, as many reload a more powerful cartridge than produced by the ammunition companies. They may use a different shape and weight of bullet and a greater powder charge, but I have no means of knowing just what these special loads are and in this section only factory loads will be mentioned.

The cartridges recommended for hunting are the .45 Colt, .44 Winchester, .38 Winchester, .45 Automatic, .38 Automatic, .44 S. & W. Special, .38 S. & W., and Colt Special, not forgetting that little partridge load, the .22 Long Rifle. The 9 mm. Luger, 7.63 Mauser, and 7.65 Luger, while little used in this country, and shooting a very light bullet, may be mentioned as possible game cartridges.

To my mind the .45 caliber Colt cartridge heads the list as the finest cartridge for hunting with the hand gun. The smokeless powder charge with two hundred and fifty grain bullet, seven hundred and seventy feet per second, and a striking force of three hundred and thirty pounds added to the shape of the bullet is sufficient for almost any purpose that a hunting arm would be used for. With the black powder load it is the most powerful hand gun bullet on the market, a velocity of nine hundred and ten feet per second and a striking force of four hundred and sixty pounds.

I use in my .45 caliber revolvers two black powder cartridges and four smokeless powder cartridges and find this combination satisfactory whether on a hunting trip or in peace times. Andrew J. Palmer of Bridgeport, Connecticut, gave me some black powder cartridges, .45 Colt, a short time ago that registered five hundred twenty-five pounds' striking force and made my favorite two-inch forty-five revolvers very nervous.

The .44 Winchester is next on the list. While it has not quite as long a range as the .38 Winchester cartridge, it does have a larger and heavier bullet and I consider it a better game cartridge. Bullet weight for the .44 Winchester cartridge is 200 grains, velocity 919 feet per second at muzzle, and muzzle energy 375 foot-pounds, and the .38 Winchester with a bullet of 180 grains, muzzle velocity 950 feet per second, and muzzle energy of 360 foot-pounds. The last two named are very close in power and performance. The .45 Colt automatic 230-grain bullet has a muzzle velocity 809 feet per second, muzzle energy 335 foot-pounds. The 200-grain bullet has a muzzle velocity of 910 feet per second, muzzle energy 368 foot-pounds. The .38 automatic has a muzzle velocity of 1146 to 1200 feet per second and a muzzle energy of 379 to 410 foot-pounds. I hope now that a real pistol for this cartridge is on the market that the ammunition companies will increase the velocity to at least 1250 feet per second and come forward with a real hollow point bullet and other bullets adaptable for game shooting. We would then have a long range pistol cartridge with penetration accuracy, and stopping power to suit the most exacting.

I know I am going to hear some comments about putting the .44 Special cartridge away down here, but it is universally used with smokeless powder and a 246-grain bullet only has a muzzle velocity of 770 feet per second and a muzzle energy of 320 foot-pounds. If black powder were used it would have a muzzle velocity of 820 feet per second and a muzzle energy of 370 foot-pounds.

The .38 Colt and S. & W. Special bullet weighing 158 grains using black powder has a muzzle velocity of 960 feet per second and a muzzle energy of 320 foot-pounds. Using smokeless powder it has a muzzle velocity of 860 feet per second and a muzzle energy of 260 foot-pounds. The 9 mm. Luger bullet weighing 124 grains has a muzzle velocity of 1040 feet per second and a muzzle energy of 300 foot-pounds. The 7.63 Mauser 85-grain bullet has a muzzle velocity of 1397 feet per second and a muzzle energy of 373 foot-pounds. The 7.65 Luger bullet weighing 93 grains has a muzzle velocity of 1225 feet per second and a muzzle energy of 310 foot-pounds.

A cartridge which should be well up on the list is the .455 cartridge bullet weighing 265 grains, with a muzzle velocity of 758 feet per second and a muzzle energy of 337 foot-pounds. We must not forget the little .22 Long Rifle bullet weighing 40 grains, with a velocity of 910 feet per second and muzzle energy of 58 foot-pounds. This last mentioned cartridge is much used in both revolvers and automatic pistols by trappers and hunters for small game shooting. It may be procured with a hollow point.

Hunting is a matter of practice on moving objects and I feel that if any one, after a reasonable amount of preparation, should take his favorite side arm into the woods instead of a rifle he would be pleased with the result. I prefer two revolvers to any of my rifles when hunting (I never go after mountain goats). Two .45 caliber revolvers will make any bear wish he had lived a better life if the hunter does not get bear fever.

Camp Perry practice for running deer and running man shooting is presided over by Colonel Critchfield and it is excellent practice. I could see surprise written on many faces because of the misses with both rifle and revolver when the moving targets were first tried, but after a short period of practice the smiles came back and they were registering hits with the revolvers and rifles at fifty yards.

The following ballistic tables will show the comparative power of the different cartridges and the proper placing of bullets is the answer to the full or empty game bag. I have derived more pleasure in hunting with revolvers and automatic pistols then I ever experienced when carrying a rifle and on stormy days the arms were dry when I arrived in camp.

TABLES OF BALLISTICS
WESTERN REVOLVER AND PISTOL CARTRIDGES

Velocity energy and penetration are based on smokeless powder results. In the table on instrumental velocity, where two figures are shown, the first one indicates black powder velocity, and the second, smokeless powder velocity.

Name of Cartridges	Weight of Bullet in Grains	Round or Flat Nose	Length of Barrel in Arm Tested	Instrumental Velocity at 25 Feet from Muzzle	Energy at 25 Feet from Muzzle	Penetration in 7/8" Pine Boards at 20 Feet
22 Long Rifle	40 Lubaloy Ct'd	RN	6"	759 F. S.	51 Ft. Lbs.	4
22 Win. R. F. (22 Rem. Spec.)	45 Lubaloy Ct'd	FN	6"	811 F. S.	66 Ft. Lbs.	4
41 Short	130 Lubaloy Ct'd	RN	3"	390 F. S.	44 Ft. Lbs.	2
25 Auto (6.35 m/m)	50 M. C.	RN	2"	750 F. S.	62 Ft. Lbs.	4
9 m/m Luger		FN	4"	1039 F. S.	297 Ft. Lbs.	10
30 (7.65) Luger	125 S. P. and M. C.	RN	4"	1173 F. S.	285 Ft. Lbs.	10
30 (7.63) Mauser	93 S. P. and M. C.	RN	6"	1397 F. S.	373 Ft. Lbs.	11
32-20 Winchester C. F.	86 S. P. and M. C.	FN	5.5"	954 F. S.	232 Ft. Lbs.	5
32 Auto (7.65 m/m)	115 S. P. and M. C.	RN	3.5"	950 F. S.	144 Ft. Lbs.	5
32 S. W.	74 M. C.	RN	10"	725 F. S.	99 Ft. Lbs.	5
32 Long Colt	85 Lubaloy Ct'd and M. P.	RN	6"	641 F. S.	82 Ft. Lbs.	4
32 Short Colt	82 Lubaloy Ct'd	RN	6"	650-800 F. S.	119 Ft. Lbs.	4
32 S. & W. Long	80 Lubaloy Ct'd	RN	6"	740-775 F. S.	130 Ft. Lbs.	4
32 Colt N. P.	98 Lubaloy Ct'd and M. P.	RN	6"	750 F. S.	121 Ft. Lbs.	4
38 S. & W.	98 Lubaloy Ct'd and M. P.	RN	10"	725-750 F. S.	181 Ft. Lbs.	6
38 Auto	145 Lubaloy Ct'd and M. P.	RN	6"	1100 F. S.	352 Ft. Lbs.	12
380 Auto	130 M. C.	RN	3.5"	855 F. S.	154 Ft. Lbs.	4
38 Colt N. P.	95 M. C.	RN	6"	625 F. S.	130 Ft. Lbs.	5
38 Short Colt	150 Lubaloy Ct'd	RN	6"	608-775 F. S.	173 Ft. Lbs.	5
38 Long Colt	130 Lubaloy Ct'd	RN	6"	750 F. S.	186 Ft. Lbs.	6
38 Special	150 Lubaloy Ct'd	RN	6"	825 F. S.	239 Ft. Lbs.	7
38 Special Mid. R.	158 Lubaloy Ct'd	RN	6"	750 F. S.	185 Ft. Lbs.	5
38-40 Winchester	148 Lubaloy Ct'd	"Clean Cutter"	6"	975 F. S.	380 Ft. Lbs.	6
41 Short Colt	180 Lubaloy Coated, M. C. and S. P.	FN	5"	625-665 F. S.	157 Ft. Lbs.	4
41 Long Colt	160 Lubaloy Ct'd	RN	6"	725 F. S.	235 Ft. Lbs.	5
44 S. & W. Special	200 Lubaloy Ct'd	RN	7.5"	760 F. S.	315 Ft. Lbs.	9
44 S. & W. American	246 Lubaloy Ct'd	RN	7.5"	675 F. S.	207 Ft. Lbs.	7
44 S. & W. Russian	205 Lubaloy Ct'd	RN	7.5"	750 F. S.	324 Ft. Lbs.	7
44 Winchester C. F.	246 Lubaloy Ct'd	FN	7.5"	975 F. S.	422 Ft. Lbs.	6
45 Auto	200 Lubaloy Coated, S. P. and M. C.	RN	5"	900 F. S.	360 Ft. Lbs.	8
45 Colt	230 M. C.	RN	5"	825 F. S.	384 Ft. Lbs.	6
	255 Lubaloy Ct'd					

WESTERN CARTRIDGE CO.

Center Fire Cartridges — Revolver and Pistol Ballistics

	Barrel Length Inches	Bullet Weight Grs.	Velocities Feet per Second		Energies Foot-Pounds		Penetration in ⅞″ Pine Boards		
			Muzzle	100 Yds.	Muzzle	100 Yds.	Lead	S. P. or H. P.	M. C. or M. P.
.25 A. C. P., Smo., S. P. and M. C.	2	50	745	650	61	46	..	..	4
.30 Luger, Smo., S. P. (7.65 m/m) and M. C.	4½	93	1173	1031	284	174	..	..	10
.32 Short Colt and Smo.	6	82	680	611	82	68	4	..	..
.32 Long Colt.	6	82	690	610	86	67	5	..	..
.32 Long Colt, Smo.	6	82	720	636	94	72	5	..	..
.32 Colt, N. P. and Smo.	4	100	730	660	117	96	4	..	..
.32 A. C. P., Smo., S. P. (7.65 Br.) and M. C.	3½	73	965	847	151	113	..	..	5
.32 S. & W., Smo.	4	85	635	560	76	59	4	..	..
.32 S. & W., Long and Smo.	4	98	720	650	112	92	4	..	..
.32/20 and Smo., Lead, S. P. and M. C.	6	100	954	874	232	169	5	..	..
9 m/m Luger, Smo., M. C. and H. P.	4	125	1040	930	300	240	..	..	10
.35 S. & W., Auto., Smo., S. P. and M. P.	3¼	76	809	..	111	..	..	4	..
.38 S. & W., and Smo.	4	146	700	632	159	129	6	..	..
.38 S. & W., Special and Smo.	6	158	860	798	258	218	7	..	..
.38 S. & W., Special Mid-Range, W.C.	6	147	755	..	187	..	4	..	..
.38 Colt, N. P. and Smo.	4	150	700	641	163	137	6	..	..
.38 Short Colt and Smo.	6	125	630	563	107	88	4	..	..
.38 Long Colt and Smo.	6	150	800	735	213	180	8	..	..
.38 Long Colt, D. A., Mid-Range	6	150	660	..	145	..	6	..	..
.380 A. C. P., Smo., S. P. and M. C.	5	95	1190	1026	408	303	..	..	12
.38 A. C. P., Smo., S. P. and M. C.	3½	130	900	789	171	131	..	..	5
.38 Colt Special	6	158	860	798	258	218	7	..	..
.38 Win. (38/40), Smo., S. P. and M. C.	5½	180	985	867	389	300	7	..	..
.41 Short Colt and Smo.	6	160	710	636	179	143	4	..	..
.41 Long Colt and Smo.	6	196	715	654	222	186	5	..	..
.44 S. & W., American	6	205	682	625	212	177	6	..	..
.44 S. & W., Russian	6	246	712	659	277	237	7	..	..
.44 S. W. Special	6	246	780	724	332	286	6	..	..
.44 Win. (44/40), Smo., S. P. and M. C.	5½	200	918	808	375	290	6	..	..
.45 Colt.	5½	255	790	729	353	301	5	..	..
.45 A. C. P., M. C., Smo., 200 Gr.	5	200	910	847	368	319	..	..	8
.45 A. C. P., M. C., Smo., 230 Gr.	5	230	809	761	335	295	..	..	7
.45 Auto Rim, M. C., Smo., 230 Gr.	5½	230	809	761	335	295	..	..	7
.45 Auto., Rim, Lead, Smo.	5	255	740	682	310	263	5	..	..

PETERS CARTRIDGE CO.

Ballistics on Remington Oil-Proof Pistol and Revolver Cartridges

Cartridges		Type of Bullet	Weight of Bullet	Muzzle Velocity	Approx. Muzzle Energy	Barrel Length Inches
5.5 m/m Velo Dog	Kleanbore	M. C.	45	750	56	2
.25 (6.35 m/m) Automatic Pistol	Kleanbore	M. C.	50	735	60	3 1/8
.30 (7.63 m/m) Mauser Automatic Pistol	Kleanbore	M. C.	85	1280	310	6
.30 (7.63 m/m) Mauser Automatic Pistol	Kleanbore	S. P.	85	1280	310	6
.30 (7.65 m/m) Luger Automatic Pistol	Kleanbore	M. C.	93	1180	290	4 1/2
.30 (7.65 m/m) Luger Automatic Pistol	Kleanbore	S. P.	93	1180	290	4 1/2
.30 (7.65 m/m) Luger Automatic Pistol	Kleanbore	H. Pt.	93	1180	290	4 1/2
.32 Smith & Wesson		Lead	88	730	100	4
.32 Smith & Wesson	Kleanbore	Lead	88	710	100	4
.32 Smith & Wesson	Kleanbore	M. Pt.	88	710	100	4
.32 Smith & Wesson, Long		Lead	98	820	150	5 3/4
.32 Smith & Wesson, Long	Kleanbore	Lead	98	790	140	5 3/4
.32 Smith & Wesson, Long	Kleanbore	M. Pt.	98	790	140	5 3/4
.32 Short Colt		Lead	80	750	100	4
.32 Short Colt	Kleanbore	Lead	80	670	80	4
.32 Long Colt		Lead	83	810	120	4
.32 Long Colt	Kleanbore	Lead	81	770	110	4
.32 Colt New Police (Police Positive)		Lead	100	760	130	4
.32 Colt New Police (Police Positive)	Kleanbore	Lead	100	730	120	4
.32 Colt New Police (Police Positive)	Kleanbore	M. Pt.	100	730	120	4
.32 Colt New Police, Mid Range	Kleanbore	Lead	100	670	100	4
.32 (7.65 m/m) Automatic Pistol	Kleanbore	M. C.	71	950	140	4
.35 Smith & Wesson Automatic	Kleanbore	M. Pt.	76	830	120	3 1/2
9 m/m Luger Auto Pistol	Kleanbore	M. C.	124	1210	400	8
9 m/m Luger Auto Pistol	Kleanbore	H. Pt.	124	1210	400	8
.380 (9 m/m) Automatic Pistol	Kleanbore	M. C.	95	850	150	3 3/4
.38 Super Automatic Colt Pistol	Kleanbore	M. C.	130	1200	417	6
.38 Smith & Wesson		Lead	146	750	180	6
.38 Smith & Wesson	Kleanbore	Lead	146	730	170	6
.38 Smith & Wesson	Kleanbore	M. Pt.	146	730	170	6
.38 Smith & Wesson, Special		Lead	158	960	320	6
.38 Smith & Wesson, Special	Kleanbore	Lead	158	860	260	6
.38 Smith & Wesson, Special	Kleanbore	M. Pt.	158	860	260	6
.38 S. & W. Special Mid Range, Sharp Shoulder Bullet	Kleanbore	Lead	146	760	190	6
.38 S. & W. Special Target, 50 Yards	Kleanbore	Lead	130	750	160	6
.38 Colt New Police (Police Positive)	Kleanbore	Lead	150	710	170	4

Cartridge					
.38 Colt New Police (Police Positive)	Kleanbore	Lead	150	710	170	4
.38 Short Colt		Lead	125	650	120	6
.38 Short Colt	Kleanbore	Lead	125	710	140	6
.38 Long Colt		Lead	152	860	250	6
.38 Long Colt	Kleanbore	Lead	148	780	200	6
.38 Colt Special		Lead	158	960	320	6
.38 Colt Special	Kleanbore	Lead	158	860	260	6
.41 Short Colt		Lead	163	660	160	6
.41 Short Colt	Kleanbore	Lead	163	660	160	6
.41 Long Colt		Lead	195	850	310	6
.41 Long Colt	Kleanbore	Lead	195	720	220	6
.44 Smith & Wesson, American		Lead	218	650	200	6½
.44 Smith & Wesson, Russian		Lead	246	830	380	6½
.44 Smith & Wesson, Russian	Kleanbore	Lead	246	780	330	6½
.44 Smith & Wesson, Special		Lead	246	820	370	6
.44 Smith & Wesson, Special	Kleanbore	Lead	246	770	320	6
.44 Smith & Wesson, Special	Kleanbore	M. Pt.	246	770	320	6
.44 Colt, Old Model		Lead	210	660	200	6
.44 Webley		Lead	200	560	140	4½
.44 Bull Dog		Lead	170	460	80	4½
.45 Webley		Lead	230	550	150	6½
.45 Smith & Wesson		Lead	250	710	280	7
.45 Colt		Lead	250	910	460	6
.45 Colt	Kleanbore	Lead	250	770	330	6
.45 Colt Auto Pistol	Kleanbore	M. C.	230	810	340	5
.45 Auto Rim	Kleanbore	M. C.	230	810	340	5½
.45 Auto Rim	Kleanbore	Lead	230	810	340	5½
.450 Revolver		Lead	226	590	170	6
.455 Webley Mark II	Kleanbore	Lead	275	600	220	6½

REMINGTON ARMS CO.

Revolver Ballistics of Winchester Rim Fire Cartridges

Name of Cartridge	Barrel Length, Inches	Weight of Bullet, Grains	Velocities of Bullet, Feet per Second at Muzzle	Energies of Bullet, Ft. Lbs. at Muzzle
.22 Short, Staynless	6	30	850	48
.22 Long, Staynless	6	30	870	50
.22 Long Rifle, Staynless	6	40	815	59
.22 W. R. F., Staynless	6	45	810	66

Revolver and Pistol Ballistics of Winchester Center Fire Staynless Cartridges

Caliber	Bullet Weight Grains	Muzzle Vel. Ft. per Sec.	Muzzle Energy Ft. Lbs.	Penetration at 15 Ft. in ⅞ in. Soft Pine Boards
.25 Auto Colt	50	755	63	3
.32 S. & W. Lead	85	700	93	3
.32 S. & W. F. P. Lead Bearing	85	700	93	3.5
.32 S. & W. Long	98	810	143	4
.32 S. & W. Long F. P. Lead Bearing	98	810	143	4.5
7.63 Mauser	86	1397	373	11
7.65 Luger	93	1225	310	11
.32 Short Colt	80	700	90	3
.32 Long Colt Inside Lub	82	705	91	3
.32 Colt N. P.	98	706	109	3
.32 Auto Colt	74	965	152	5
.32 Win. Lead	100	974	210	5
.32 Win. M. P.	115	954	232	6
.35 S. & W. Auto	76	809	110	—
9 m/m Luger	125	1040	300	10
.38 Short Colt	130	705	144	4
.38 Colt N. P.	150	675	152	4
.38 Colt Spl.	158	858	258	6.5
.38 Long Colt	150	772	198	6
.38 Long F. P.	150	772	198	6.5
.38 Auto Colt	130	1190	410	10
.380 Auto Colt	95	890	168	5.5
.38 S. & W. Lead	145	700	158	4
.38 S. & W. F. P. Lead Bearing	145	700	158	4.5
.38 S. & W. Spl. Lead	158	857	258	7
.38 S. & W. Spl. F. P. Lead Bearing	158	857	258	7.5
.38 S. & W. Spl. Mid Range Sharp Corner	148	750	185	—
.38 Win. M. P.	180	986	389	7
.41 Short Colt	160	707	178	4
.41 Long Colt	196	706	217	5
.44 S. & W. Amer.	205	682	212	4
.44 S. & W. Russian	246	680	252	4
.44 S. & W. Special Lead	246	755	312	7.5
.44 S. & W. Spl. F. P. Lead Bearing	246	755	312	8
.44 Win. M. P.	200	919	375	7
.45 Colt	255	771	336	5
.45 Auto Colt	230	809	335	6
.45 Colt	265	757	337	5

WINCHESTER REPEATING ARMS CO.

BALLISTICS FOR AUTOMATIC PISTOL AND REVOLVER CARTRIDGES, U. S. CARTRIDGE CO.

Cartridge	Bullet Weight Grains	Muzzle Velocity Foot Second	Muzzle Energy Ft. Lbs.	Barrel Length Inches
.25 Colt Auto	50	750	63.	3.1
.32 Colt Auto	75	950	150.3	3.7
.38 Colt Auto	130	1190	410.	5.
.380 Colt Auto	95	870	159.7	3.7
.45 Colt Auto	230	800	327.0	5.
7.63 m/m Mauser	86	1377	373.	5.5
7.65 m/m Luger	94	1200	297.5	4.7
9 m/m Luger	125	1050	306.1	4.
.32 S. & W.	87	650	81.64	3.
.32 S. & W. Long	98	800	139.3	6.
.38 S. & W.	150	715	170.3	5.
.38 S. & W. Special	164	850	258.	6.
.38 S. & W. Special M-R	147	650	123.7	6.
.44 S. & W. American	207	680	212.6	6.5
.44 S. & W. Russian	246	775	328.2	6.5
.44 S. & W. Special	246	775	328.2	6.5
.32 Short Colt	80	700	87.	6.
.32 Long Colt	87	700	94.7	6.
.32 Colt New Police	100	700	106.	6.
.38 Short Colt	128	750	160.	6.
.38 Long Colt	148	775	197.4	6.
.38 Colt Special	164	800	233.1	6.
.38 Colt New Police	150	715	170.2	5.
.38 Colt New Police	150	800	213.2	6.
.41 Short Colt	167	650	156.7	6.
.41 Long Colt	200	700	220.9	6.
.44 Bull Dog	164	450	73.7	2.5
.44 Webley	200	500	111.1	2.5
.44 Colt	210	700	228.6	8.
.45 Colt	250	765	336.	5.5

BALLISTICS FOR .22 LONG RIFLE N. R. A. CARTRIDGE FIRED IN .22 COLT AUTOMATIC PISTOL

Arm used: Colt Auto Pistol with 6 5/8" Barrel.
Bullet Weight: 40 Grains.
Penetration at 15 feet 1" Pine Boards, 3.7".

Range Yards	Velocity Ft. Sec.	Energy Ft. Lbs.	Time Flight Sec.	Drop at Target Inches
0	940	78.5	....	...
25	914	74.1	.080	1.2
50	889	70.2	.164	5.2
75	866	66.6	.249	11.8
100	843	63.0	.338	21.5
150	801	57.0	.711	50.0
200	760	51.3	1.132	91.0

UNITED STATES CARTRIDGE CO.

SECTION 32
COMPARING VARIOUS BULLETS AS MAN STOPPERS

In considering the stopping power of bullets it must be taken into consideration that a .22 caliber bullet in some parts of the head or body is just as deadly as the well-known .45 Colt. In using a revolver for protection every second counts. A bullet from a light caliber gun may eventually stop a man, but will it stop him before he can shoot you? This is what must be considered. From one extreme to the other a .22 caliber bullet with a striking force of about forty-eight foot-pounds may be compared, as it strikes the arm or leg and part of the body, to a blow from the small end of a heavy whip; while the .45 Colt, with its energy of three hundred and thirty foot-pounds in smokeless powder and four hundred and sixty foot-pounds in black powder, may be compared to a blow from the butt end of a heavy whip. In other words the .45 Colt strikes a blow, whether in arm, leg or body that will temporarily disable the prisoner, therefore probably saving one man's life.

I know when this is read that many of my readers will remember cases where this did not occur and they are right; it is not always the case. Sometimes a man will hold a heap of lead and still keep on shooting, but as Colonel Chandler, first Superintendent of the New York State Troopers, used to say: "If you shoot a man with a .45 Colt and he doesn't go down, just walk around back of him and see what is holding him up."

In speaking in this article of bullets as man stoppers the thought is of the man in a place where speed, accuracy, and the hitting power of his revolver is the only thing that will save his life. His bullet must disable his opponent instantly to the extent that he will not be able to shoot back.

It is true that extreme accuracy and the small caliber bullets will cause this result, but ninety per cent of the man's shooting to protect his life is at night and a hit in any part of the body is very accurate shooting when sights cannot be seen. Personally I do not believe that any bullet with less than one hundred and fifty pounds' muzzle energy is heavy enough for protective or police purposes. The .25 Colt Auto Cartridge bullet has a striking force of sixty foot-pounds and the .32 Police Positive bullet has a striking force of one hundred foot-pounds.

It must be taken into consideration that some men will carry off more lead than others. I could cite several cases where two men have stood not over five feet apart and emptied their revolvers, chambered for the .38 Colt Special and S. & W. Special cartridge, into each other's body, both dying later, but that is not the idea. Either by accurately placing the shots and instantly disabling the opponent with the small caliber revolvers, or by using the large caliber arms that greatly increase the man's chances, can the desired result be accomplished. We cannot afford to trade a good citizen or an officer for a crook. Miniature arms for protection are better than the larger arms, due to weight, as long as they are not needed to protect the owner's life, but the sense of security derived from the more powerful arm is well worth the carrying of added weight. But, however powerful the arm used as to stopping power, a hit must be registered; misses do not count.

I believe it would be impossible for any physician to describe the effect of bullets in certain parts of the body that would apply to every one. The outdoor man with approximately twenty-five per cent more vitality than the office man, and the fighter who will go through as long as he is able to move, are all different. A friend of mine some years ago was called to his door one evening and without warning was shot one-half inch below the heart with a .38 Colt Police Positive cartridge. He went back into the house, ran through three rooms, found his shotgun, ran back through the house and out into the yard, and ran nearly fifty yards before he fell. At least ninety per cent of men shot in the same way would have fallen in the door. This argument of bullets as man stoppers can never be settled, as cases may be cited where men who have been wounded have performed almost unbelievable feats.

The man-stopping qualities, of course, do not interest target shooters, but they do interest the man who wishes to use his favorite side arm for hunting. We sometimes receive a photograph of bear, moose, and other household pets being killed with a .22 revolver or pistol. Such things have happened, but if the bear has his mind on his work it may fail and at a time when there are no small trees to climb. There are bears and bears. If you ever meet a grizzly and have only a .22, don't argue; find a small tree that the bear cannot climb and, when nicely out of reach, try out the .22.

This reminds me of an experience which happened in the Iver-Johnson Sporting Goods Stores some years ago when I was employed there. A young man weighing about one hundred and twenty-five pounds came in and informed me that he was going down in Maine to shoot bear and deer. I showed him a .30/30 Winchester carbine ¾-magazine, checked pistol grip,—a nicely finished arm. He said: "If you don't know what a man wants to shoot bear and deer with I can go somewhere else and trade." Then I knew my customer and told him I had just what he wanted. I sold him an eleven millimeter Mauser and eighty cartridges imported and loaded with Cordite powder. After a little persuasion and the assurance that after a couple of shots he wouldn't mind the recoil, the young man shook hands with me and told me he would come in when he came back and report. The motto of all this is: If you are entirely unfamiliar with firearms either take a friend along who does know them or allow the clerk whose business it is to equip hunting parties to help choose the outfit. The same thing is true about automatics and revolvers. The man with a very small hand may have trouble in using a .45 New Service with speed and accuracy, wherein he may accomplish the desired result with a .38 caliber arm or a .45 or .38 caliber automatic pistol.

I am a great believer in large caliber revolvers or pistols for protection or as a game weapon and believe it carries a certain security that is missing in the smaller calibers.

I have always been a firm believer in the .41 caliber Colt cartridge and still am. With a bullet of approximately two hundred and fifteen grains in front of the correct charge of smokeless powder, a revolver with barrel correctly fitting said bullet and a cylinder built along the same lines as the .38 Colt cylinder to accommodate this .41 Special cartridge; what a prize that would be for hunting, protection, etc. And who would without trying it say that it would not be accurate? The shape of the old .41 bullet at front end could not be improved on as a man or game stopper, and another advantage is the size of the revolver in which this cartridge could be used. For instance, the Official Police revolver in two, four or six inch barrel and from thirty-one to thirty-four ounces, and with a stopping power great enough to place this combination well up in the list, is one of the hardest hitting hand guns in the world.

I have shot thousands of the old black powder .41 cartridges loaded with the very hollow base bullets. When the explosion occurred the base would expand against the sides of the chamber and barrel, consequently unbalancing the bullet. While some degree of accuracy could be attained by this method it never was satisfactory. Then came the smokeless powder but still the hollow-base bullet and large barrel, and this combination sounded the death knell of the cartridge that never had a chance. Perhaps we should let the dead rest in peace, but I can look into the crystal and see the value of such an arm. Thousands of hunters, police officers, and gun lovers have discarded the larger caliber revolvers for the .38, sacrificing stopping power and possibly their lives because they did not wish to carry a few extra ounces of metal. I believe I would lay aside my constant companions, two .45 New Service 2-inch barrels, for a pair of the two-inch .41 Specia's.

Every gun lover, I am sure, wants to see a light-weight, high-power combination in his collection. All gun-bugs are sane on most subjects but who can tell by looking at them what new idea they are planning to harass the poor abused manufacturers of arms and ammunition with. But how else do improvements originate in firearms and ammunition except through the needs of the users. Actual use and experience bring forth our needs. No man sitting behind a desk, unless he has had actual experience or has profited by the experience of others, can tell what weapon is best suited for a certain purpose.

The sharp shoulder bullet in .38 caliber is an excellent bullet if backed by a full charge instead of mid-range loads. We cannot have the one revolver for all uses any more than we can have one golf club for all purposes; therefore, we must consider before purchasing an arm just how big the game is that we are going to shoot or if the arm is going to be used for protection, whether it is to be carried or used at home. My own two pocket guns with short barrels are sufficiently powerful so that I feel at all times prepared for a hunting trip or constant protection whether home or traveling. They are accurate enough to place ten consecutive bullets in an eight-inch black at twenty-five yards and would place said ten bullets in the ten ring at this distance if I could hold them.

SECTION 33

SINGLE AND DOUBLE ACTION SHOOTING

Single or double action shooting? This has been the controversy among the shooters. Let us first take the claims of the single-action converts. They claim that more accuracy can be attained in this way. Now we are speaking of police work and not target shooting and we must all agree that if an officer must fire a shot in self-defense the bullet has no effect until it strikes his opponent. An officer's life is in very little danger except at short range (by short range I mean inside of fifteen feet) and at this distance extreme accuracy is not as important as speed. The question has been asked me many times: "Why do you instruct the police to practice double-action shooting?" My answer to this is: "Because in fast shooting every officer will shoot double action." Imagine yourself with a double-action revolver in your hand at short range, knowing that your life depended upon your speed, cocking your revolver for each shot. Double action is one motion as you draw your revolver and point it, pull the trigger and your first bullet is on its way. Single action, draw the revolver, find the low hammer used on all double-action revolvers, draw it to the rearward position until it locks, with the chance of your thumb slipping off the hammer as you cock it, especially in cold weather.

The double action was placed in revolvers to use and as an improvement over the old single action. While single action is correct for slow fire and long range shooting it is incorrect where speed is desired. Ninety per cent of effective police shooting is inside of ten feet and less than two seconds to get into action. Any one who will practice double-action shooting will be surprised at the accuracy. Target men will shake their heads and tell you it can't be done. It is done, and I can name officers who use this double action in matches where plenty of time is allowed for single-action shooting, and they are making good scores.

The way you practice is the way you will shoot when you are protecting your life; if you have always practiced slow, deliberate fire you will know no other way.

And now I know I am going to hear from the lovers of the "Old Peace Maker," the single-action army, "How about us?" The single action is a wonderful arm; always the favorite of the old-timers and in a class by itself. For the man who has lived with the single action and who has practiced with it until he has mastered the art of quick draw and getting the first shot away it is a wonderful arm; but for the officer of today who has never taken the time to become familiar with any revolver he will find that he can master the later double-action revolvers in less time then he can the single action, which would in most cases be too heavy for his work.

The double action has its advantages for many occasions where the officer must carry his revolver ready for instant use, as in entering a house or room in which he has every reason to believe a criminal is hiding. If he should enter the house with his revolver cocked, a loud noise, as the slamming of a door or the throwing of some article, may cause him to fire a shot because less than one-eighth of an inch pull will release the hammer. On the other hand, if the revolver is carried with the finger near the trigger ready for double-action shooting five-eighths of an inch is required to fire the shot and for a quick shot it is not necessary to have the finger on the trigger, but just outside ready to slip inside the guard.

I have heard many senseless arguments why double actions should not be used. I remember the Pennsylvania State Police Team coming to Camp Perry and shooting double action in the matches. The old target men said it couldn't be done, but they did it and did it well at twenty-five yards. I do not recommend double action in this work, but I do recommend it for police shooting at close range. One reason that single action and target shooting was taught to police departments in years past is the fact that some one in that town or city, known as a good shot, either offered his services or was asked to instruct the officers. If he had never practiced in any way except at a target at regulation distance he would, of course, teach target shooting.

Target shooting or any other kind of revolver shooting will help the officer, but what he must eventually have is rough and tumble shooting, using speed rather than extreme accuracy. The idea is submitted through the motion pictures and western stories that no arms are used in the West except the single action. This is not true, and thousands of .38 and .45 caliber double-action revolvers and .38 and .45 caliber automatic pistols are used.

Many advance the idea that the single action is more dependable than the double-action revolvers; that if they were to locate in some out-of-the-way place or explore darkest Africa where a repair shop could not be reached for six months they would take the single action. I do not agree with this; the modern double-action revolvers will fire more shots and still remain in working order longer than the single action. I know I will hear from this statement but, nevertheless, it is true. Don't get discouraged, single-action men; you still have your pets and this statement will only make you love them more than ever.

CHAPTER 34

THE SHOOTERS' SECTION

Building a Championship Team

By Capt. J. H. Young

Just a few words of advice to those who wish to develop a good, strong revolver team.

First, check up on the timber you have to work with, or, in other words, have every man report for practice who wishes to try and make the team. Be sure to reject any man who does not want to shoot on the team, regardless of how good a marksman he may be. One unwilling member on a team, who does not think he can be told anything, will spoil a whole team. A team coach must have the good-will and confidence of every member on the team or he will make no progress.

Now let's assume that you have fifteen men to try for the team. Start them shooting, and note carefully the men who have the steadiest nerve and the best eye. You can soon dismiss several and save ammunition. As soon as you can tell who the most promising shots are, you can thin them down to about twice the size of your team. Then after a little more practice and instruction, hold an elimination contest, say about twelve matches. This will give you an idea of what competition will do to each man. You can then readily select your team with a couple of alternates and start your real training in earnest.

A great deal can be said about the way to train a team, but I will try to touch lightly on some of the most important points.

First, start your men in dry snapping. This is to a revolver shooter what running the scales on a piano is to a student of music, as you can watch the barrel of his revolver and see how much flip it has when the hammer falls. This you could not do if the gun was fired. Instruct each man to aim carefully, as if he were shooting in a match, and squeeze gently until the hammer falls, but still hold the gun on the bull's-eye for some moments after the hammer falls. If the gun has a barrel flip when the trigger releases, the student hasn't just the proper hold on the stock of the gun, or he has jerked on the trigger, or perhaps he has squeezed the stock with his whole hand, which is wrong. The trigger must be squeezed with the index finger. However, you may lay the thumb up along the frame of the piece and as you squeeze with the index finger press the thumb against the gun slightly. This will steady the gun and prevent the barrel flip.

After all of your team understand the trigger pull, take up the position of the body. Every man will have some peculiarity about his position, and he will insist on using it, because he made the team that way, but you must insist on correcting the position and see that it is done, but do it by reasoning with the student rather than by strict discipline, as here is where you get the confidence and good-will of your team. Now about the position of the body. Teach each man to face at an angle of about forty-five degrees from the target, and insist on this because if he faces squarely to one side at an angle of ninety degrees, he will have to turn his head to the right so much that he is likely to hamper the circulation of the blood through the jugular vein. On the other hand, if the student faces toward the target he will have to bring his hand over in front of the body, which puts the sights nearer the eye and also gives him an awkward position.

Now about the distance. The feet should be apart, which depends altogether on the comformation of the man. A tall man with long legs must stand with a greater stride than the shorter man. The left hand may be placed on the hip or in the trousers pocket, or left hanging naturally by the side as the student wishes. The head must be held erect, not reared backward or stooped forward, for if the student keeps shooting he some day will have to shoot with glasses, and if taught to hold his head in the proper position, it will come natural for him to see the sights through the center of his glasses, which one must do to get correct vision.

After you have the team trained on the position, the trigger pull and the proper grip on the handle, see that they do not slight any of these details, and each time you fall in for practice make your team dry snap a few minutes. This will steady their nerves and give you a chance to check on all positions and correct any error that they might make before they start shooting. Keep a record of all scores shot by your team so you can tell how they are improving. Begin with the slow fire first, and fire nothing else until they can make a good score. Then take up the time fire, but be sure to do some more dry snapping, timing the men, or have some one else do the timing while you check all other details and correct any errors.

After your men have learned the time fire, take up the rapid fire in the same manner, letting the team shoot together. You might run a little over the alloted time for rapid fire until the scores begin improving, then cut down the time to the regular ten seconds. Much time must be spent on the rapid fire so as to get the men accustomed to the allotted time.

Now you have your team working nicely, and it is up to you to guard against any discord among the team, such as jealousy or ill-will toward each other. Study each man's disposition carefully and coach him accordingly, as every man is different when he is firing. While one man may be talked to between shots or between strings of shots, another must not be spoken to at all while he is firing his score; never speak to any one while he is aiming, but correct his error between shots. But if he has had the proper instruction in practice he will not have to be corrected while firing for record. Do not allow your man to figure what score he or any one else is making if you are shooting a match, say thirty shots per man. Each competitor has only one thing to think about and that must be thought about thirty times, and this one thing is the shot he is firing. Just ease the trigger off at 6 o'clock when that shot is scored, forget it and start thinking about the next one and let the coach attend to all other details, such as spotting and challenging of shots. Be sure that your men know the number of the target they are to shoot on and see that they shoot on no other, for many an important match has been lost by firing on the wrong target.

And let me say once more, above all things, do not allow any animosity to arise among your team members; just remember that harmony is the strength of all organizations.

Camp Perry
1918 to 1928

By Major H. L. Harker

Away back about 1911, towards the close of one of those beautiful Indian summer days, while ascending a very long, steep hill full of tangled greenbrier and other matted undergrowth, seeking the wary cotton-tail rabbit with dog and gun, I arrived at the conclusion, that, if it was shooting I was looking for, it was to be in some other form. I had shot small rifle at stationary and moving targets for many years, so I thought I would try revolver shooting. Before very long I purchased a .38 D. A. Army Colt and sought acquaintance with some National Guard officers in whose armory there was a three-target range.

Among those who shot in this range were Major S. J. Fort and Sergt. W. A. Renehan. It was through these two men that I first learned of Camp Perry, but I didn't know what it was all about at that time. As the winter season approached, all hands being members of the Baltimore Revolver Club, we entered the indoor matches of the United States Revolver Association and shot successfully through these matches for several seasons. The World War was now shortly to come on and when it finally broke, and likelihood of this nation becoming involved, there was a great stimulus in revolver and military shooting.

After our government entered the conflict, it was found, notwithstanding we prided ourselves "A Nation of Riflemen," that we were far short of sufficient instructors in the regular service to properly train the men of the National Army who were to represent us at the front. Hence, in the spring of 1918 the Small Arms Firing School was organized at Camp Perry, Ohio, and by reason of our qualifications with the revolver, Major Fort and myself were commissioned and ordered to report to the commandant, Lieut. Col. Morton C. Mumma, at Camp Perry, Ohio, where we were to teach the revolver and automatic pistol. Thus was I formally introduced to Camp Perry, upon which I desire to write, and where I have spent many pleasant hours and made acquaintance with many fine men from all over the United States and its possessions. It is these men, the shooting clan, that I select as my colleagues, whether it be in peace, war or shooting holes in paper targets.

Upon arrival and officially reporting, we next secured quarters, some securing berths in the clubhouse and others being assigned to tents near by; however, near enough so we could hear that familiar early morning cry—"Roll call, everybody out." This took place in the basement of the clubhouse. Colonel Mumma usually presided, assisted by Major Brookhart and Major Libby. You will realize that there was lots to be worked out before classes could be properly handled. A plan of operation was drafted and a refresher course put on with us, who were to offer the instruction to the students. When I say that this was some band of shooting nuts, I am putting it mildly; even the little frame house now occupied as a range house for the pistol was named "Squirrel Inn."

There were about seventy-two in the personnel of the school, forty-two of whom were instructors. They included some Britishers, who had seen service across and who exerted their efforts in the snipers' section. Captain Richards, now with the Winchester Company, was with the snipers.

Major S. J. Fort was in charge of the Pistol Section and had, for his assistants, Captain Thomas LeBoutellier and Lieut. John Dietz, both from New York, and the writer. The other instructors were known as Rifle Instructors, who were assigned about thirty men to whom they taught the rifle from the beginning of its manufacture to the completed human element—"The Expert Rifleman."

One hour out of each day these rifle instructors marched their groups to the pistol ranges or to some designated spot, generally in the shade of those fine old trees on Sandy Kerr's lawn, where we proceeded to expound to them the mysteries of the 1917 revolvers and the Colt's automatic pistol, both of caliber .45. At first the pistol firing was conducted on the east end of the present 200-yard rifle butt; later, on a temporary range of twenty targets installed on the beach near the clubhouse. This was in charge of Lieutenant Dietz and generally referred to by the Colonel as the "Jon Dietz Range." The groups moved to and from these two ranges every hour of the working day. The pistol ranges were indeed very busy places. There were five classes in all that passed through the school from its opening in April to the early part of October, 1918, each class spending about five weeks there. The students consisted entirely of officers, from second lieutenants to colonels, and were assembled from the many posts throughout the government's possessions. These men, being far above the average, learned quickly and became very good instructors. After receiving a Certificate of Graduation from the school, they were returned to their respective stations to instruct the men of their commands.

In September, 1918, and in the midst of the work with our last class the National Matches were staged. As the war was still on and many of the country's best shots engaged in the training of men, the matches were not very well attended, except by those of the class and a few outsiders who had not been gobbled up in the draft. The pistol match, I do recall, was a record breaker for attendance, the number shooting being more than 1,100 and taking twenty-three relays to run it off. It was won by Mr. Frank Parmly of Kansas in the last relay.

The matches being over, the work of finishing up the last class again demanded attention, and I recall vividly the day for pistol qualifications. The day came in cloudy and overcast, and about the time the relays were all squadded a hard, driving rain set in. The work had to be completed that day and the several delays on account of torrential downfalls put the last squad through at dark, and every one soaked to the hide and some hungry. I think I turned in after taking a good hot shower and without supper. It now being October, the cold days began to put in their appearance along the shores of Lake Erie, making it undesirable for school purposes, which meant a change. It was rumored that we were to be grouped into instruction units, composed of a major in command, six riflemen, and a pistolman, and sent to six of the large cantonments. You can imagine the anxiety with which we watched the hand of Colonel Mumma, which held the chalk from which was to flow the names to comprise the units and where sent. I did not have long to wait, for the very first cantonment listed was Camp Travis, San Antonio, Texas; then the names, Major Krembs, and then mine. In a day or two our orders came through and we all went our several ways, planning to meet at the large hotel on the Plaza in San Antonio next to the Alamo on the morning of the 14th day of October, 1918. Once assembled and after breakfast we went to camp headquarters, presented our orders, and were assigned quarters. Then began the work of organization and some pupils to work on. This being something new to this camp, we had hard sledding for awhile, as it seemed that everybody was too busy with the new recruits, putting them through their "squads right," with no time left for shooting. However, I was detailed by the Major to scrape together a pistol class, while he and the others worked for the rifle.

I soon located by settling on the artillery. Now, every one knows when it comes time for the Field Artillery to use pistols things are very desperate, and it is about time for all hands to wish they were home under the kitchen stove. However, they were to be taught, so that ended any argument. Next, I inquired about their pistols. Well, it so happened that none had been issued, so the Colonel got busy and borrowed some from the 35th Infantry, then in camp, which enabled us to get started. After a few days this Colonel became very friendly and he had his chauffeur call for me at each session of firing, and at the close of the day I enjoyed the privilege of riding with him in the rear seat, much to the chagrin of my Major, who said he couldn't even get a jitney to take him to town.

In a week or so a school of two hundred and fifty-one was organized and we all proceeded to Camp Bullis, a target and combat range about twenty miles from Travis. It was while we were at this camp that the Armistice was signed and at the time when we were in the midst of our instructions. I recall very well the Sunday afternoon following the Armistice, I put through the class in pistol firing for qualifications. Shortly after this we were ordered to Camp Benning (now Fort Benning), Georgia, where we formed the nucleus of the Small Arms Division of the Camp and had under instruction at that time one hundred and thirteen men from West Point Academy. After this class, there being no urgent need for our services as instructors, we were assigned to the several points where arms from demobilized troops were sent for inspection, cleaning and packing, after which most of us accepted our discharge or went into the Reserve Corps.

In 1920, Col. Morton C. Mumma, having been selected as Commandant of the National Matches, surrounded himself with as many of the personnel of his old school as was possible and requisite, and with others I was asked to serve as range officer at my same old stand, "The Pistol Range." This reunion with the boys of the school was a very pleasant one.

It was at this match that I first made the acquaintance of Mr. J. Henry FitzGerald of the Colt Company, better known by his old friends as "Fitz," and easily told at great distances by his size and his ten-gallon hat which he invariably wears. This year, Commercial Row was along the east side of the main street entering camp at a point where Paddy O'Hare is now located. Fitz did not do quite as much repairing on the line in those days and at night the Colt tent was usually packed to "busting" to accommodate those who wanted repairs made and also with those who came to tell the latest jokes, good and otherwise, that could be gathered from all over the world; while Fitz was busy toiling in the rays of the old "Gasoline Lantern," taking out "creeps" and carefully placing them in a tin box to prevent them from getting in some other gun; and substituting "crickets" for sear springs when the customer was not watching. The only reason the crickets didn't work was when their frail legs would break. With all the work he always found time to come in on the laugh of a good joke and offering one in his turn. Many of the old timers will recall these pleasant evenings.

The next year found Commercial Row on the west side of the same street. It was this year that we had quite a lot of rain and several heavy blows from the lake. On one occasion most of the front row tents were blown down and General Phillips, then Secretary of the N. R. A., found himself wandering around in the rain all dressed up in his pajamas, his tent having gone skyward. There was at least six inches of water in the area occupied by the competitors; the boys had to undress atop of their cots and, during the night, through twisting and turning, some of the wearing apparel usually fell overboard. It was a common thing to hear some fellow ask: "See anything of my shoes floating around here?" and after all this they were ready to go at 7.30.

As I have been on duty on the Pistol Range every year since 1920, I have seen Camp Perry grow from a normal shooting camp to the one we have just passed, the largest ever, and in this time have made the acquaintance of the majority of the pistol shooters of the country, many of whom I know intimately. There is, of course, like in every group of human beings, the fellow who becomes a pest in some form or other. Some will insist on firing the last shot on the range, whether or not it is too dark to see the target or whether it is raining so hard the pasters slip off, which gives him a chance to claim all the open tens. Then we have the fellow who, after all rifle action has ceased, makes a run for the pistol range, only to find all the targets taken down except, possibly, the Instruction Target, setting off on the flank: "Say, Captain, can I take just one shot at that one?" One fellow came along with his .45 automatic and picked up a trigger weight to weigh in, cocked the gun, and hooked on the weight—"bingo" right by Colonel Rumsey's ear. He forgot about the one in the barrel. Another fellow only got off four shots in a ten second string: "Captain, can't I shoot six next time?" Then we have the fellow who gets nervous waiting for the targets to appear and proceeds to scratch the side of his head with the cocked pistol: "Say, cut that out, and stand at 'raised pistol'; if that gun goes off the bullet will ricochet off your dome and kill some one." While I am pretty well used to all these tricks, occasionally some fellow pulls a new one; so just keep smiling, take things as they come, and order up the next relay.

Keeping the pistol game going at Perry, with only fifteen operated targets, always presented quite a problem with 600 pistol shooters in camp. Shooting on the temporary ranges is really the best practice, as a man has the advantage of viewing his own shot groups; but, inasmuch as it was necessary to hold the major matches on the rifle butts, it was hardly fair to the men who had to practice on the non-operated ranges, owing to the line of fire being at quite an angle above the horizontal. This will all be obviated now, as the new pistol range of seventy targets, started in 1928, will likely be in shape for the 1929 matches, when it is hoped we will have sufficient targets to take care of all the matches and practice. There is a great stimulus in pistol shooting throughout the country. This is reflected in the National Match, the entries totaling 619 in 1928. Competition is keener than ever before and the man who wins in any event deserves his honor.

Fitz is the outstanding figure of the hand-gun clan and being a practical shot in any position, slow or rapid fire, quick draw and whatever else there is, he understands their very needs and the boys come from far and near to bring him their ills, whether real or imaginary. Long before he arrives in camp I am asked: "When is Fitz coming?" and those who are not acquainted, say: "Where can I find Mr. FitzGerald?" Well, pretty soon Fitz drives along in the family coach dragging the trailer which contains all usually found in a first-class hotel and a gun factory combined, and takes possession in No. 1, Governors Row, Squaw Camp. As soon as I notice this movement I get in touch with the Camp Director and have a tent put up in the rear of the pistol firing line where he can be near at hand and attend to the shooters promptly. Fitz formerly opened shop under a large wagon umbrella, but his popularity and need for his service caused the change to more commodious quarters; hence the tent. From the time he first opens his tool-kit until after the National Team Match he is a man to be pitied and well deserves a reprieve to grow some new skin on his finger tips that are about worn through. We are all glad when the last shot is fired, but before the snow of the following winter has disappeared, we are eagerly looking forward and scanning the pages of the "American Rifleman" for the announcement of the date of the next National Match.

Above illustration is the famous Shooters' Supply House of P. J. O'Hare, Camp Perry, Ohio, distributor of fine telescopes and shooters' accessories. Mr. O'Hare knows the shooters' needs and supplies them with the best, whether at his home, 552 Irvington Avenue, Maplewood, N. J., or at Camp Perry.

SECTION 35
EVIDENCE AND EXPERT TESTIMONY

Valuable evidence is often destroyed by carelessness on the part of the investigator. Many things which ordinarily would be of no consequence are very important when found at the scene of a crime. An empty shell lying on the sidewalk or in a room would have no significance, but if the dead body of a man or woman was found a few feet away from the shell that shell would be very important as it might be traced to the pistol or revolver used.

Nearly every shell whether fired in a revolver or automatic pistol has identification marks which, if the arm used is found, will mark other shells in the same manner.

In the following pages are photomicrograph pictures by Captain William A. Jones, Firearms Expert and Expert Photographer of New York City, which will explain some of these identifications marks on shells and bullets.

Of utmost importance on finding a body, as mentioned above, is to disturb nothing until a thorough investigation has been made for finger prints, pistol, knife, revolver or other weapons, bullets, shells, position of body, and, if possible, photographs should be taken before anything is disturbed. No two cases are exactly alike and notes should be taken that can later be used in court of everything connected with the case. It does not necessarily mean because a body is found with a revolver or pistol grasped in the hand that it is a case of suicide. The weapon may have been placed under the hand by the murderer.

Powder stains, burns and scorches on clothing and body may determine whether the wound was self-inflicted or not. I remember a case on which I was called where an officer was killed with his service revolver. The officer was called to the house to subdue a drunken man. In the scuffle the policeman was shot. One bullet fired through the side of the coat near the bottom did no damage except to make four holes in the coat and sweater; the fatal bullet entered the body high up on the chest. Both bullets were fired from an angle that would make it impossible for the officer to fire either shot himself. This was a case where neither bullet, shell, nor revolver figured; only the position of bullet holes in body and clothing would be of assistance as far as firearms evidence was concerned. A conviction was secured.

Bullets found in the body or imbedded in any material at the scene of a crime are very important, as not only can the caliber, make, and weight be determined, but they can in nearly every case be traced to the revolver or pistol from which they were fired if the arm can be found. The land and groove marks on the bullets will in many cases determine the make of the arm used and will reveal the peculiarities of that particular arm.

I remember a case I was called on some years ago. The man who killed an officer rode a motorcycle and the arm used was a Colt New Service .45 caliber. He used an open holster open at the bottom and short enough to allow the muzzle of the revolver to extend below the leather. As he rode the muzzle would continually strike on the frame or guard of the motorcycle. This continual pounding caused the muzzle to be flattened in such a manner as to force a part of the steel at the muzzle inward until it extended beyond the surface of the barrel cavity. Every bullet fired through this barrel was marked in the same way with a very clear identification mark. Many cases are encountered where some peculiarity in the revolver or pistol in evidence may be noted and classed as a factory mark. We also have the identification marks which are caused by conditions over which the factory has no control, due to accidents, dropping and not cleaning properly. Corrosion or rust in the barrel may mark the bullet or any number of bullets in the same way. Erosion marks may be visible and traced to several bullets. A bullet stuck in the barrel and forced out by putting a piece of heavy wire or other steel instrument in the barrel at the muzzle may raise a furrow of steel at some point in the barrel that would mark every bullet exactly the same. I appeared in a case some years ago where this was the condition and it left a positive identification mark. Bullets may be classed as lead, metal cased, and soft point, and these all register the peculiarities of the particular arm through which it is fired.

Great care must be taken in this work of matching bullets in evidence with bullets fired through the suspected revolver or pistol. It is not safe to jump at conclusions; be sure you are right and then go ahead. Only a careful examination with a good magnifying glass or microscope will reveal the facts to the expert, who possesses the ability through years of experiments and practice to compare the identification marks on bullets and shells fired from the same and different pistols and revolvers. Without this experience mistakes can be made with the microscope as well as with the magnifying glass. A seven-power glass is very accurate and as high as ten power in the magnifying glasses and ten to twenty-one power in the microscope is usually powerful enough for this work.

The question is many times asked me, would two barrels, coming one after the other from the rifling machine, carry identification marks by which the bullets could be traced to the barrels they were fired from? While two barrels may be rifled consecutively a slight difference may be found in the diameter of the lands and grooves. The bore diameter may vary one or two thousandths of an inch; the grooves may be deeper in one barrel than in the other; condition of the barrels after use may be such that the bullets may easily be checked as coming from one or the other barrel. A slight difference in the steel used in the barrels may cause a slight roughness in one that would not be found in the other. Two pistols or revolvers may be numbered consecutively, but that would not mean that the barrels were manufactured on the same machine or in rotation. Where mention is made in this article of defective tools or difference in grade of steel no particular make of arms are thought of, as both high-grade arms and those of inferior make and material are encountered in cases where firearms were used either to kill or wound, and the cheap, inferior arms of foreign manufacture are easier to trace a bullet to than the high-grade arms.

In a case which I had some years ago a man was killed with a .32 Smith & Wesson short bullet and the man who was arrested for the crime a short distance away was carrying a .32 Colt automatic pistol. The revolver shell was found near the body. It seemed a perfect alibi until the jury and court were shown that the .32 caliber Smith & Wesson short cartridge could be placed in the chamber of the .32 Colt automatic pistol and fired from it usually ejecting the empty shell, and allowing an automatic cartridge to be carried into the chamber and cocking the pistol. The bullet in this case could be traced to pistol in evidence and the shell plainly showed that it was not fired from a revolver.

It would be a long story to go into details of evidence encountered in thirty-five years of experimental work and then only a small part of what may be encountered in the gathering of evidence would be covered. We live and learn; we can only tell what we by experience know to be a fact and tell it in a way that it will be perfectly clear and understood by the court and jury. I believe that a very clear way to show identification marks on the bullets and shells is by the comparison microscope, as it shows clearly one-half of each two bullets compared and even persons not familiar with the work can easily see the identification marks or lines on lands and grooves if they exist. A complete outfit of high-priced microscopes are, of course, very helpful in expert work but equipment without experience means nothing. In a great many cases valuable evidence is lost by careless handling of the exhibits. One question: Why will an officer push a pencil or knife through a bullet hole in cloth, wood or other substance? I give it up, why will he?

A very serious trouble in the identification of bullets is the difference in the diameter of each bullet even in the same box. This is overcome in revolver bullets, which are usually made of lead. A lead bullet will mold itself into the corners of the lands and grooves in the barrel where the metal-cased bullets are of harder material and will not always fill the corners of the grooves. Right and left hand twist and width of lands and groove will many times determine the make of revolver from which a certain bullet was shot. The primer will usually identify the pistol or revolvers from which it was fired.

The firing pin identification is not always to be relied upon because of the kick back of the anvil in the primer, which will change the bottom of the firing pin indentation. In some automatic pistols the firing pin is the ejector and in this case the shell is rotating on the end of the firing pin from the instant the pistol starts to open until the shell is released. Many hard primers are encountered especially in the foreign cartridges and in these the lines and marks will not be so pronounced.

Many bullets recovered from a body and those which have come in contact with hard substances are deformed and some to the extent that only one or two lands and grooves are visible. If these happen to carry identification marks that can be traced to test bullets fired from the same revolver then fortune favors the expert. Sometimes identification is positive in a very few minutes and again several hours may be spent before a decision is reached. In any case the expert should be sure before rendering a decision.

My outfit consists of a Spencer Comparison Microscope; a Zeiss Binocular Microscope, with different objectives and eye pieces; a Zeiss Turmon Monocular, with 10X, 12X, 16X, and 20X supplementary lenses; a Hardy Binocular Loupe; a 10X Bausch & Lomb Hastings Triplet; a 7X of the same; an 8X and a 30X Hensholdt Glass and an 8-power Zeiss Microscope.

Powder stains, scorches and burns on clothing or on the body are very important in connection with the bullet wound and may be classified as contact shots, near contact shots where powder stains, scorches or burns are found on the body or clothing, and the distance shots outside the zone of powder stains. The contact shot may be readily determined as, for instance, the revolver or pistol held against the side of the head as the shot is fired. If the muzzle is loosely pressed against the skin a large, ragged wound about the size of the muzzle of the pistol will be the result and the edge of the wound will appear to be forced outward. If the muzzle is held tightly against the skin the powder gases will follow the bullet into the wound a short ways and will cause a swelling around the wound about the size of a dollar and the edge of the wound will be ragged and forced outward. A contact shot shows a small burn or scorch on edge of wound. By using the same kind of a pistol or revolver and ammunition a very accurate estimate may be given of the distance between the muzzle and the wound, also the direction of the bullet in relation to the wound may be determined by the location of the wound and the powder stains or scorch on the body or clothing.

Many times the question arises as to how far away the shot can be fired and powder stains and burns appear on body or clothing? To answer this the kind of powder used must be known and also its condition, whether black or smokeless, whether the shooting was done in a strong wind, and, if so, whether against the wind or with it. Many conditions enter into the correct analysis of the evidence presented.

Bullet identification and other evidence brought out by expert testimony is positive and only doubted by those who do not understand it. I heard a man testify, in a case I was called in upon several years ago, that he could see the flash from a 6-inch .32/20 Colt revolver twenty-four inches long. When asked how far the powder would burn from the same arm he answered eighteen inches. He was then asked what burned to show the flash that last six inches and then he decided that three years' experience as a gunsmith did not teach him all he should know.

Great stress has been laid on the fact that experts disagree, so do doctors and professional men and people in all walks of life. It lays with the judge and jury to determine the honesty of a witness, whether he be an expert or just a witness, and a disagreement of experts does not mean in all cases that one of them is dishonest; experience and judgment may enter into the case. We can only testify to what we can see.

Many more interesting facts might be added to this section if we were sure that the book would only reach the hands of those who would use them for lawful purposes. The fascinating part of expert testimony is that no two cases are the same. In consultations and testimony relating to hundreds of cases I have found this true; such aids as trick photographs and manufactured evidence is never resorted to by the honest expert. He has no interest in the poor devil being tried; he is only interested in his work and the stating of plain facts as he sees them.

Capt. William A. Jones, Mr. Albert W. Foster, Jr., and myself have appeared in many cases and examined hundreds of bullets and firearms together. I cannot recall one case where we have disagreed in our diagnosis of a case.

I have appeared at different times with Capt. Van Amberg, Boston, Mass., James Burns, Ballistic Engineer, Remington Arms Co., and Murton Robinson, Winchester Repeating Arms Co.,—men with years of experience and a thorough understanding of the value of bullet identification.

EMPTY SHELLS FROM TWO PISTOLS

The empty shells in this picture came from a pair of .25 Colt's Automatic Pistols. The three at top came from one pistol, while those at the bottom came from the other. Note difference in markings on primers.

TWO SHELLS AT LEFT ARE FATAL SHELLS
SHELL AT RIGHT IS A TEST SHELL

At Top: Two shells fired from one .25 Automatic Pistol.
At Bottom: Two shells fired from another .25 Automatic Pistol.
Note VI at top of primer on two bottom shells. This mark is distinctive and could not be identified with any mark or lines appearing on the two shells at top.

TRANSPOSING A PART OF FATAL BULLET TO THE TEST
BULLET SHOWS IDENTICAL LINES ON LANDS AND GROOVES

TRANSPOSURE OF PART OF ONE RIFLE BULLET TO ANOTHER
AND IDENTIFIED AS COMING FROM THE SAME RIFLE

CAPT. WM. A. JONES
Firearms Expert, New York City

COMPARISON MICROSCOPE.
Used by Capt. Wm. A. Jones, with bullets in place for comparison

MR. ALBERT FOSTER, JR.
Connoisseur of antique and modern arms
and firearms expert

SECTION 36

HOW TO BECOME A FIREARMS EXPERT

The first requirement is a knowledge of firearms and ammunition covering all the latest arms and cartridges and also the older models. Many old model arms now laying in some trunk or drawer will appear at the scene of a crime and a working knowledge of the arms is necessary. Whenever an unfamiliar revolver or pistol appears study it, take it apart, and make notes on the direction of twist, width of lands and grooves, peculiarities of breech block, construction of chamber, action, grips, frame, etc. It does not follow that an expert cannot correctly testify about an arm of a make that he has never seen before. The land and groove marks of a bullet fired from the unfamiliar model will compare with the land and groove marks on another bullet fired from the same revolver or pistol if the barrel is of a size that fits the bullets. I mention this fact because in my experience I have encountered many times a modern cartridge loaded with smokeless powder and with a bullet too small to fit some of the older model arms. In fact one old model revolver of .38 caliber with a barrel designed to shoot the black powder, hollow base bullet is so large that the modern bullet .38 S. & W. or Colt Special will drop through the barrel.

If a modern bullet is shot in this revolver it is almost impossible to identify it due to the bullet striking first on one side and then on the other on its journey through the barrel. I was on such a case a few years ago. We had the confession and the owner of the revolver admitted that was the revolver used in the shooting, also that he had fired the shot, but I could not identify the bullet for the above reason and therefore did not testify.

It makes no difference what proof is submitted through other sources the expert must by his own efforts build up his case. As the fatal bullet is received examine it for identification marks. In a recent case a bullet was submitted to me that had been carried by some one in the pocket or case for a period of time and all identification marks were erased. It was just a lump of lead and could not be identified. If our coroners and attorneys would use more care in the handling of bullets and shells our work would be easier. The proper way to preserve bullets and shells is to roll them in cotton, each one separately, and place cotton and exhibits in a serviceable box for future use.

Identification marks may be placed on bullets and shells for use in court if it is properly done without erasing marks in evidence. The bullets may be marked on base or rear end,—a straight line for number one bullet, two lines for number two bullet, and so on until each bullet has an individual mark. These marks should be registered in a notebook with the other material pertaining to the case and after each mark explain fully where bullet was found and everything relating to it,—date, hour, and minute it was found, names of those examining it, place it was kept from that time until the trial, and names of persons having access to it between those dates.

The shells, while not as easily damaged as the bullets, should be handled with the same care and marked at the open end either inside or out in a way that will not interfere with identification marks.

We are now back to the bullet. It may be first examined with a seven, eight, or ten power microscope, and in many cases this is powerful enough to discover prominent marks. If these are discovered the bullet is then placed in the comparison microscope with the prominent marks up or toward the glass. These marks may also be found by placing the bullet in the microscope without examination with a small glass.

With the revolver as received, fire a shot using the same make of ammunition and shape of bullet. This may be easily accomplished by purchasing a pound box of absorbent cotton; open the end of box, stand it up on the floor and fire a shot into the open end, being careful to fire the bullet straight into the cotton about halfway between center of cotton and edge of box; otherwise the entire roll of cotton must be opened and if the exact center of the cotton is hit the bullet may follow end of paper and cotton to the bottom of the roll. This package of cotton will stop revolver or automatic bullets, but will *not* stop rifle bullets. It is an added precaution to fire this shot in the basement, but it is not absolutely necessary. After the bullet is recovered it may be examined with small glass or put directly into the microscope with the prominent marks toward glass if they are found. Then adjust comparison eyepiece and the microscope to view one-half of each bullet. If the fatal bullet is badly defaced and parts of prominent identification marks are missing, then other marks may be used in comparison. Capt. William A. Jones was the owner of the first successful comparison microscope used in this work. A microscope of this kind is a very positive way of comparing bullets and shells.

The shell identification is similar to the bullet identification except that shells are stood on end and primers are compared, exposing one-half of each primer in microscope and comparing the markings on surface. Ejector and extractor marks on automatic shells are important and easily compared.

It is not necessary to go to the expense of purchasing a comparison microscope for ordinary cases, but it is the most accurate road to correct identification. Another addition which may be used in connection with comparison microscope is a camera, mounted on a standard without lens, that may be inverted and placed above microscope taking a picture of what you see. This picture may be enlarged to desired size and used in court work. I have used a binocular microscope, a monocular microscope, and several others for this work and while they will answer the purpose the comparison marks must be carried in the mind from one bullet to the other. Only in very low power glass can both bullets be seen at the same time. Finger prints and small objects may also be compared correct'y with the comparison microscope. The proper lighting is very essential and the same power light used at each bullet.

The binocular microscope with horseshoe base is of great assistance in the examination of bullet holes, blood, powder stains, finger prints, and other material connected with a case, and in investigation work. It is an image-erecting scope and useful in many ways. The high-grade pocket magnifying glasses are very useful and easily carried.

The comparison of bullets and shells is very important and equally so is the effect of bullets on the human body, the body of an animal, wood, metal, glass and other substances. The contact shot is one which requires much study, for the effect of a contact shot is different in different parts of the body.

We will first analize the effect of a shot so fired with a cartridge loaded with smokeless powder. If the muzzle of the revolver or pistol is held tight against the side of the head as the shot is fired the effect will be a hole several sizes larger than the bullet, with the edges blackened and scorched and turned outward. A gas pocket about the size of a dollar will be formed around the bullet hole between flesh and bone in which will be found particles of powder and powder residue. As the bullet passes through the flesh and encounters the bone it is slowed up by the bone resistance and this hesitation of the bullet in its flight will tend to stop the onrushing gases, causing them to spread and form a gas pocket. A large per cent of the remaining gases will follow the bullet into the wound, sometimes tearing the tissue and causing a frightful wound inside the head. The outrushing blood will wash out some of the powder residue, particles of powder, and discoloration and will tend to cover the rest to the extent that a casual observation would create the idea that it was a clean wound. The revolver or pistol so fired may not have any bloodstains upon it because the onrushing gases following the bullet will check the flow of blood until the forward pressure of gas is released by the recoil of the revolver or pistol, which forces the muzzle away from the wound and upward. The hand holding the weapon would not be liable to show bloodstains for the same reason. The weapon may be found several feet away, if shot was fired when the person was standing up.

The effect of above shot fired from revolver and automatic pistols of different calibers and powers will differ as to size of wound, gas pocket, tearing of wound, etc., but the general characteristics will be the same. While smokeless powder is spoken of in this explanation of contact shots, there are different kinds of smokeless powder. Many revolver and all automatic cartridges are loaded with a flash powder, which is nearly all burned in the shell, while .32/20, .38/40, and .44/40 cartridges used in both rifle and revolver are usually loaded with a slower burning powder. This may be proved by laying a white paper on the ground or floor ten or twelve feet long and with revolver parallel with and six inches above the paper fire a shot. Unburned grains of powder will be found along the paper sometimes ten feet away. This will be especially true in the case of the .38/40 and .44/40 cartridges. The effect of gases from above-named cartridges on the wound described would be different from the description given and would give nearly the same results as black powder.

A contact shot when black powder is loaded in the cartridge will produce different results than that obtained with smokeless powder. The force of the gases is greater and the wound will be slightly larger, the edges more ragged or torn, the gas pocket larger, and a greater amount of powder and powder residue will be noted in pocket. The destruction of tissue will be greater in many cases, the flesh will be torn in several directions, from one-half to one and one-half inches in length.

If the contact shot is fired with the weapon against the forehead the tearing of the flesh may be greater than when it is fired against the side of the head, due to the flesh being drawn tighter across forehead and curve of the bone. If the muzzle of the weapon is one-quarter of an inch away from the flesh and shot is fired no gas pocket will be found. The powder grains and residue will be found on the outside of the wound. As the distance increases the size of the circle containing powder grains and residue will increase and by using the same kind of cartridges, with powder in same condition, the distance at which a shot was fired can be estimated correctly to within one-half inch.

If a contact shot is fired with clothing, coat, vest or trousers between the muzzle of the gun and the body the gas pocket will in nearly all cases be absent, as gases escape through cloth leaving a ragged hole in the garment, but powder residue will be visible around the wound. Smokeless powder residue will be visible around the wound or on clothing at a distance of one-quarter inch to fifteen inches. The .32/20, .38/40, and .44/40 cartridges loaded with slow-burning smokeless powder will have powder residue visible if the shot is fired from one-quarter inch to twenty inches; black powder is visible from one-quarter inch to four feet, depending on the condition of the powder. If the cartridges have been kept in a damp place and the particles of powder have become caked or stuck together, this ball or mass of powder will go out of the barrel as a projectile and will cause powder stains up to the distance stated,—four feet.

Formulas of different powders would not assist the expert because many powders are blended or made for special requirements and would have to be analyzed to determine the ingredients. The most successful results are accomplished by procuring ammunition of the same make, powder, and bullet; also date of manufacture, if possible, and perform experiments until the desired results are obtained.

A room in which a crime is committed by shooting should be thoroughly searched for bullet holes, powder stains, finger prints, etc., as every clue is important.

When appearing on a case, after viewing the exhibits go over the tesitmony with the attorney and give him a clear understanding of your deductions, also give him an outline of your qualifications in expert work on a card or paper that he can refer to when you are called to testify. The following are the qualifications which I use in court work:

Q. What is your name?
A. J. Henry FitzGerald.
Q. Where do you reside?
A. Hartford, Connecticut.
Q. What is your occupation?
A. The study of firearms, their construction and uses; the investigation of cases where firearms were used either to kill or to wound; police instructor; and giving expert testimony in trials where firearms were used.

Q. How many years have you experimented with firearms?
A. Thirty-nine years.
Q. How many experiments have you performed with firearms?
A. Over 150,000 experiments with different arms.
Q. Why were these experiments performed?
A. To gain the knowledge of firearms and their uses and also the knowledge of ammunition used in firearms.
Q. What is the nature of your testimony in regard to firearms?
A. The external effect of bullets on the human body and other substances, powder stains, scorches and burns on the human body and other substances. The direction of bullets, the comparison of land and groove marks in the different revolvers and pistols, the comparison of land and groove marks on bullets fired from the same and different revolvers and pistols, and the comparison of primers and shells fired in the same and different revolvers and pistols.
Q. Name some of the police departments you have instructed and are connected with.
A. I am shooting instructor of the New York State Police and a member of that organization; a member of the faculty and firearms inspector instructor in the New York State Police School; and a Member of the New York State Police Chief's Association. I have instructed the state police of Pennsylvania, Maine, Maryland, Delaware, New Jersey, and several other state departments, and the city police of Washington, D. C., Minneapolis, St. Paul, St. Joseph, Des Moines, Kansas City, Omaha, Louisville, Indianapolis, Montreal, Ottawa, and hundreds of banks and police departments in the United States and Canada.

Q. How many trials have you testified in where firearms were used.
A. About 265 trials where firearms were used and I have been consulted in between 1200 and 1500 cases relating to arms and ammunition.

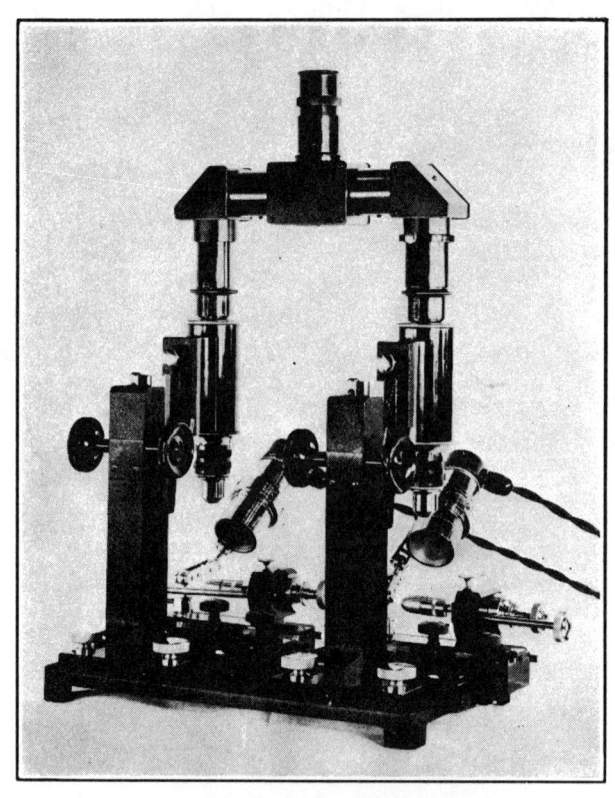

COMPARISON MICROSCOPE
As manufactured by Spencer Lens Co., Buffalo, N. Y.

Cut No. 1

FRONT OF PORK RIND OF CONTACT SHOT

With .38 Colt's special cartridge loaded with black powder. Note torn skin around bullet hole.

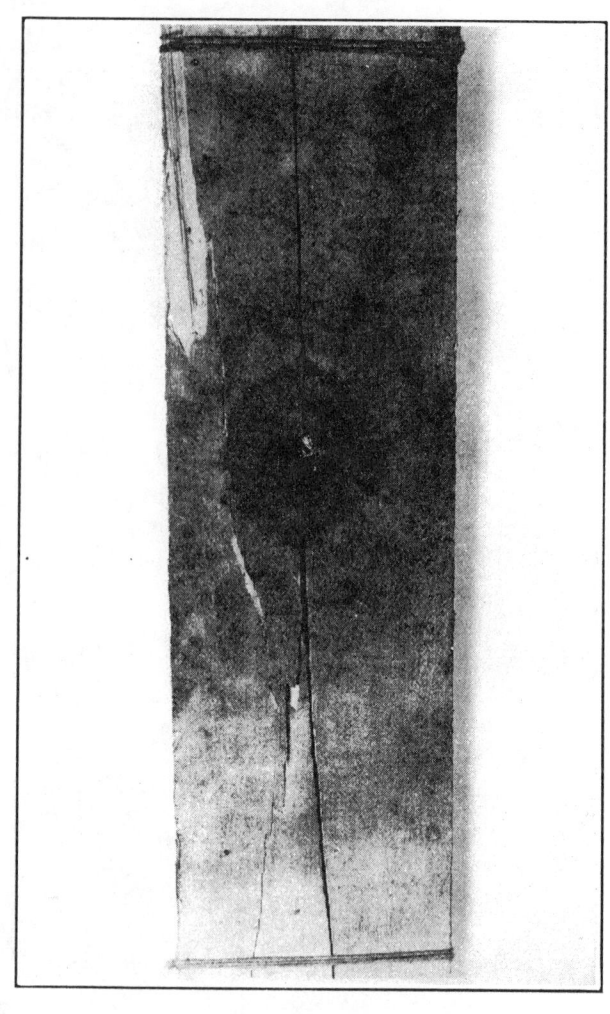

Cut No. 2
BOARD OF CONTACT SHOT
Placed behind pork rind in Cut No. 1. Note deep stain around bullet hole.

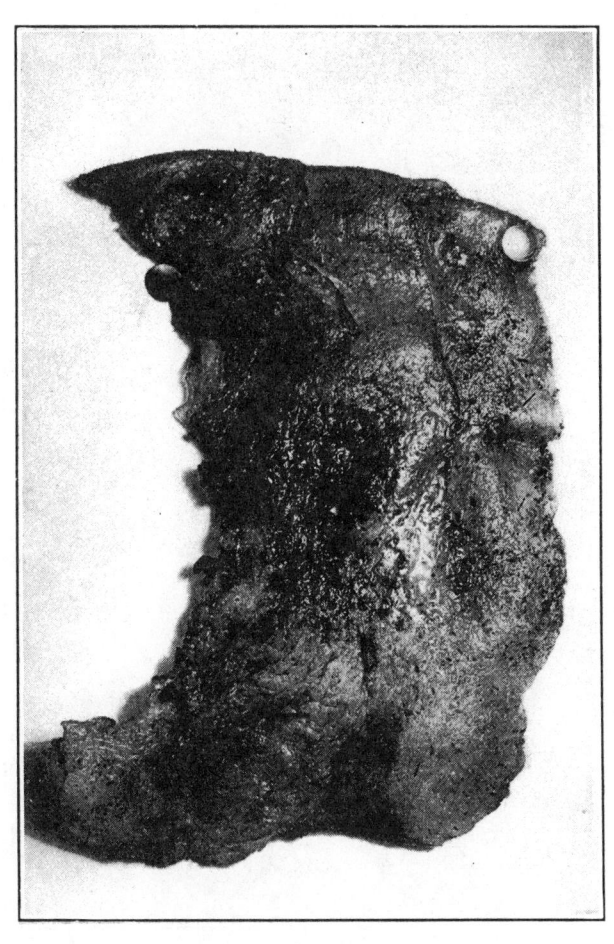

Cut No. 3
BACK OF PORK RIND, CONTACT SHOT
Note powder residue around bullet hole.

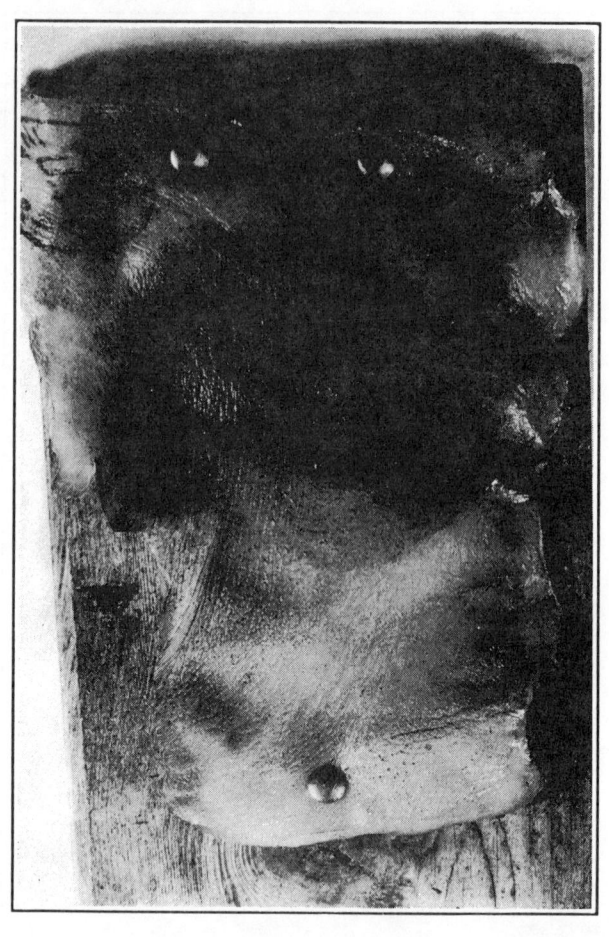

Cut No. 4
FRONT OF PORK RIND, ONE-FOURTH INCH DISTANCE SHOT
Note powder residue around bullet hole.

Cut No. 5
BOARD OF ONE-FOURTH INCH DISTANCE SHOT
Note absence of powder residue around bullet hole in board.

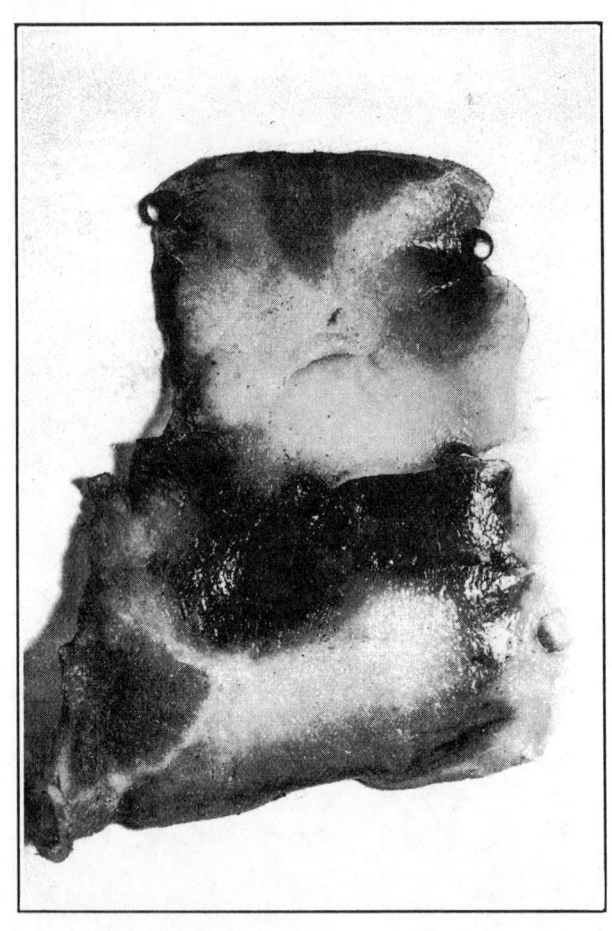

Cut No. 6
BACK OF PORK RIND, ONE-FOURTH INCH DISTANCE SHOT
Note absence of powder residue around bullet hole on side next to board.

PREFACE FOR POLICE AND BANK SECTIONS

In the following Police and Bank Sections I have endeavored to outline a protective system of shooting covering all emergencies which might arise.

It is not founded upon theory, as every situation is covered by rules and instructions that have been successfully used in bank and police circles. The fundamentals are speed and accuracy of fire when it shall become necessary to use a revolver in self-defense or to protect the lives and property of others. At that time the peace officer, through study and practice of the following system, will be able not only to save his own life but to apprehend the criminal or at least discourage his activities in that locality.

We must meet the present situation of lawlessness with an adequate system of protection. The police are outnumbered many times by those who resort to crime as a means of gaining a livelihood and only by superior skill and training may the officer hope to succeed in his chosen profession.

SECTION 37

PRACTICAL POLICE AND DEFENSE SHOOTING

Practical police and defense shooting applies to the necessary shooting by police officers, bank guards and armored car guards in discharge of their duty, and, in fact, every one whose occupation it is to protect money and property.

By practical shooting I mean being able to shoot quick and straight. Target shooting is that branch of shooting where the object is to place your shots in the center of a small target and the penalty for not doing so is a poor score. Practical shooting is the placing of your bullets in a human target in such a manner that said human will be unable to shoot at you. The penalty of not being able to do this is the loss of your own life.

We may as well look at this in the true light for target shooting is not sufficient, as that is an advanced stage in the art of shooting. Some of the best quick-draw shots in the world never shot at a target and couldn't hit one if they did. It is at short range that your life is in danger and at short range that you must be able to place your shots. You may carry a revolver for months and years without knowing how to use it and never have any trouble, and then again you may have trouble the first day or week. If you do not know how to use your revolver you will either forget that you have it and freeze in your tracks, or you will draw it and perforate some innocent bystander, scattering your shots in all directions and no one will be safe, not even yourself.

I have heard the remark, "No one knows what he will do in a gun fight." This is not correct, because the man who is a practical shot will always give a good account of himself as he has confidence in his ability. He knows just what he can do and he knows that the chances are one hundred to one that his opponent has not his confidence or knowledge, and this confidence and knowledge will be the means of developing a system of self-preservation and defense that is priceless.

I firmly believe that if this system of police shooting becomes universal that crime will decrease fifty per cent. But it must be more than one or two men in a department; all should practice until they are at least fair shots. It does not take months and years to become a fair shot, as it does in target work; it may be accomplished in a very short time.

You have a large target in front of you and the natural qualification of being able to point your finger at a certain object; by handling your revolver a short time you will be able to point the barrel of the revolver as you would your finger, pulling the trigger double action as the barrel swings into line with the target. When you have accomplished this you have the principle of quick shooting at short range and quick draw will be taken up later.

I know a great many officers who never shot at a regular target in their life but who, when their time came to bring in their man, did it with no trouble whatever. I have been called upon many times to instruct a police department of forty or fifty men with a time limit of two or three days placed upon the job. Only one thing can be done in that length of time. Place a Colt's Silhouette target at five, ten and fifteen yards, and instruct the men in hitting it both single and double action with the right and left hand. All the courses are timed with a watch that times to one one-hundredth or one-fifth part of a second and, in scoring, one-third of the time is subtracted from the scores.

We have heard that little saying that slow and steady wins the race, but quick and steady wins a gun fight, and the quotation that "Colts make all men equal" doesn't mean that the man who has had practice and knows how to shoot is not the master of the man who doesn't.

A short time ago I visited a police department and knowing the lieutenant well wished to speak a good word for him to the chief. I said: "Lieutenant S—— is a good man for you, Chief, and a fine revolver shot." The chief said: "Yes, a h—— of a fine revolver shot. Missed a man six times the other night who was crawling out of a window twenty-five feet away. I was with him." Now, I know that this particular lieutenant was a fine shot as far as target shooting was concerned, but he was not a rapid fire shot, and therefore was as wild as any amateur when trying something he was not familiar with.

I have several times been shown revolvers that were used by officers in a shooting bee, with the complaint that the arm did not work properly. I found nothing wrong except that when the first shot was fired the trigger was not released and, of course, the next shot could not be fired. I instructed the guards in one of our large banks a short time ago and one of the officials, in the course of our talk, pointed out one of the guards and told me that he was a coward. When I asked the reason he said that a short time ago they had a little scare and a couple of shots were fired, and that the man in question stood in the middle of the floor and never even drew his revolver. I then asked if the man had ever been instructed in the use of a revolver and the official said he had not. I explained to the official that a a man should not be branded a coward until, after proper instruction, he had failed in his duty. A man who has never fired a revolver is probably more afraid of his own revolver than he is of the one in the hands of a gunman.

One of my greatest troubles is teaching officers not to swing their revolvers up over their shoulders and head before bringing it down on the object they want to hit like the movie method. This method makes it unsafe for every one in the range and valuable time is lost, and, as I heard Colonel Rumsey tell one of the shooters at Camp Perry, "The bullet may bounce off your head and hurt somebody." A close second to the over-the-shoulder and around-the-head variety of getting ready is to aim the revolver at the feet. You are liable to spoil a good pair of shoes, if you persist in this, and it doesn't improve the foot any, either. Keep the muzzle of the revolver pointed *toward* the *target* at all times and keep your mind on what you are doing. Another dangerous proceeding is to turn around at the firing point with a loaded revolver in your hand. Some years ago at Perry on the firing line the contestant on my right asked me if I could see with my glass where his last shot went. I turned around and found that he was aiming his .45 automatic at my belt buckle. I side-stepped and told him that I couldn't see where his last shot went, but that I knew where my next one would go if he didn't swing his pistol toward the target.

It seems that I am always quoting something that I have heard at Camp Perry, but one cannot help it who has been fortunate enough to visit the camp during the National Matches. I am glad to see that, while the Police Team and Individual Matches are the big matches, the practical matches are not forgotten. Bobbing targets, running man, running deer, gas attacks and jiu-jitsu are all taught, and this work is of more importance in police work than the target shooting.

One or two lessons will not bring about the desired result, but continual practice will. I have been asked: When is an officer proficient in the use of a revolver? That is when he can handle his revolver with the same speed and sureness of action that the driver handles his car. A car suddenly appears out of a side street without any preliminaries. The brakes go on and the car comes to a stop. Now the policeman comes along the same street, and instead of a car coming out of the side street a burglar appears with a revolver in his hand thirty feet away; can the policeman get into action with the same sure, swift motion that the autoist did? I wonder! The revolver is probably carried under the coat and, being unfamiliar with drawing it, valuable time is lost here; if he is unfamiliar with drawing his revolver he is also unfamiliar with using it when he gets it. We may say three seconds gone and all this time the burglar may be shooting at him because the officer is trying to do something he is not accustomed to do, namely:

To shoot quick and straight and not at a paper target but at a living target capable of shooting back; we know the answer. Fortunate is the inexperienced officer who emerges from this situation alive and if he does the reason is that the other man was as poor a shot as he was. On the other hand place an officer in this position who has mastered the art of quick drawing and quick, accurate shooting; with his trained eye and gun hand, he is master of the situation, even getting his first shot away accurately before the inexperienced man can raise his pistol and fire a shot that has only one chance in one hundred of registering a hit. The difference between inexperienced and experienced officers is that word is passed among the burglar's friends to keep away from that town, as the bulls there can shoot. The officer who can shoot is a credit to his department and to himself. This question may be asked by some of my readers: Suppose the policeman made a mistake; suppose this was the man who owned the house looking for a burglar? If he was he would not have raised his revolver to shoot the officer, as all officers are plainly marked even to the shiny badge locating his heart.

Many otherwise good officers are killed every year because they do not know how to shoot. It is the cheapest kind of insurance and pays big dividends because it teaches when to shoot and when not to shoot. The inexperienced officer may shoot for no reason at all. The man coming out of the driveway may be in direct line with the house where it would not be safe to miss; the expert would take all this in at first glance and would not miss. I have heard several officers say they would not shoot a man. If this is the case they do not value their own life or their oath to uphold the law. At the present time there is too much shooting by the crook and not enough by the police.

It is just as necessary to know when not to use the revolver as it is to know when to use it. For instance, on a crowded street conditions may arise when it would be dangerous to fire a shot even at six feet. The power of the revolver used must be taken into consideration. It must be remembered that a .38 caliber bullet or larger striking the arm, leg, or parts of the body where no bone is encountered may go straight through and wound some innocent bystander. It is better to let the criminal escape than to have this occur. The officer who does not know how to use his revolver is dangerous because he will either draw his revolver and shoot before the proper time or will be so slow in getting into action that he will lose his own life or be unable to protect the life and property of others. It is not a pleasant subject to speak of shooting a human being, but if we must choose between losing a good officer or a known crook even our sob sisters must agree that the officer should live. The officer is always at a disadvantage as he is known to the crook by his uniform. The crook is not always known unless he breaks a law, which he will not do unless it appears to him that he will be successful and his get-away is assured.

Disarming Holds by Captain Langrish and Lieutenant McGann

The following explanations and illustrations will show the disarming holds practiced by Captain Langrish and Lieutenant McGann.

Positions 1, 2 and 3.

From hands up position drop left hand, thumb on cylinder, turn revolver away from body.

With right hand grasp opponent's right wrist, force revolver away at an angle that will cause opponenet to loosen hold on revolver.

Continue pressure until opponent's finger is caught by trigger guard. Always practice with revolver empty.

Positions 4 and 5.

Opponent using revolver as club, revolver grasped by barrel. Raise right arm in front of head, catch opponent's wrist with right hand as he attempts to strike.

Force arm backward, lock left forearm inside opponent's elbow, grasp your right wrist with left hand, step forward, increase pressure on opponent's arm until revolver is released, then throw him over your right hip.

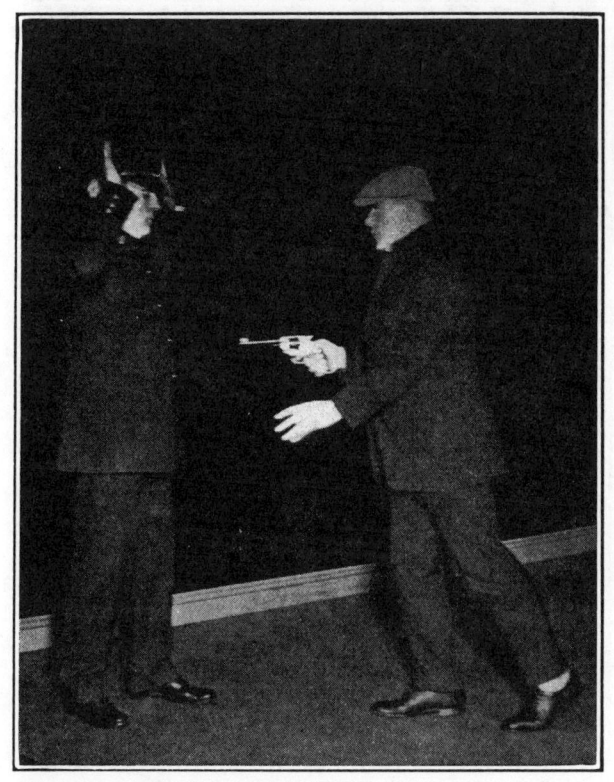

POSITION No. 1
(See description on page 308)

POSITION No. 2
(See description on page 308)

POSITION No. 3
(See description on page 308)

POSITION No. 4
(See description on page 308)

POSITION No. 5
(See description on page 308)

SECTION 38

THE MAGIC OF KNOWING THAT YOU CAN SHOOT QUICK AND STRAIGHT

The magic of knowing that you can shoot quick and straight is a life-saver and when you acquire it you will place more dependence in your revolver than you will in any three friends you have. You know what you can do with it and you have confidence in yourself. You not only know this yourself, but your brother officer knows it and consequently every gunman in your city, and they will let you alone and pick on some other officer whom they know will not be dangerous if they should exchange shots with him.

Knowing your own capabilities will cause you to work out in your own mind certain ways and means by which to overcome every possible emergency which might arise. If you are going into a house or hall after a prisoner you will work out certain lines of safety, such as not going into a house with gloves on and your revolver tucked away in your hip pocket under several coats and sweaters. I once saw an officer go after his revolver and after opening several layers of coats and sweaters take a bundle out of his hip pocket. It was the leg of his wife's stocking sewed up at the bottom, inside of which he kept his revolver. He asked me to suggest a better place to carry it. I told him I could name several and that even going home after it when it was needed would have its advantages over standing on the street and trying to get it, that is, if you went fast enough the first hundred yards. One gentleman told me some time ago that he carried his revolver in his back pocket and his coat buttoned up so that no one could get it, and my answer to him was, "Neither can you get it if you need it."

To all officers who carry their revolver in out-of-the-way places I will only ask them to step in front of a looking-glass and go after their revolver; see yourself as others see you. An instance that happened years ago when my labors consisted of selling revolvers for the Iver-Johnson Sporting Goods Company in Boston, Massachusetts, may be cited here. Two men came in, and in the course of the conversation informed me that they were secret-service men, that their life depended on their ability to use their revolvers, and that they both felt sorry for me because I only sold revolvers and didn't know how to use them. I told them I was glad they came in and asked them if they would show me just how fast an up-to-date officer could get his revolver or pistol into action. They agreed to show me and we placed our hands on the showcase, fingers touching and at the word "Go" we all three went after our arms. I don't like to talk about myself but before either of the secret-service men had reached his hip pocket they were looking into the business end of two .45 New Service revolvers. I asked them to show me the arms they carried and both proceeded to take out handkerchiefs, keys, etc., and finally a little buckskin pocketbook with clasp at the top. After opening this, they tried to take out a .25 Colt automatic. I say tried because both pistols were rusted and stuck to the felt lining. We finally succeeded in getting them out of the cases and the arms were so rusted that they could not be opened easily. I recommended a thorough cleaning and a different holster. One of the men remarked that my revolvers were cannons and should have wheels and asked me why the .25 automatic did not have a higher front sight. I told him that it was built that way, so that when it was taken away from him and shoved down his throat it would not hurt him so badly.

I have listened to many officers explaining how good they could shoot and when they got on the firing line they couldn't hit a cow in the head with a snow shovel. I remember a two-gun man, an officer, never mind where, who informed me that twelve shots meant twelve dead men. I put up two silhouette targets and he started after his peace-makers. I agreed with him that twelve men might be killed, but whether they would be killed in front, behind, or on either side I was not sure; neither were others in the range, as we were alone when the exhibition was over. I believe I gave a fine exhibition of escaping from a drink-crazed fleet of hornets. I told him to always stand in the middle of anything he wanted to hit, as neither target showed any signs of distress.

I visited a friend of mine who ran a small manufacturing plant and as it was after-hours we went upstairs to the office. We were there only a short time when we heard a heavy tread on the stairs and finally the officer on that beat opened the office door and came in. He said, "Oh, it's you, is it, Frank? I thought it might be burglars when I saw the light up here." He came in with his heavy gloves on and several layers of coats and sweaters over his hip pocket. I asked the officer why, if he thought there were burglars in the office, he did not come prepared. He said he was and proceeded to go after his revolver. It took him two minutes and eleven seconds to get his revolver out ready for business.

A police chief once told me that a little incident which happened two days before had convinced him that his men and himself should learn how to shoot. He said he was going home through the park when he discovered one of his men chasing a burglar. He joined in the chase. While running he caught his foot on a root and, as he was carrying his revolver with finger on the trigger, he fired a shot, perforating a perfectly good park bench, and striking his head against a tree. He was unconscious and his men carried him back to the station before they found that he had not been shot.

It is a grand and glorious feeling to know that you can shoot quick and straight, but don't fool yourself, be sure you can do it.

SECTION 39

POLICE REVOLVERS

The first thing an officer requires is a serviceable revolver, one that is safe and reliable, and will function perfectly when his life is in danger. He may carry any caliber from .32 to .45, but if he can place his shots and place them quickly all calibers of arms are effective. The heavy calibers are, of course, preferable and safer for the officer to use, as a slightly misplaced shot will cause the desired result. As the old saying goes: "In a gun fight the little arms will hide under the thumb nail, but you feel like a he-man with a .45 in your hand."

It is well to remember that the gunmen of today are carrying .38 and .45 caliber arms; in many cases the .45 automatic pistol. It is true that small caliber arms will kill but will they kill quick enough to prevent the criminal from killing the officer? It is all very well to speak of placing the shots. This can be done in good light and favorable conditions, but many times the officer is forced to shoot when a hit in any part of the body is good shooting and the caliber used should be large enough to slow up the criminal if hit in any part of the body.

The .38 Official Police six-inch barrel and the .45 New Service five and one-half inch barrel revolvers are the favorites with state troopers and officers employed in protecting rural and outlying districts, the longer barrel because of the more open country and the chance for long range shooting, and by all means the arm should be worn on the outside. The two-inch and four-inch barrels are recommended for inside holster use and for use in the side pockets, as these barrels are long enough for any shooting which an officer will be called upon to do, and is faster on the draw than the longer barrel revolvers. Every inch added to the length of the barrel adds to the time required to place the first shot.

The most effective, fastest and lightest revolver made in a medium power arm is the Police Special, with a two-inch barrel. In close quarters this arm is supreme because of its power and because of the short barrel. If this revolver is grasped by an opponent he would be unable to twist it out of the officer's hand as he could easily do with the longer barrel because of the greater leverage. I have always been an advocate of short barrels for pocket and inside holster arms because of the speed of draw. I have heard complaints about a two-inch barrel being inaccurate, but I find that many of the men who say they cannot hit anything with it cannot do much better with any revolver, and the men who can shoot find no fault with the short barrel.

The officer's revolver should be equipped with a positive safety, so that in case it is dropped upon the floor or pavement it positively will not explode the cartridge. Many officers have been killed or wounded or have been the cause of wounding others by dropping their revolver. And this is liable to happen if the men are equipped with any revolver not having a positive safety. A police revolver should be one that will give long service and stand up under rough, hard usage. A police revolver should be tested at the factory to shoot double action. This is very important, as a large per cent of police shooting is double action. The gun should be tested with different kinds of ammunition and be tested for accuracy offhand as the officer will use it.

Many officers are carrying old-style revolvers to protect their lives; this is not economy, as the best and safest revolver is what every officer should carry. One is carrying a revolver probably for years and practicing with it for what? To be ready for that few seconds when a perfect working revolver and clear head and steady hand will be your only chance of escaping with your life.

Some police departments carry the same arms for fifteen or twenty years. I do not believe this is economy. The arms of twenty years ago are not as good and never were as the arms of today. We would not think of using automobiles even eight or ten years. Why expect a revolver to last forever? In speaking of firearms improvements take, for instance, the sights. Twenty years ago the front sights on police revolvers were of the knife-edge variety with a very fine rear notch. It is safe to say that one-half of the police officers in the United States could not see this combination of sights clearly either twenty years ago or today and without good sights it is impossible to place the shots.

The point will arise that a great many shots fired by police officers are at night and this is true, but the only way that a police officer can shoot well at night is in knowing by the feel of his revolver when the arm is pointing in the desired direction. He can only perfect this kind of shooting by constant practice in good light and with sights that he can see plainly. Then he will develop the feel of the revolver that will enable him to shoot well at night. Captain Machelli, instructor of the New York Police Department, is a firm believer in wide, square sights for police revolvers, $1/10$ and $1/8$ inch sights, even on the service revolver with four-inch barrel. These sights can be seen in lights when the ordinary narrow sights would be invisible. Such sights will stand a great deal more abuse than the narrow variety.

Now, the subject of grips. The old-style hard rubber grips, which would surely break if the arm was dropped and sometimes when the arms were fired, are no longer furnished to police departments; in their place has come the checked wood stocks or grips roughly checked and practically unbreakable. They are superior in every way to pearl, ivory, or any kind of composition grips yet invented for service. It is true that if the arm is carried on the inside it will wear the coat lining or vest, but the proper holster will eliminate much of this wear and a piece of leather attached to coat lining will eliminate the rest. If stocks seem too rough for the hand a fine piece of sandpaper will remove this objection. Even the triggers have been improved on the modern arms. They are now furnished on police revolvers and target arms roughly checked and this prevents all slippage of the fingers when firing. Sights are roughened or sandblasted, which is an aid when shooting in a strong light and the mechanism is greatly improved over the older type of arm.

I do not wish to discourage police departments with old arms they may be using, but with the other up-to-date articles of police equipment it is not fair to endanger an officer's life by equipping him with an old out-of-date revolver. It is well to take into consideration when buying new revolvers the size of the average officer's hands. If the men all have large hands, then the larger, heavier model would be more acceptable. The smaller models, if properly held, while not as comfortable as the larger arms, will fit the hand nicely, and are, of course, lighter to carry.

The mainspring in the police revolver is heavier than is practical in a target revolver and for this reason police revolvers are used double action; whether double or single is used the spring must be heavy enough to explode the cartridge. After the revolver is shot three or four hundred shots the spring may be lightened, as at that time the mechanism is working with less friction than when the arm is new. It is well to carry six or twelve extra cartridges, as one never can tell how many may be used. Full charge ammunition should always be carried in the arm as the sights are corrected for the full load and it will not be accurate with a reduced charge. It is advisable to always look at the revolver before going on duty; see that the side-plate screws are tight, hammer nose in working order, and the arm fully loaded. It may surprise the officer on one of these inspections to find that either through the cleaning process or in showing the arm to a friend he had neglected to load the arm.

The revolver is the king of protective weapons and, instead of passing laws to prohibit its use, every good citizen should be the owner of a revolver and know how to use it. What else may we have in the house to protect the family and our worldly possessions from the sneak thief, who cares for neither God, man, nor the devil, and who carries a revolver to protect himself from the police and will use it on women and children if they cross his path? What else may we take in an automobile or on camping trips for protection but a reliable revolver or automatic?

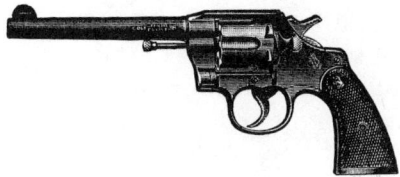

.38 COLT'S OFFICIAL POLICE MODEL
Made in 4, 5 and 6 inch barrels and also in .22 caliber, 6-inch barrel.

.38 COLT'S OFFICER'S MODEL
Made in 4, 6 and 7½ inch barrels and also in .22 caliber, 6-inch barrel.

SECTION 40
INSPECTION OF POLICE REVOLVERS

It is very important that a police officer should know how to care for his revolver. First, *unload* the revolver, look once to see that the revolver *is* unloaded and then look again to see that you did not make a mistake. *Do this first* and *look again; be sure.* See that it is clean and that the side-plate screws and all other screws are tight; otherwise the revolver will not function properly. See that firing pin is not broken; this very rarely happens, but it doesn't take long to look. Swing cylinder out and pull the trigger; hold up to the light and see that the firing pin comes through the recoil plate; see that the barrel is clean and no obstruction in it. Rub the finger across the firing-pin hole in the recoil plate and see that no burr has been thrown up by the firing-pin coming through the recoil plate, as this will sometimes cause a jam and the condition may be easily corrected with a small, fine file. It is a condition which only exists after an arm has been fired or snapped many times and cannot always be detected at the factory.

Always try the bullets to see that they are not loose in the shells, for if this should be the case the loose bullets will jump forward as a shot is fired, extending beyond the end of the cylinder and catching on the end of the barrel causing a jam. See that no lint, paper, or other substances have fallen between the hammer and frame to stop the firing pin from striking the primer.

Snap the arm a few times to see that all springs and parts are working properly. This would be a fine time for some dry shooting. Stand before the mirror, hands at the side, revolver in its accustomed place; draw five times and snap at the man in the glass; if time permits aim and snap ten times at some small object on the wall. Load the revolver and you are ready for any emergency.

SECTION 41

MATCH SHOOTING AND POLICE WORK

By Captain Edward J. Langrish

As a diversion from the serious work of the officer when on duty, he may turn to the more pleasant branch of revolver work,—target shooting. This is a very profitable pastime for the officer because, while it may not teach him the art of quick draw, it does teach him to accurately place his shots and to safely handle firearms.

The benefits derived from a trip to Camp Perry may better be understood by the officer who is fortunate enough to make the trip. At this camp is a police school maintained by the government with capable instructors who teach jiu-jitsu, the proper handling of tear gas, target shooting and, in fact, many branches valuable in police work.

There is an individual running-man police revolver match for police officers only. This match has developed into a team match with five men on a team. The running-man match is fired on the Colt Silhouette target at fifty yards. The target appears from cover and travels across the field at right angles to the shooter. It travels about twenty-three yards in five seconds, then disappears again. The officers are to fire three shots at the target on its first trip across and two shots on the return trip. Each shot counts that strikes in the black figure in a match of this kind. In shooting a match of this kind it is better to lead about three inches from the left elbow of the silhouette and on the return trip aim for the elbow of the arm with hand in the pocket. This kind of shooting is just the kind that the police want to get used to as it teaches the officer to shoot at a moving object.

Another very fine match is the bobbing surprise targe match. The police officer walks out on to the field with his revolver cocked and in raised pistol position. The target is operated from a control pit back of the shooter at various distances and different angles. The limit of distance is sixty yards away and the nearer the target is to the shooter the less of the body of the target is exposed. Five targets are fired at in a match and the target is exposed for three seconds for each shot. The object is to aim at the center of the figure and to use all the time possible to ease off the trigger and not jerk it. The police officer must keep walking until the target is exposed, then stop walking to fire the shot.

The target shooting at the police school is at the same distance as in the regular police matches and the practice obtained here will condition the officers for the big matches. The Police Individual Match is fired under the following condition: ten shots at fifty yards on a Standard American target, ten minutes allowed for the ten shots; ten shots each five in twenty seconds at twenty-five yards on the Standard American fifty-yard target with ten and nine ring black; ten shots each five in ten seconds at twenty-five yards with the same target. In the Police Team Match all shooting is at twenty-five yards timed the same as the individual match and the twenty-five yard target is used in all three stages.

The time is very important and only by constant practice may the officer learn to use the time allowed to within one second. For this I use the Eastman Photographic Timer shown in another section, and instruct my men in its use. The author of this book, whom I have known for many years, is very good at guessing his time; in fact, I have timed him in many matches to as near as two-fifths of a second of the allowed time. This is accomplished by practice and dry shooting.

The best practice for winter is the Telegraph Match. These matches are shot on twelve-yard police targets as furnished by the Colt's Patent Fire Arms Company and these targets must be signed by the captains of each team and exchanged by them. It costs very little to conduct these matches for each team shoots on its own range and telegraphs the score after the match is completed. A member of a local revolver club may referee the match and sign the targets as a witness. The practice obtained in these matches is of great assistance to the officer in the coming outdoor matches at Perry or elsewhere. I have seen the old, cool, and collected officer, such as Sergeant J. H. Young of Portland, Oregon, stand on the firing line allowing nothing to interfere with a score up to his average or better, while the young officer who is making his first trip away from his home range will become over-anxious and will work himself into a state which will surely lower his scores. It is not a good practice to watch the different score boards when shooting in a match.

For several years at Camp Perry we have heard much discussion in regard to gadgets, or fitting the space between rear of trigger guard and front of grip with plastic wood, metal, etc. I favor plastic wood for my own revolver and the picture of a revolver so changed will appear elsewhere in this book (Section 6). I believe in my own case it is an advantage, especially in ten second work for it allows me to cock the hammer straight back and the trigger finger lays in a more direct line with the trigger, also the revolver comes back to the same position each time.

The following Closed Home Notice created by Captain Langrish is worthy of consideration by every police department, insurance company and householder.

CLOSED HOME NOTICE

Street	No.
Name	House Telephone
Will close house	Will open house
In case of necessity address mail	
Telegraph	Telephone
Has anyone in town a key?	Name
Address	Telephone

Will anyone such as laundress or gardener be at house any time during summer? (Give names and purpose.)

Before leaving put valuables in safe deposit. See that windows and doors are all locked.

FIRST POLICE PRECINCT, HARTFORD, CONN.

If house is found open, officer will make detailed report on back of this card.

CAPTAIN EDWARD J. LANGRISH AND HIS TARGET

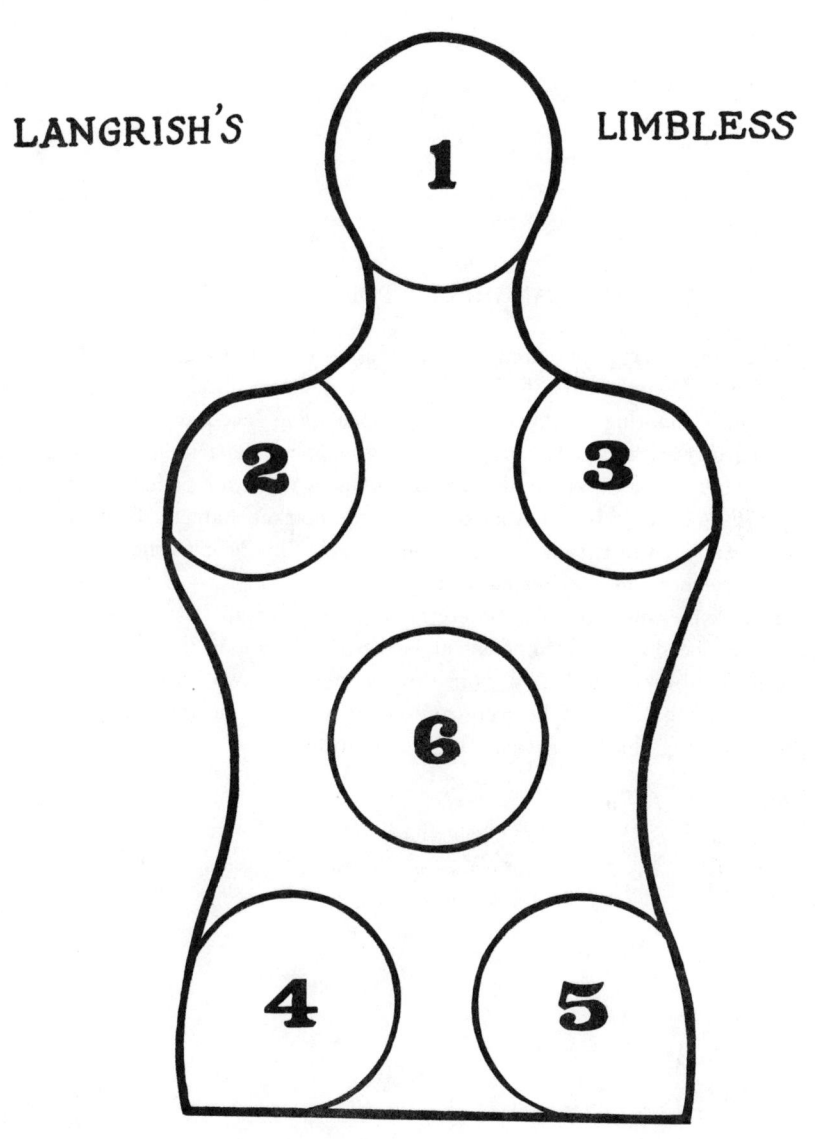

CAPTAIN LANGRISH'S POLICE TARGET

The police target invented by Captain Edward J. Langrish of the Hartford (Connecticut) Police Department is a wonderful target for police shooting. It teaches both speed and accuracy and the placing of the shots. I would advise every police department to use this target at least part of the time as it has a value for police shooting that is covered by no other target on the market, namely the placing of six shots in the circles from one to six. This teaches the officer to place every shot he fires accurately.

It is a pleasure to hold the stop watch on Captain Langrish and note the speed with which he can make a perfect score on this target,—six perfect hits at twelve yards in three to four and two-fifths seconds, double action. It may be seen from this time that the requirements of the scoring chart may easily be accomplished.

—THE AUTHOR

Manufactured by
CASE, LOCKWOOD & BRAINERD,
Hartford, Conn.

Scoring chart for rapid-fire revolver shooting on Captain Langrish's Limbless Police Target.

Seconds	1 Head 100	2 Right Shoulder 200	3 Left Shoulder 300	4 Right Hip 400	5 Left Hip 500	6 Stomach 600
3	16.6	33.3	50.	66.6	83.3	100.
3 1/5	15.6	31.2	46.8	62.5	78.1	93.7
3 2/5	14.7	29.4	44.1	58.8	73.5	88.2
3 3/5	13.8	27.7	41.6	55.5	69.4	83.3
3 4/5	13.1	26.3	39.4	52.6	65.7	78.9
4	12.5	25.	37.5	50.	62.5	75.
4 1/5	11.9	23.8	35.7	47.6	59.5	71.4
4 2/5	11.3	22.7	34.	45.4	56.8	68.1
4 3/5	10.8	21.7	32.6	43.4	54.3	65.2
4 4/5	10.4	20.8	31.2	41.6	52.	62.5
5	10.	20.	30.	40.	50.	60.
5 1/5	9.6	19.2	28.8	38.4	48.	57.6
5 2/5	9.2	18.5	27.7	37.	46.2	55.5
5 3/5	8.9	17.8	26.7	35.7	44.6	53.5
5 4/5	8.6	17.2	25.8	34.4	43.1	51.7
6	8.3	16.6	25.	33.3	41.6	50.
6 1/5	8.	16.1	24.1	32.2	40.3	48.3
6 2/5	7.8	15.6	23.4	31.2	39.	46.8
6 3/5	7.5	15.1	22.7	30.3	37.8	45.4
6 4/5	7.3	14.7	22.	29.4	36.7	44.1
7	7.1	14.2	21.4	28.5	35.7	42.8
7 1/5	6.9	13.8	20.8	27.7	34.7	41.6
7 2/5	6.7	13.5	20.2	27.	33.7	40.5
7 3/5	6.5	13.1	19.7	26.3	32.8	39.4
7 4/5	6.4	12.8	19.2	25.6	32.	38.4
8	6.2	12.5	18.7	25.	31.2	37.5
8 1/5	6.0	12.1	18.2	24.3	30.4	36.5
8 2/5	5.9	11.9	17.8	23.8	29.7	35.7
8 3/5	5.8	11.6	17.4	23.2	29.	34.8
8 4/5	5.6	11.3	17.	22.7	28.4	34.
9	5.5	11.1	16.6	22.2	27.7	33.3
9 1/5	5.4	10.8	16.3	21.7	27.1	32.6
9 2/5	5.3	10.6	15.9	21.2	26.5	31.9
9 3/5	5.2	10.4	15.6	20.8	26.	31.2
9 4/5	5.1	10.2	15.3	20.4	25.5	30.6
10	5.	10.	15.	20.	25.	30.

SECTION 42

THE COLT'S SILHOUETTE TARGET

The Colt's Police Target now in use for several years is a very popular target with police departments, banks, armored car service and, in fact, with every body of men whose profession is the protection of life and property.

The silhouette figure, life size, is more practical and more realistic than the ordinary bull's-eye target, which is not only too small for quick-draw rough-and-tumble police shooting, but also is not the object which an officer will see when his life is in danger. This target represents what may be a fugitive or felon forcibly resisting arrest and attempting to shoot, stab, or run away from the officer. The position of the figure is that of a man standing in front of the officer and with right hand in the position of drawing a weapon from the hip pocket.

Two methods of scoring are possible with the target, namely, a killing and a disabling series. If it is desired to kill the fugitive, then the fatal zones (head, heart, lungs and stomach) are given count of highest value (K-5). Shots in other parts of the target, while not strictly killing shots, are given a value in the killing series of their approximate worth, such as the zone outside the K-5 zone, or rest of the body, will count K-4, the right arm will count K-3, and the left arm will count K-2. The possible score for six shots is thirty points minus one-third of one point deducted for each second used from the command FIRE until the six shots are fired. It is possible to draw and fire so fast that even with this life-size target six misses may be registered at ten feet, so not only must speed be used in getting into action but judgment in placing the shots. A perfect score cannot be made on this target because of the deduction of one-third of one point for each second used.

It is not the idea of this instruction to teach officers to kill. Only as a last resort is this course recommended. If an officer is facing two or more men who have their hands on their weapons no other course is open to him and he must then pick the man whom he thinks will get into action first. The usual purpose of an officer is to wound or disable a fugitive so as to bring him in without the necessity of a fatal or killing shot. This requires the highest type of proficiency in the handling of a revolver—hence, if the officer decides to shoot a disabling course the most effective disabling shot or one of highest count is the right shoulder (D-5) or the right arm or wrist; left arm if a left-handed man. If the fugitive is in the act of drawing a knife or revolver a head shot that may not penetrate, but graze the skull, also counts (D-5).

The next value or D-4 is left arm, including wrist, hand, and shoulder, as the fugitive may be shot through the right arm and still be able to shoot left-handed. D-3 is the outside of body and D-2 or low count the center of body and portion of legs. Only a small part of the legs are shown, as it is not practical to shoot at the legs either in a standing or running position. Shooting at the legs of a standing man, even a hit, does not disable him if he is armed, and it is not safe to shoot at the legs of a running man if other people are on the street or if the streets are of cement or any hard surface. A wound from a glancing bullet is sometimes more dangerous than a direct shot and it may glance at an angle of forty-five degrees. It is very dangerous to miss the person that is shot at, not only for yourself but also for every one within range of the bullet, which may be anywhere within five hundred yards, depending upon the angle of departure.

Years ago when my police instruction was confined to the bull's-eye target and I would spend a week with a department of fifty or seventy-five men I went home discouraged and I know the officers felt the same as I did. That number of men cannot be taught target shooting in a week and neither can one man become a target shot in a week, but with the silhouette target that number of men can be taught to hit the target with right and left hand, double action at fifteen feet, inside of which distance ninety per cent of police shooting is done.

When I first began to instruct police in the use of firearms the only available targets were designed for fine target shooting and then we had the shapeless silhouettes. I found that while a group of ten shots may appear to be very poor shooting, counting between fifty and sixty, that they all registered in the figure of a man. I then designed the target now known as the Colt Silhouette target and with the advent of this target my troubles were over as far as police and bank instruction was concerned. The men could all hit this target and they were taught the appearance of a criminal when their life was in danger. Scores could be shot on this target, either killing or disabling, and all members of the department could be taught to be at least fair shots and their shooting on this kind of target inspired confidence. Silhouette targets are now universally used by police departments and a larger per cent of fast, straight shooting police officers are the result.

The Colt Silhouette target is used in the running man match at Camp Perry, and I think that the same match using the Langrish Limbless target would be of great assistance to officers attending the big shoot. One criticism I have heard of the Colt Silhouette target is that the sights are difficult to see against the dark background. I never heard of a crook wearing a white aiming point on his coat to aid the officer and this target is supposed to represent conditions as they are; however, if a white aiming point is desired a white circle may be pasted on the desired spot on the target. This will aid in grouping the shots in the target, but will retard the speed of fire which is more necessary than a fine group in police work.

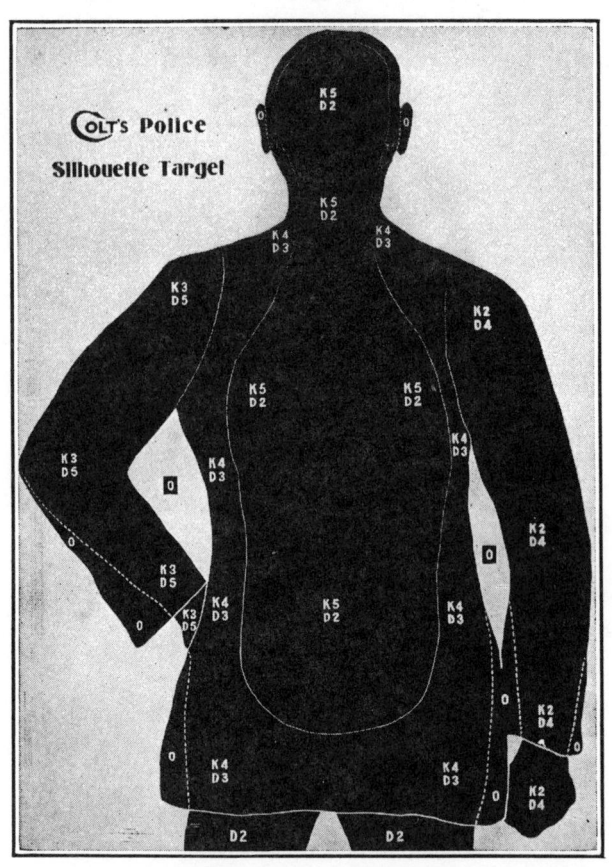

COLT'S POLICE SILHOUETTE TARGET
(See description on pages 334 and 335)

SECTION 43

THE NEW YORK STATE POLICE REVOLVER COURSE IN SHOOTING

The following course in practical police shooting has been used for many years by the New York State Troopers and is taught by the author at the New York State Police School. This organization was the first to use the Colt's Silhouette target. When Captain Albert B. Moore and I visited all the barracks in the state and taught the officers this new course in the shooting, the valuable suggestions of Captain Moore were of great assistance in compiling the course, which has the sanction of former superintendent, Colonel George Chandler, and the present superintendent, Major John A. Warner.

The Colt Silhouette target is used because it is the shape and size of target which must be hit in an emergency.

Course I

6 shots single action
10 yards distance
2 Colt Silhouette targets used
3 shots with right hand
3 shots with left hand
Not timed
K zone to count

The object of this slow-fire course is to familiarize each officer with sights, position, recoil, and general shooting instructions, also to teach him the use of right and left hand, a very important accomplishment for any officer. Two targets are used to determine proficiency with each hand.

Course II

    6 shots double action
    15 feet distance
    2 Colt Silhouette targets

Position: Hands at side, revolver in holster. At command FIRE, draw and fire 3 shots with right hand at right hand target; change revolver to left hand and fire 3 shots with left hand at left hand target.

K zone to count.

Timed from command FIRE to last shot.

This course teaches quick draw, double action with right and left hand and shooting with speed and accuracy.

Course III

    6 shots double action
    1 Colt Silhouette target
    15 feet distance

Stand, hands at side, revolver in holster. At command FIRE, draw and fire 1 shot; return revolver to holster, arms at side. Without command, draw and fire second shot; return revolver to holster, hands at side. Repeat until 6 shots are fired.

Timed from command FIRE to last shot.

K zone to count.

This course teaches quick draw with favorite gun hand and placing the first shot accurately.

Course IV

    6 shots single and double action
    25 yards distance
    2 Colt Silhouette targets

Stand on 25-yard line, revolver in holster, hands at side. At command FIRE, draw and fire 1 shot, single action, at each silhouette target. Run to 12 yards (carrying revolver safely while running, finger out of the trigger guard, arm at side) and, holding revolver in both hands (place gun hand in palm of the other hand, closing fingers around gun hand), fire 1 shot at each target. Drop to mat and holding revolver with both hands fire 1 shot at each target.

Timed from command FIRE to last shot.

K zone to count.

This course teaches twenty-five yard shooting, how to carry a revolver when running, to stop when firing, to steady a revolver with both hands after a run, and to drop to the ground when fired upon (making a target one-sixth the size of a standing man), and to fire accurately from a prone position.

Course V

6 shots double action
10 feet distance
2 Colt Silhouette targets

Position: Revolver in holster, hands at side. At command FIRE, draw and fire 1 shot at the center zone of each target; return revolver to holster, hand to side. At command FIRE, draw and fire 1 shot at each head; return revolver to holster, hand to side. At command FIRE, draw and fire 1 shot at each right arm (bent arm).

Each 2 shots are timed.

No hits to count except those in part of silhouette target stated in command. Body hit from bottom of center zone to separating line in neck. Head hit from separating line in neck to top of head. Arm hit from white line at shoulder to body at side. Sleeve zone marked O does not count.

All hits count 5.

This course teaches the quick, accurate placing of shots at short range and they are considered the six most important shots that any officer can perfect himself in. Two targets are used in the above courses to teach the officer the accurate placing of shots in two targets without loss of time or accuracy.

Many other courses may be created with the Colt Silhouette target and different distances may be used.

Target Shooting

Target shooting is very essential to a police officer in the discharge of his duty, and is especially beneficial where long range shooting is necessary. For this work I consider the Camp Perry Police Course at twenty-five and fifty yards the most helpful.

> 10 shots slow fire, 1 minute per shot
> 10 shots each 5 in 20 seconds
> 10 shots each 5 in 10 seconds

The three essentials for police shooting are: the officer who is willing to learn, good ammunition, and an accurate, serviceable, and reliable revolver.

NAME	No. 1		No. 2		No. 3		No. 4		BODY		No. 5 HEAD		ARM		TOTAL	
	Score	Time	Score	Time	Score	Time	Score	Time	Score	Time	Score	Time	Score	Time	Score	Time

Sample Score Sheet for use in Police Course

New York State Police School
TROY, N.Y.
Class of Feb. 1930

- Corp. W. E. Caskin, Identification Instructor
- Capt. A. B. Moore, Director
- Corp. E. R. Miller, Physical Training Instructor
- J. H. Fitzgerald, Firearms Instructor
- Lieut. G. M. Searle, Executive Instructor
- Dr. S. McC. Martin, Medical Officer
- Fr. Hoerchner, First Aid Instructor
- R. Dixon, Sec.
- J. J. Fitzpatrick, Police Instructor

SECTION 44
THE INSTRUCTOR

It is the instructor's duty to first see that the range is safe and to explain to the men SAFETY ON THE RANGE, which may be handled in different ways.

The officers may be instructed to leave their revolvers in their holsters until called to the firing line or a still safer way is to ask each officer as he enters the range to step to the firing line, unload his revolver and deposit all ammunition in his possession there. Another very good way is to place a table in the range and, as each recruit comes in, to see that he places his revolver and all ammunition in his possession on the table. Count to see that all are accounted for; too much cannot be said about safety, not only to others in the range but to the officer receiving instructions.

AND STILL ANOTHER SAFETY NOTE. If revolvers are not unloaded at the firing line as each officer enters the range, every one must keep his hands away from his revolver. I mention this as I have been present when several different officers or guards have unthinkingly placed their hands on their revolvers and fired a shot through the holster. Another accident which frequently happens is when a guard unloads his revolver, cleans and oils it, loads it again and, after holding the revolver in his hands for a few minutes while talking to some friends, deliberately aims at a target on the wall and drives a bullet through it. Whenever your hands are near your revolver keep your mind on what you are doing until you take them away again. Day dreaming and handling a loaded revolver bring a smile to no one's face but the undertaker's.

The beginner is bound to aim the pistol at his feet or swing the muzzle over his shoulder, making all parts of the range unsafe. The first instructions should be with the revolver empty for a single-action shooting. New men should be taught how to stand, how to aim, the use of sights, trigger squeeze, holding the breath, flinching, and the value of dry shooting. The instructor should note every man's errors, but not call the attention of the firing squad to any one man; he should make the correction general. The instructor should give short and interesting talks on "Lack of Interest," and if you find some of the men that do not show interest in this branch of police work you will find them careless in other things connected with their duties as a police officer.

Again I am going to mention safety, as that is a subject that an instructor cannot talk about too often. In fact, while he is talking to his men, he can look along the line and see some one with his revolver pointing at his own feet or at his neighbors. Remember a firearm is always dangerous unless the cylinder is open and out of line with the hammer, if it is a revolver; and slide open or fastened in a rearward position and magazine out of pistol, if an automatic is used.

The instructor will find some of the men who will hold well until the instant they squeeze the trigger. Then they will take a death grip on the arm, close their eyes, shut their teeth, and pull down on the arm as the explosion occurs, shaking the bullets out instead of shooting them, consequently a wild shot. A very good way to show the beginner his error is to slip an empty shell into his revolver if he is flinching or pulling down, for he will do the same with an empty shell. Or, the revolver may be taken by the instructor who, without the knowledge of the pupil, will set the cylinder back so that the hammer will fall on an empty shell. This will show clearly what happens when the explosion and recoil are expected. Flinching can easily be overcome if the shooter will only take the advice of the instructor.

The instructor can easily instruct the men in the proper way to stand and this may be varied slightly by men of different size and build. If instructing for practical police shooting then the position is: revolver in holster, hands at side, and in standing or walking position.

Beginners should be placed near enough to the target so they can hit it and can more easily see their errors. This is more essential in police work than in any other kind of shooting, as most of their service shooting is at short range.

At the shooting class practice some of the men will show marked improvement over others, so these men should be put in an advanced squad, shooting a harder course and at different ranges. The result is—more interest will be shown by the advanced squad, as they know they are improving; more interest will be shown by the men in the novice squad for they will use renewed efforts to reach the advanced class. Ten, twelve, fifteen, and twenty-five yards have proven the popular distances for police work.

Both silhouette and target shooting will give the officer experience, confidence in himself, and confidence in his revolver, all of which is necessary for a successful officer. One hundred yard target shooting and one hundred yard silhouette shooting should be practiced by the officer, who will then know the possibilities of his revolver. While the revolver has always been considered a short range weapon, an experienced shot can easily demonstrate that it is very accurate at one hundred yards and that the silhouettes may easily be hit at two hundred yards.

A good shot is an honor to any force and is known to the crook as well as to his brother officers. An officer succeeds in his chosen profession by being able to handle himself and the arm he carries. He creates a respect that will live as long as he is connected with police work.

Every officer will ask himself after a few weeks: "Am I improving?" If he has faithfully followed the rules of practical police shooting he has and can prove it to his own satisfaction. If he has taken it up in a half-hearted manner he has improved very little. If he has said to himself that he does not need practical police shooting, that he does not have to listen to the instructor, he will regret it the first time he is called upon to defend himself.

SECTION 45

OUTGUESSING THE CRIMINAL

Never take a chance. An officer should remember this and keep it constantly in his mind. Every officer is at a disadvantage, because only by observation and the study of human beings can he hope to succeed in his chosen profession. The officer who finds a man under suspicious circumstances arrests him. The man tells the officer that he has done nothing and will go peaceably, why should the officer believe him and why should he take a chance? Put yourself in the place of the criminal. What would you do if you knew you were wanted for murder? Would you not take the first chance offered to escape? You would, knowing that the penalty is the same for killing one or ten.

Any man questioned by an officer who is suspicious of him may be wanted for murder in some other city or town. Many times an officer will arrest a man in a place where he feels he has not time to search him and the only solution is to handcuff his hands behind his back; the officer is then reasonably safe, because if the prisoner should have a weapon where he can then reach it he must at least turn halfway around and cannot see just where the bullet or knife will strike if he tries to use it. If he is handcuffed in front he has every chance to use a weapon if he has one.

Many officers lose their lives through the careless handling of prisoners. Another time-worn excuse is the request to change clothes before going to the station. If I wanted to kill a prisoner I would give him just that chance and let him go to a bureau drawer or closet for the articles he needed. Two very careful detectives some years ago went to a house and found their man. He had on neither vest nor coat and he asked if he might put them on. One officer carefully searched coat and vest and handed them to him. He put them on and all three started for the door. As they reached it, the prisoner put his hand to his hip pocket and said, "I have no handkerchief; may I go and get one out of that bureau drawer?" One of the detectives told him he could and as the drawer was opened he whipped out a .32 automatic and shot both officers and got away. The same thing happened at another time except that the officers were careful in searching and getting all articles needed and they had taken the prisoner out on the sidewalk. He looked down and said: "Wait a minute; I want to tie my shoestring." He knelt down to tie the shoestring, took a .38 caliber revolver out of his stocking, shot both officers, and got away. That was the one place they forgot to search.

A short time ago two experienced officers were killed because they allowed a prisoner to go upstairs and change his clothes, while one officer stood in the yard and the other stood near the front stairs waiting for him. The prisoner used a single barrel shotgun, first killing the one on the outside and then, running to the stairs, killing the other officer as he started up the stairs. Two officers whom I knew arrested a man wanted for murder and put him in the back seat of their car, while they both rode in the front seat, and one officer was killed on the way to the police station.

Years ago the policeman's uniform and badge commanded a certain amount of respect for the law but those days have gone forever. Hundreds of cases may be mentioned where officers have lost their lives through carelessness. I may cite the case of an officer who saved his life because he went into a building sidewise to expose the body as little as possible. Three shots were fired at him; one went through the front of his coat from right to left, two more went through his coat at the back. If he had gone through the door in a natural manner all three bullets would have entered his body. How many have opened a door and stepped in without first swinging the door open until it came in contact with the wall and have been killed by some one behind it.

I can see a reason for this carelessness in the fact that practically all of the people whom the officer encounters in his course of duty are law-abiding. Possibly one in ten thousand may be dangerous to him and the large per cent of peace-loving citizens will cause carelessness on the part of the officer and when that one bad man or crank comes along the officer is not ready for the trick that will not be started until everything favors a perfect get-away. Watch his hands instead of listening to his alibis. Becoming a good revolver shot in practical police shooting will do more to create a system of watchfulness and the ability to outguess the criminal than all other instructions in self-preservation. The officer who can shoot (I do not mean the one who thinks he can shoot) knows to a fraction of a second just how long it will take him to get into action and just what he can do when he does go into action and he also knows when not to shoot and this is very important. Read this twice: A revolver is an officer's best friend, if he knows how to use it. It may also get him into more trouble in two seconds than he can get out of in ten years. The day is fast approaching when the public and the courts will not look kindly upon promiscuous shooting by inexperienced police officers.

We read in the papers of many persons being shot in an automobile because they did not stop immediately when a hand was held up or a whistle blown, and sometimes by an officer not in uniform. Is this a crime that calls for several bullets being fired into a car? It is not, unless the officer is positive that a felony has been committed by some one in that car. It is better to let one or two criminals get away for the time being than to kill some innocent person. The man who is inexperienced in the use of firearms is very liable to make a blunder that will not be a credit to himself or his department. Just thinking that he is a good shot will not make any one capable of handling firearms properly. I have met several men who carry two revolvers and feel they are well protected, when they were not capable of handling one. There are very few two-gun men and by many thousand too few one-gun men that are enforcing law and order. At no time in the history of our country has the need for fast, straight-shooting officers, who are versed in every trick used to evade the law, become so apparent as at the present time.

SECTION 46
DOUBLE-ACTION REVOLVER VERSUS AUTOMATIC

I have continually spoken of a revolver when police shooting was mentioned and I will here give my reasons. The automatic is fast if the user has by practice become accustomed to its use; still it is almost an impossible accomplishment to instruct a large force and feel that every man can handle the arm safely. The automatic is just as safe as the revolver if properly handled, but if unfamiliar with its use it is not.

It is not as fast for the first shot as the revolver fired double action, for that is one motion to draw and pull the trigger and the bullet is on its way. With the automatic there is the one added motion of pressing down the safety and more time is consumed than with the revolver. If revolver is fired single action there is very little difference in the time of first shot but, after the first shot, the automatic is faster than the revolver for the remaining shots. The automatic is very accurate in fast shooting due to the natural grip and pointing feature as you would point your finger.

The failure to fire through jams in the present-day high-grade automatics of American make may be traced to neglect through failure to keep chamber and barrel clean and free from rust; otherwise, a jam or misfire may be traced to oil-soaked cartridge, which will cause trouble in either revolver or automatic. In Fitz Safety Rules will be found the safe way to handle the automatic.

If an automatic is carried it should, at all times for police work, have a cartridge in the chamber and safety in place because an officer may have but one hand at liberty when the time to shoot arrives and the automatic requires two hands to place the first cartridge in the chamber. The arm should be carried ready for use at all times. I have noted that many departments carry only five cartridges in the revolver. Any revolver with a police positive safety is perfectly safe with six cartridges and that sixth cartridge may save a life.

I am a firm believer in double action with the revolver at short range and, for speed of first shot, the revolver double action is supreme. If I hear from the single-action lovers through this statement it is because they have not put in the days and years of practice with the double-action revolver that they have with their favorite peace maker.

SECTION 47

PRONE SHOOTING

If an officer is fired upon by one or more persons, especially in open country or on the street where no shelter is available and the space is clear between him and his assailants, he should drop to the ground, head toward the enemy, resting both elbows on the ground much in the same manner as a rifleman except the body should be straight with the target, then use both hands to steady the revolver as in two hand shooting. The officer is one-sixth the size prone that he is standing and a very hard object to hit.

The prone manner of shooting is recommended for long range work. At night-time all objects will be brought above the sky line and the officer will appear to be wounded as he drops to the ground. In night shooting roll over after every shot.

At the New York State Police School at Troy, New York, a few years ago this subject of prone shooting was explained to the students and they were taught to shoot in this position on the range. About six weeks after the school closed, Captain Moore, director of the school, received a letter from one of his students stating that prone shooting saved his life. It seems that the officer was covering his beat late at night when he saw two men coming out of a jewelry store and one of them, seeing the officer, fired at him. The officer immediately fell to the ground getting his revolver as he fell. He heard one of the men say, "Got the damn bull the first time; come on, let's finish him." They started toward the officer and it is needless to say he had no difficulty in getting both men.

At the Pennsylvania State Police School some years ago

Captain Mauck and his men were firing at a silhouette target at one hundred yards with a .30/30 Winchester Carbine. After the rifle practice was over I asked the same men to shoot at the same targets and distance with their revolvers and the scores averaged nearly as well as with the rifle. This not only showed the extreme accuracy of the revolver at one hundred yards, but also the accuracy which may be attained in the prone position.

Years of long-range shooting with a revolver has taught me the value of this position and years of police instruction has taught me the value of this position in the saving of an officer's life and the accurate placing of bullets. As in other protective shooting, use double action at short range (up to ten yards) and single action at the longer ranges. At night when the flash will reveal your exact position get away from behind the flash after every shot. In this position the sights may be more readily seen at night due to raising objects above the sky line. It is by taking advantages of these short cuts to safety that the officer may prolong his life and the knowledge will add to his confidence in his own prowess.

CAPTAIN ALBERT B. MOORE
New York State Police
Prone Position

SECTION 48

CARRYING A REVOLVER WHEN RUNNING

It is very important that an officer be properly taught how to carry his revolver when running. Here is a safe and sane way: Carry the revolver with muzzle toward the object to be shot at, elbow held close to the side, and the forearm pointing straight ahead. Never raise the hammer of the revolver while running. Never place the finger in the trigger guard or on the trigger; in this way you will eliminate the possibility of stumbling and shooting yourself or some innocent bystander.

I have known several cases where officers have fired accidental shots in this manner and safety first is the best preventive. It is agreed that the best place to carry a revolver when it may be needed instantly is in the hand, but it must be carried safely. An incident related to me by a police lieutenant may be repeated to show the up-to-date firearms knowledge possessed by some police officers. It seems that in a burglary scare a couple of shots were fired. The lieutenant was standing in a doorway a short time afterward, when one of his men came along, revolver in his hand and cocked ready for business. "Here!" called the Lieutenant. "What's the idea of that revolver carried that way; you know that the war is over."

"Oh, yes, sir, I know, but I cocked this revolver and I am going up to the station to have some one let the hammer down for me."

Think of a man carrying a loaded and cocked revolver around for a half hour on the street not knowing what to press to let the hammer down. Whew! some men have all the luck.

CAPTAIN ALBERT B. MOORE
New York State Police
Showing position to carry a revolver safely while running

SECTION 49
STOP WHEN FIRING

Never fire a shot at any object while running; STOP. You cannot shoot accurately unless you have had a great deal of practice and then only at a large object at short range. Your bullets travel many times faster than your target, and you cannot hope to place your shots accurately unless you do stop. You are endangering the lives of every one on the street if you do not take this precaution, to say nothing of plate glass, electric signs, etc. A few seconds may be lost in stopping, but the result will be satisfactory.

CAPTAIN ALBERT B. MOORE
New York State Police
Firing Position

SECTION 50
TWO-HAND SHOOTING

After running a short distance the officer may find as he stops to shoot that he is trembling badly and cannot take steady aim. In that case place the hand holding the revolver firmly in the palm of the other hand, the first finger of the outside hand to be just under the trigger guard and the thumb over the thumb of the hand holding the revolver. Use pressure enough to steady the revolver and if inside of fifteen yards use double action; if at a longer range and time permits cock the hammer with the thumb of the outside hand and shoot single action. Very accurate shooting may be done in this manner and the officer will find that he can shoot faster and with more accuracy after a run if the arm is held in this manner.

In this shooting if the revolver is held in the right hand and both placed in the left, the left foot should be placed ahead of the right and slightly to the left or nearly the position of the feet for left-hand shooting. If arm is held first in the left hand the position would be reversed and right foot would be ahead of the left. A little practice using both hands will convince the officer of the value of two-hand shooting.

TWO-HAND SHOOTING

SECTION 51
NIGHT SHOOTING

It is very important for a police officer when firing at night to move either to right or left after each shot. Many times an officer will go into a dark alleyway or a building after a criminal, where it is too dark to see any one hiding there. If a shot is fired by his opponent he is ready to fire at the flash and the criminal will be just as ready to fire at the flash of the officer's revolver; therefore, he must move immediately after each shot. One course in the New York State Trooper's School instructed the men in firing at twelve yards at two silhouette targets, alternating targets after each shot.

It is easy to tell in what direction the shot is fired by the flash. If a streak of fire from eight to twenty inches long should be seen going toward the left or right, then the officer who should see it knows that he is not the one being fired at. If he should see an oval flash about the shape of a Rugby football, then the bullet is coming in his direction. If lying on the ground, roll over after firing; get away from that flash. In night shooting neither sights nor revolver can be seen, and it is then the officer who by constant practice knows by the feel of his revolver when it is pointing as he would point his finger that will shoot with any degree of accuracy.

If a prisoner is caught in a place as above-mentioned and there is no chance to search properly, handcuff his hands behind his back. It will keep him out of temptation and the officer may get out alive. In night shooting each officer should know the position of the other officers, as it is easy to make a mistake in the dark.

SECTION 52

RIGHT AND LEFT HAND SHOOTING

Every officer should practice shooting with right and left hand and should carry his revolver where he can get it with either hand. You never know what your favorite gun hand will be doing when you decide to draw your revolver. A few hours of practice with either hand may net you big results. You use both hands to subdue a prisoner who is unarmed. This is not as important as being able to use either hand when your life is in danger. A bullet through your right arm or shoulder and you are at the mercy of your assailant unless you can use your left hand. You may be leading a prisoner with your right hand and his friends interfere; if you release him while you reach for your revolver valuable time is lost and you may lose your man.

It is not the idea of this book to teach officers to use their revolvers unless absolutely necessary. The officer who knows his revolver and knows how to handle it knows to a fraction of a second how long it will take him to get into action and is not liable to make a mistake as one who is not familar with firearms.

I have stated many times that if an officer who has never fired a shot (and there are several of them) will stand fifteen feet from a silhouette target and do as he is told for five minutes, he can then fire three shots with right hand and three shots with left hand and all will hit the target at a speed of about nine seconds. In future trials he will hit the target and decrease the time until it is between three and four seconds. Who cares to argue with a man who can, with either hand, hit you six times in three seconds? I'll bite; who does?

Many police departments are at the present time practicing with right and left hand. The six hundred New York State Troopers are all two-hand men. Buffalo and many other departments have used both hands in their shooting course, and all are benefited thereby. Even officers who are fair shots with the right hand will, on the first trial with right and left hand, make just as good a score with one hand as the other on the silhouette target.

New Jersey State Police qualify with right and left hand on their adopted shooting course.

SECTION 53
USING TWO REVOLVERS

Using a revolver in the right and left hand at the same time is the last word in practical police shooting and is, of course, for short range only. It is mentioned in the police section of this book because of the many cases where the gunman uses two revolvers or pistols. When two or more crooks are encountered by the officer at the same time it is very practical, if the officer has had experience in two-gun shooting.

The side draw is the same, except both hands move at the same time. The cross-stomach draw must be made one at a time or by swinging one elbow and arm outward to allow the other arm to move on the inside. In firing at two Colt Silhouette targets six feet apart and eight feet away the revolvers are pointed as one would point his finger and both triggers pulled at the same time. The sights are not used at this distance. A few shots fired in this manner will convince any one that this is a very practical way to shoot if occasion requires the use of two revolvers. A man with two revolvers and necessary experience is just twice as dangerous as one man with one revolver.

Anything the size of a man is, of course, a large target at eight to twelve feet and very easy to hit with two revolvers. This is, of course, double action and pointing, no sights used, the arm stiffened when the muzzle is pointed in the right direction.

I have had many of the gun-bugs look at me and shake their heads when I mentioned shooting two guns, but after a trial or two they ceased to feel sorry for me. In the settling of the West many two-gun men were developed and either gun would command **respect**.

I am not advising every officer to carry two revolvers, but I know a great many who do, especially in cold weather. One small revolver, usually a two-inch barrel, is carried in the outside overcoat pocket. Two revolvers are also carried by many hunters and trappers who may not be able to reach a repair shop for many months. Accidents will happen and usually do when you are in a position to want a bullet or two mighty bad.

I may speak of a case where an old friend of mine in the game country fired his last shot from one of his revolvers and as he was only a few yards from his cabin decided he would go inside before reloading. As he stepped inside and closed the door he encountered one of the largest cats he had ever seen. He told me afterward that the second revolver saved his life, got him a fine pelt, and wrecked his pet coffee pot.

Another little incident happened to a police officer whom I know, who chased a couple of crooks into a blind alley. In the exchange of shots he emptied his revolver. As the sixth shot was fired by him they both rushed toward where he was standing before he could reload. They didn't know that he carried another revolver and they are serving ten years each to pay for their blunder.

SERGEANT WILLIAM E. CASHIN
New York State Troupers
Firing Position

SECTION 54

DRAWING FROM THE SIDE OR FRONT POCKET

The outside overcoat is one of the very best places to carry a small revolver. An officer may walk along with his hand in his pocket and no one on the street would know that he had a revolver in his hand—this, of course, if he felt he might have occasion to use it. Some police departments object to the officer placing his hands in his pockets, but the usual time when this would be necessary would be at night in dark, unfrequented streets.

As an officer acquires the art of handling his revolver properly he will be able to scent trouble and as certain conditions appear to him he will prepare himself for quick action, which means in extreme cases the quick, accurate use of his revolver. How many officers have lost their lives because they were not prepared,—an unlocked door, the officer investigating without first taking all necessary precautions. First, if necessary, call help. Both sides of the building should be watched. Next, draw your revolver and enter building carefully, first noiselessly swinging door open slowly, forcing it back until it rests against the wall. This is to convince yourself that no one is behind it when you enter. Try to enter without casting a shadow of your body into the building. Wait in the shadow until your eyes have become accustomed to the inside darkness, otherwise you will only notify the intruder of your presence. It is not an act of bravery to walk headlong into danger unprepared.

In a small city where I had previously given firearm instruction to the police an officer came to me and said: "You remember on your last visit you told us about carrying a revolver in the outside overcoat pocket?" I told him I did. "Well, that instruction saved my life. I was standing on the corner late one night when a man crossed the street and came toward me. It was cold and I had my hands in my pockets, my revolver under my right hand, when about ten feet away he stopped and drawing a revolver fired at me. I felt the blow of the bullet but fired my own revolver before he could fire the second shot and I stopped him." The bullet fired by the officer's assailant struck and imbedded itself in his heavy hunting-case watch which I was shown. The officer had a miraculous escape from the first bullet, but his speed of getting into action and the accuracy of his first shot saved his life. This could not have been possible with a revolver carried under several coats and in either hip pocket or holster. We rarely need a revolver to protect our lives, but when we do need it we need it badly.

A leather pocket built in the police coat would be a good place to carry the light model revolvers and the front trousers pockets are also much used for carrying small revolvers by plain clothes men, always remembering to place thumb over the hammer when drawing the arm to avoid catching in the cloth. It is not claimed that the pocket draw is faster than the properly carried holster, but it is fast enough to beat the inexperienced or those who persist in carrying their arms in the hip pocket.

SECTION 55

FITZ TRICK HOLDS AND PERSUADERS

Many surprise holds are used upon a prisoner or for protection by the civilian. A few of these that I have taught and used in police work I will illustrate. The day of promiscuous head breaking with clubs is passed except in certain cases where all other methods fail. It does not increase the popularity of a police department to hammer a prisoner into insensibility on a crowded street and at all costs he must get his man; therefore, the seemingly milder method which to the onlooker seems more humane is in reality more painful than the club.

A course in jiu-jitsu consists of twenty-five to thirty-five holds, but it is unnecessary for an officer or civilian to learn all these; three or four holds at his finger ends is better than the entire list because a surprise hold must be applied instantly and with pressure enough to enforce submission. A strong man may be subdued if hold is applied before he has time to set his muscles against it even by a much weaker antagonist.

The Lip Hold is very effective on wild women and some little men and consists of catching the loose flesh of lower lip between first finger and thumb, pulling outward and twisting if the straight pull should fail. Usually this hold is sufficient to lead a prisoner wherever necessary. It is usually as severe as before-mentioned lady will care to endure and may be the means of cutting short a needless conversation.

A very fine hold for the civilian to use in case of a hold-up, where arm of hold-up gentleman is concealed in the outside coat pocket and pointed through the cloth, is, as the arms go up at command, with right hand grasp the shoulder of assailant turning him toward the right. Grasp his left wrist with your left hand, swinging his left hand behind his back and up between the shoulder blades—the Hammer Lock. In the meantime slide right hand from the shoulder to the wrist and hand concealed in the pocket before it can be withdrawn, being careful at all times to keep his body between yourself and the suspected pocket. With this hold he can easily be held until help arrives. If no help is in sight place right leg and hip in front and throw him on his face, being careful not to loosen the hammer lock; as he goes down in this position the weapon in pocket may be safely reached. Enough pressure may be applied to break the arm in the hammer lock if necessary.

The Hand Hold, palm up, is very effective and consists of grasping the fingers of opponent's left or right hand and raising them above his head, palm up, exerting a downward pressure on the ends of his fingers. The more pressure applied the less desire he will have to strike you with the other hand. Any pressure or any hold applied against the natural direction in which joints and muscles are supposed to move is effective if properly applied.

The Coat Arm Lock is applied by throwing an open coat downward from shoulders and halfway between shoulders and elbow; both arms are then held at the side.

Many still believe that the under hold or arms around body under the arms is a good hold and it would be if the opponent's arms were included with the body; otherwise three very effective ways to break this hold are left open: the chin is grasped with one hand, then forced upward, or chin is grasped with one hand, back of head with the other, then head is twisted until hold under arms is broken. A quick snap will break the neck.

The Nose Hold will also break the underarm hold. Place heel of hand under the nose and force quickly upward; this is an effective way to have the face lifted. If the hold is around arms and body, bring hands together at front and force them upward between opponent's body and your own until the hold is broken; then apply a hold of your own.

The Adam's Apple Blow is striking the opponent with side of hand or fist on the Adam's apple. A sharp blow will bring results, usually dropping the person so struck.

The Stomach Blow is very effective. The bigger they are the harder they fall. This consists of a short, sharp blow at about the third button on the vest; a six-inch blow will be effective.

The Finger Hold consists of bending any of the fingers inward toward the palm, thumb on end of finger, and first finger under second joint.

A successful way to break the Throat Hold is, instead of trying to pull the entire hand away, take one finger at a time, bending it over backward until it breaks.

The Belt Hold consists of grasping opponent's belt at center of back and pushing him forward; very effective in forcing a prisoner along as he cannot turn around.

The Arm Grip, palm up, consists of grasping opponent's hand, palm up, and then with other arm under elbow grasp opponent's coat on the opposite side from where you are standing. Then force opponent's hand downward, holding your own arm under his elbow.

A very effective way to throw an opponent over the head is to cross the hands, grasping a lapel of the opponent's coat in each hand; turn quarter round and pull forward, crouch or drop to one knee. Scarcely any strength is required to perform this feat and, if necessary, the fall may be as severe as required.

The Ear Pressure Hold consists of forcing thumb between the two bones just under the ear. This may be applied to both sides at the same time, if necessary, grasping collar with three fingers to hold the prisoner's head and body in position and the pressure may then be applied.

The Hair Hold consists of grasping the hair at back of head and lifting upward, if opponent refuses to rise. The Cheek Hold consists of forcing the thumb against side of face halfway between eye and mouth; very effective if opponent refuses to go through a door and hands are braced on door jambs to prevent being pushed through. Still I am inclined to favor grasping both legs and pulling his feet away from door; then he will get a fall he will never forget.

The Hip Lock is a hold every one knows and consists of throwing opponent over the hip.

The ladies can be taught one very effective hold, or protection measure, consisting of forcing one or two fingers into the opponent's eyes when grasped by him.

Now comes the dangerous part of defense work,—foiling the gunman. If held up and opponent's revolver is placed muzzle against stomach, with command of "Hands up," put them up at once. If opponent is holding revolver in right hand, drop right hand quickly on cylinder of revolver, at the same time holding body against muzzle. Turn to left to force barrel out of line with body. The hand on cylinder will prevent trigger being pulled if a revolver is not cocked; if it is an automatic, turning the body will prevent being struck by the bullet and if slide is held the empty shell will remain in the chamber of automatic. Then force muzzle of either quickly upward to vertical position and push the revolver or pistol in this position sharply downward. This will break opponent's trigger finger at second joint. There are many ways to disarm a man who places a revolver against stomach and they are all good, but most of them require two hands. This requires one hand and is very effective. I have used it for years and have yet to find a man who could snap the arm, with muzzle still toward any part of the body, if he waited until he saw me move, even after he knew what I was going to do. I have been asked many times if it were not possible to put a revolver against a man's stomach in such a manner that he could not take it away. My answer is to push the revolver in about three inches and he will not try to disarm you.

A man with experience would not get close enough to be disarmed in this way. He would stand about six feet away and, when hands were up, order his man to turn and face the wall; then, with his own revolver well back at the side, search the prisoner, first trying him out by placing finger in his back. He might turn around and try to take what he believed to be the revolver away from you while said revolver is safe at side in the other hand. In nearly every case any one who came up from behind would place the revolver against the back instead of the finger. The difference can be told by pressing the back slightly against the muzzle or finger. In case it is the revolver, swing the body sharply around, knocking the muzzle out of line with the elbow and grasping cylinder with right hand as you turn; then proceed to break finger as before. An effective addition to this hands-up, revolver-in-stomach get-away, is to grasp the hat brim with left hand, while hands are up, and slap the opponent across the face as hands are dropped.

In all holds and all tricks watch the opponent's feet as well as his hands. Some men are as clever with their feet as they are with their hands and may get in a decisive blow with either foot or knee. Many men have found this out when too late to avoid losing a prisoner.

For an officer to search thoroughly constitutes nearly disrobing the prisoner. I have been searched by officers who even missed two .45 revolvers and allowed me, because they did not find them, to keep gas pencils, small automatics, pencil pistols, knife in shoes, knife at back of neck, revolver in hose and many other hide-outs after searching me to their satisfaction.

In leading a man to the police station extreme care must be taken, as your prisoner may know all the tricks of eluding his captor and, if so, he is dangerous at all parts of the journey. I favor the belt hold with revolver in the hand, or where it can be reached instantly.

But a man must be his own judge as to the amount of force to use and what precautions to take in getting his man, but never take a chance.

POSITION No. 1

SEARCHING FROM THE REAR

Revolver is held in a position to avoid having it taken away by prisoner. Finger in back to represent muzzle of revolver, thus tempting prisoner to turn, and attempt to disarm.

POSITION No. 2
COAT DOWN TO BIND PRISONER'S ARMS WHEN
APPROACHING FROM FRONT

In lowering coat, search around collar and at middle of back for possible weapons. Watch prisoner's hands and keep them away from belt and pockets.

POSITION No. 3
SEARCHING FROM THE FRONT

Coat, binding arms and hip, toward prisoner to avoid prisoner's knee or foot. Note revolver found in waist band.

POSITION No. 1
REVOLVER MUZZLE AGAINST STOMACH IN HOLD-UP

POSITION No. 2

As cylinder is grasped to prevent turning, revolver is bent backward to break finger and disarm. Left hand is in position to guard against blow from opponent and hip turned to prevent kick in vital part.

POSITION No. 1
REVOLVER MUZZLE AGAINST BACK

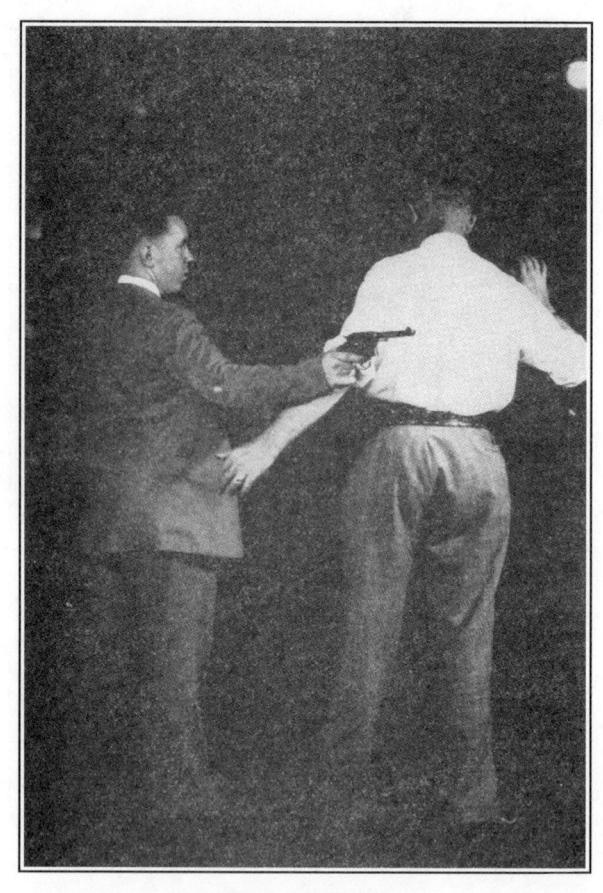

POSITION No. 2
REVOLVER FORCED OUT OF LINE WITH BODY

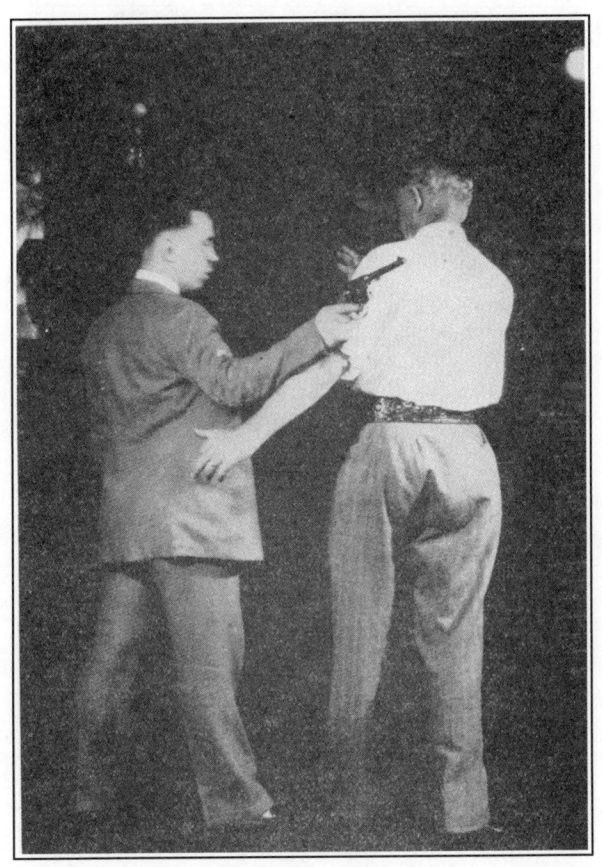

POSITION No. 3

Body turned and right hand preparing to grasp revolver for final disarming.

POSITION No. 4

Revolver grasped with right hand and bent over in position to break finger of opponent in disarming process.

SECTION 56

SHOOTING FROM MOTORCYCLE OR HORSE

The same rule applies to this shooting as to shooting from the running-board of a moving car. Take the vibration below the knees combined with the ability to shoot instantly when the sights are in proper position.

The old idea of throwing down on the object to be fired at will not count for as many hits on the target as bringing the arm up to a level with the target. In quick-draw work, when bringing the arm down on an object it must first be raised, then moved downward, obstructing the view of the object to be hit. Usually a low shot is the result, because when the object is seen clearly the sights must be below it. The idea of throwing down originated with the single action, as the coming down allowed the weight of the revolver to aid in cocking the piece. I know many of the old-timers with a single-action complex will object to any system of shooting except that which they have always used and I do not blame them. I may say here that a person, by constant practice, will become very fast in his own particular style of firing the first shot, but will he attain accuracy as well? Speed without accuracy means nothing. I have seen many of the otherwise fast men snap a revolver out with a speed that the eye could not follow and then perforate the atmosphere in six different places several feet apart. Distance reduces the speed and sights must be used to attain accuracy at over ten yards whether on foot or mounted.

Let us go back to the system of drawing revolver from holster and raising it until sights are on a level with the bull's-eye. In this way no time is lost, as the shot is fired when the sights reach the proper level. The object fired at is in plain view at all times and any movement may be noted if animal or human is being fired at. All side arms are sighted to hold at six o'clock and the arm is stopped below the object.

Shooting from a motorcycle or horse may be classed as snap shooting and accurate enough for shooting at a target the size of a dog up to fifty yards. The dimensions of this dog vary with different men; try it out and determine the size of the dog you can hit at fifty yards.

The following is a course from the New York State Police School:

MOTORCYCLE COURSE (Indoors). Six shots, fifteen yards, seated on motorcycle. Hands on handle-bars, revolver in holster. At word "FIRE," draw and double action fire first at right target, then at left target, consecutively until six shots are fired. K zone to count, using favorite gun hand. This course teaches the officer to shoot accurately when seated. If course is shot outdoors and space permits, three targets are placed on right side of road and three on left side of road twenty-five yards apart; this constitutes a course one hundred and fifty yards long. First target is placed twenty-five yards ahead of firing line. As the officer crosses the firing line at twenty miles per hour he may draw and fire at first target and then at the other targets until six shots are fired. A firing line should be placed ten yards from each target and all shots should be fired before crossing this line. Be sure the range is safe.

Neither this section nor any other in this book is written with the idea of starting a controversy in papers or magazines over the different ways and means of attaining perfection with the revolver and pistols and if such is started it will not be answered by me. I have noted many such, as Bolt vs. Lever Action, which ended just where it started, at the end of a long, long trail. I wish all the hand-gun shooters much pleasure and success with their chosen systems and I know they wish me the same.

SECTION 57

SHOOTING FROM A MOTOR CAR

It may happen at any time in the course of duty that an officer is obliged to jump on the running-board of a passing car and pursue another car containing a criminal. It may be the object to puncture the gas tank. If this is so, the bullet must enter the tank near the bottom, otherwise a long chase may be expected. Hit the tank not over three inches from the bottom and if the distance is not too great between the cars the downward angle of the bullet shot from a greater height will nearly reach the bottom of front of tank. Shooting the tires is also a very effective way to stop a car. With the present balloon tires the target is large enough for the average police shot. It must be remembered that the bottom part of the tire below the center, if behind, is the proper place to hit. That part is rolling toward the officer, while the top half is rolling away, and a high shot may glance off the tire without penetrating.

If more strenuous methods are required, it is easy to determine the position of the driver. The best method to use to instruct in this work is to cut out black pasteboard silhouettes of two tires, about 32 x 6 inches, as seen from rear of car; gas tank, about 12 x 18 inches, with white line 3 inches from bottom. Tack on a wooden frame in position of average car. Over this at height of driver place Langrish or Colt Silhouette target. Draw an automobile up to within fifteen yards of target. Place the officer on the running board of the car near front door. Place one man behind him on the running board and one on the opposite side of car. The object is to shoot one bullet through left tire below center, one through gas tank below three-inch white line, one through right tire below center, and three through center of Langrish or Colt Silhouette target. This seems like a big order but the two extra men on the running boards, as the order is given to fire, sway the car sideways and up and down to resemble the motion of a fast-moving car over very rough ground. The target, of course, is stationary, but the car is swaying far in access of a moving car.

If the man who is shooting from the running-board has had no experience in this kind of shooting, while he may be an excellent shot from the ground, he will find trouble in hitting the targets. The secret is to bend the legs at the knees and take the sway of the car below the knees. A few shots in this manner, and very good shooting, can be done by a fair revolver shot. Care must be taken in shooting at tires and gas tank that the officer's car does not strike an obstruction in the road at the instant the shot is fired. A high shot would be the result and, as has many times happened, some one in the pursued car may be killed, where the object was only to stop the car. A glance at the road ahead before the shot is fired, and taking road shock below the knees, will eliminate any chance of shooting through the car when aiming at tires or tank.

Stopping a moving car on a highway is a part of the officer's duty, which in nearly all cases may be accomplished with no personal danger to the officer, but at some time it might mean the loss of his life if the occupants of the car were criminals escaping from justice. The only safe method is to use care at all times. Instead of stopping motorcycle ahead of the car under suspicion, stop behind the car and approach from the rear, looking in rear seat to be sure that trouble will not start from there. If satisfied as to this part of car, advance to rear of front seat and ask for license; in this way the officer is not in danger as he would be if he approached car from the front. Many officers have lost their lives by approaching a car in this manner. A usual proceeding is for the officer to stop his motorcycle ahead of stopped car, walk back to the car and demand the license, then with one foot on the running-board write the summons. How easy it would be to hit him over the head, drive against the standing motorcycle, wreck it and get away.

Another danger is in following a car too close. In this day of four-wheel brakes a reasonable distance must be allowed for safety. Sometimes the bandit's car is equipped to throw a smoke screen and if the officer is close there is no way to avoid an accident. Another reason for keeping at a safe distance, twenty to twenty-five yards, is the possibility of being fired at by some one in the car. Officers on foot should use the same care in approaching a car, as all officers look alike to the man who is trying to escape. Appearance and fine clothes are not a badge of honesty at the present time; even credentials and identification cards sometimes fail, as they may be stolen ones.

To the Citizens: Never take a man, woman, or child into a car unless they are known to you. You may lose your money, your car, and your life if you do. And the woman is the most dangerous of the three. She can tear her dress, scream, and land you in the middle of an assault case that will be hard to explain to the judge, especially if she has no criminal record. The kind-hearted motorist is traveling on the edge of a volcano, if he persists in helping out every human he encounters. Far better is it for him to distribute said kindness among the traffic officers, as a kind word here and there and the willingness to obey the officer will help to make the disagreeable task of the traffic officer a pleasure instead of the most disagreeable part of police work. The officer is there to assist you in every way, to insure your safety. He is your friend; obey him; do not meet him with a chip on your shoulder but with a smile, and your pleasure trip will have a pleasant ending.

SECTION 58
THE SCIENCE OF USING A REVOLVER AS A CLUB

A revolver may easily be rendered useless by striking some one over the head with it, if the blow is not properly executed. If a four, five, or six inch barrel is used and the muzzle should strike the object first it would be very liable to bend the best revolver barrel ever made. Also if the right side of cylinder should strike the object first it might spring the crane and force the cylinder out of line with the barrel. This might happen to any revolver whether locked at the front end of ejector rod or not.

The proper way to use a revolver as a club is to strike from the right, bringing the left side of cylinder against the head or other part of the anatomy; a needle and thread will repair all damage.

SECTION 59

POLICE BADGES AND PROTECTIVE POLICE COAT

The standard police badge of today has two distinct uses: one to denote the rank of a police officer and the other to point out the exact location of the officer's heart to the law-breaker. A badge or cap ornament may be readily seen at night in a dim light when otherwise the officer would, as far as shooting at any particular spot to shoot at, be invisible. I hope that in the near future an oxidized or dark colored badge will be adopted.

Many police departments have adopted a Sam Brown belt and holster worn on the outside, and I believe this is the proper place to wear a revolver for police use. If, however, the arm is worn on the inside, at least the two lower buttons on the coat should be snap buttons that coat may be quickly opened in case of need. If a small revolver is worn in the overcoat pocket said pocket should be lined with heavy canvas or leather and pocket so built that hammer spur will not catch as arm is drawn. The test as to whether arm is carried in a correct position for quick work or not is this: Can you stand, hands at side, revolver in holster or pocket, and get into action, firing the first shot in less than two seconds and hit what you aim at? If this can be done then the position of revolver is nearly correct. Besides position of revolver, practice enters into this demonstration, but an officer's life is not safe in case of trouble unless he can do this.

SECTION 60
TELEGRAPH MATCHES FOR BANKS AND POLICE

Telegraph matches are becoming popular with the police departments and many banks are beginning to take up this fascinating sport. It means just this, that each team can shoot on its own range under conditions that it is accustomed to. The same feeling of shooting in competition is present even if the rival team cannot be seen. They are there and sometimes loom up larger than if they were present. We cannot but wonder just what the other fellows are doing.

The Colt Patent Fire Arms Manufacturing Company has taken a great interest in this work and in the winter of 1927-28 and 29 ran a series of matches between the different police departments throughout the country. So satisfactory was the result that it will be followed for many years and will grow until not only police departments but banks and trust companies will take it up.

The matches are shot on a twelve-yard range, which nearly any bank or police department can locate in their cellar. The Camp Perry police course is used in this shooting: ten shots slow fire, one minute per shot; ten shots each five in twenty seconds; ten shots each five in ten seconds on a target one-half the size used at Camp Perry. For the teams who have had no rapid-fire experience I would advise matches with neighboring departments before entering the National Matches. First slow fire matches may be arranged and then matches with slow and twenty second courses, gradually working toward the ten second course.

If competing departments all use the light model revolvers, of course there is no advantage, but if one department should use a light model and the other the six-inch barrel revolver the lighter revolver would be badly handicapped and could only win by superior team members. Even small departments can easily use five or six of the larger revolvers for motorcycle men and extra arms and with these arms only practice is necessary to develop a good team.

The winter practice in the matches mentioned will put the men in shape for the outdoor matches and should create enough interest in each town or city to warrant the police or bank officials sending a team to the near-by contests, if not to the National Matches at Camp Perry.

The cost of equipment for an indoor range is practically nothing and the outdoor range can easily be located that will cost very little. The only outlay is for five or six revolvers suitable for this shooting.

In many cases the men who become good shots prefer to purchase their own revolvers and many load their own ammunition, which reduces the cost to less than one cent each and is just as satisfactory if properly done. These are the loading outfits which will do perfect work if properly handled,—Ideal Manufacturing Company and Schmidt's. Hand-loaded ammunition is very accurate and satisfactory. It enables the .38 and larger shooters to do nearly three times the amount of shooting for the same price invested in factory ammunition.

In other chapters I have mentioned that target shooting is not necessary for adequate protection, neither is it, but target shooting stimulates interest in the department, as each of the members outside the team will have dreams of the day when he will win a place on the team and enjoy the trips to other ranges. Each officer will put his best efforts into the work if he has something to look forward to, and every team is looking for the best material obtainable.

SECTION 61

BANK PROTECTION—THE INSTRUCTOR

Bank and police shooting are in the same class, the one difference being that the clerks behind the counter do not carry the revolver. It is placed on a shelf or on a rubber-covered steel rod to hold it in the proper position for drawing. This is preferable to the shelf. It is faster and the revolver can be grasped in proper position instantly.

We may start with a package of twelve, more or less, revolvers delivered to a bank for protection. It is unbelievable to think that a bank would hire any number of guards without employing at least one who was familiar with firearms. By being familiar I mean one who can handle firearms safely and who can impart this information to others; one who will think and study the protection of this particular bank; that is, if the bank is ever held up, how the trouble will come, and what must be done to defeat it. In every bank it will be ninety-nine per cent close work (not over twelve feet) and this eliminates long range target shooting and all kinds except silhouette target shooting, speed and accuracy at short range.

The package of revolvers is opened; the next question is what to do with them? The guard chosen for instructor should call a meeting, composed of all guards and clerks who may be called upon to use a revolver, and from a book or from his own knowledge instruct each one on the safe handling of firearms. Instruct one at a time; the others may stand at a safe distance and benefit by the instruction. The first instructions should be with the revolver empty. The trigger squeeze should be carefully practiced and the proper grip is very important. As ladies will be expected to take this course of shooting as well as gentlemen, a slight change in the prescribed grips may be used; a little higher hold on the arm will usually take care of this. The Police Positive Special four-inch barrel is the favorite for this work and in this arm the grip is perfect for either the large or small hand. With the large hand lock the little finger under grip. Start right, as it is easier to do this than to correct mistakes afterward.

The hands and wrists of bank employees are not usually as strong as the hands of the outdoor officer and the recoil from the lighter revolvers is greater than from the heavier arms. A very good plan is to purchase a .22 target revolver for the preliminary practice. Do not forget to occasionally practice with the regulation arm. The instructor should carefully instruct each shooter as to flinching. A very good way to overcome it is by dry shooting and the use of a .22 revolver.

The first actual shooting should take place after the instructor is convinced that the pupil is familiar with the foregoing instructions at short range, as bank shooting is necessarily at short range. The first actual shooting should be at fifteen feet and the Colt's Silhouette or the Langrish Limbless target used. The object is to create confidence in the shooter.

Course No. 1 (Preliminary)

Distance, 15 feet
Silhouette Target
6 shots at center of target
(See scoring of silhouette targets)
Double action

After you are able to hit the target regularly try:

Course No. 2

Distance, 15 feet
Silhouette Target
6 shots at head, single action

Correct holding of sights is very important, also trigger squeeze. Courses No. 1 and No. 2 are preparatory to the faster work that is to follow. Double action is less dangerous than single action. Your revolver will explode all perfect ammunition double action and all quick shooting at short range will be double action. In fact, a good double-action shot can do good work at all ranges and it is faster than single action at short ranges.

A table or counter should be provided to insure the safety of the shooter's feet. Too much care cannot be taken with new shooters in the safe handling of firearms.

Advanced Course No. 1 (Timed)

Guard's Course

15 yards, revolver in holster (double action)
At command "FIRE," draw and fire with favorite gun hand
2 shots at K or center zone of Silhouette Target
Run to 10 yards (carrying revolver safety finger out of trigger)
Fire 2 shots with right hand, change gun to left hand and fire 2 shots with left hand
K zone to count

Course 2 (Timed)

For employees at desk or window:

Stand behind a section of counter
Hands placed on top for Courses 2, 3, 4, 5, 6,
Revolver in position used in the bank
At command "FIRE," draw and fire
2 shots holding Colt with both hands
2 shots with right hand
2 shots with left hand

Any person unable to pull the trigger double action should fire the entire six shots, holding the arm with both hands (the gun hand placed firmly in the palm of the other hand, closing bottom hand firmly about the gun hand, in such a manner as not to interfere with pulling the trigger). Ladies with small hands may find this necessary. 1/3 of one point is deducted from all but Course No. 6 (which is slow fire) for each second used. Example: Add the scores in the first five courses and subtract 1/3 of the total of seconds used; then add score in Course No. 6 for total score.

Course 3 (Timed)

2 shots, revolver in usual position
10 feet double action
At command "FIRE," draw and fire at center of body K zone only to count

Course 4 (Timed)

Same as Course 3, except 2 shots for the head. Head only to count.

Course 5 (Timed)

Same as Course No. 3, except 2 shots for the right arm of silhouette (D) zone. Right arm to count.

Course 6 (Not Timed)

6 shots at 15 yards, slow fire, single action, at head. Head shot only to count, to top of white figures in neck. It is well for all guards to practice Course No. 2, as they may be inside the windows when trouble comes.

Note

By "Single Action" is meant cocking the hammer and squeezing the trigger for each shot. In using "Double

Action" the hammer is raised by a steady squeeze on the trigger and falls when it has reached a sufficient height to insure firing the cartridge. In timing a stop watch should be used; taking the time from the word "FIRE" to the report of the last shot. Always look at your revolver before going on duty. See that it is properly loaded and working properly, with no obstruction in the barrel and properly cleaned. Be sure that your ammunition is fresh. Oil-soaked cartridges may render your revolver useless in an emergency. It is a good plan to change cartridges every four weeks and use old ammunition for target practice. Target practice should be compulsory at least once each week.

Many other courses may be constructed from the silhouette target. See New York State Trooper's shooting courses.

I remember an instance that happened in a bank which I visited. The instructor informed me that he had four girls who could neither cock a revolver nor fire it double action. I asked if they might go to the range with us for instruction and, as he had stated, they were unable to fire the revolver. I then asked each to hold the revolver with both hands and shoot double action. They could all fire the revolver in this manner. One of the young ladies hit the silhouette six times in seven seconds,—very good shooting for one who, up to that time, had not been able to fire at all.

The point to be driven home is the fact that this work is not play and must be taken seriously. I have been asked the question: What is to be done if one is suddenly confronted at the window with a revolver and the command, "Hands up"? Only two things to do—stand still, hands up (this is dangerous for if a shot is fired in the bank, your hold-up man will shoot you), or as the hands go up drop to the floor, getting revolver as you go down.

I have tried this many times and have yet to find any one who could snap quick enough to touch me; the revolver was empty. Another question, Is it best to lock all bank doors in connection with alarm? Yes, if the guards are able to handle the situation and, whether they are or not, I believe any bank robber would hesitate before entering a bank with an alarm so constructed, with a separate secret button to open one door when police arrive.

All this practice and expense is to prepare for the one minute when lives and property are in danger and it must be done well when that minute arrives. The only way to prevent it is to be ready. The properly protected bank is never held up, as the system of protection is studied weeks in advance by the robber. Observation of the guards will locate strangers, who place themselves in advantageous positions for no apparent reason. Money should be placed on traps which, as a button or spring is pressed, will drop it into a drawer below the counter. Gas may be used in cartridges but it is a hardship for the clerks, customers, and guards as well as for the robbers.

[The following article, by Mr. Harry C. Almy, is the best on bank protection that I have ever read and I believe it covers the situation fully. Mr. Almy is not only an expert target shot but a practical shot as well, and is thoroughly versed in all branches of revolver shooting.— THE AUTHOR.]

BANK PROTECTION

By Harry C. Almy

The subject of bank protection is one that is occupying a prominent place in the minds of bankers, especially in the smaller cities and towns.

Various reasons are advanced for the increasing number of holdups. Perhaps the chief contributing cause lies in the good roads and fast automobiles, as the success of this form of outlawry depends upon the surprise of attack and the speed of escape.

The daylight holdup, as now practiced, is more or less a development of the present day. A comparatively few years ago the banker paid for burglarly insurance and robbery protection was included without extra charge. Today the robbery rate is approximately double that of burglary. Equipment has been developed to such a degree that the burglar has been baffled, but the uneasiness which he causes, is ably taken care of by the modern holdup man, who furnishes all of the thrills and lacks none of the disagreeable attributes of his predecessor.

The solution of the problem is simple,—it is to make the holdup industry so hazardous and the fruits of the labor so uncertain that those practicing the profession will be inclined to turn to more peaceful and profitable pursuits.

Just how to carry out the terms of the solution is not so simple. However, it can be done, but in the successful working out of a remedy the banks must be brought to a realization of the fact that it is chiefly their own problem and that nothing less than an earnest, aggressive, and continuous effort on their part must be put forth in cooperating with peace officers, as well as by the installation of efficient safety devices, the employment of guards, and the elimination of practices in their institutions which contribute to the ease with which robberies can be perpetrated.

It is well for the banker first to look to the customs which have become established. Man is a habit-forming creature and if not interfered with will do the same thing about the same way repeatedly; and so, because currency accumulates Monday and Tuesday, Wednesday becomes the day on which the surplus is shipped out, and month after month on the same day of the week, about the same hour of the day, the same procedure is gone through in transporting the funds to the post-office or express company, or, if the flow of currency is the other way, a regular method of handling incoming shipments usually develops. It is also true, frequently, in the manner of handling payrolls: with monotonous regularity, week after week, the same day, the same hour, the same men carry the payroll over the same route to the same factory. A smart football coach can be depended upon to figure out the signals of the opposing team in spite of a careful effort to prevent it. It is well known that advance men look over a territory when an assault is in contemplation, and it is reasonable to believe that a man who is sizing up a situation does not overlook customs which in themselves constitute invitations for attack. In many cases partition doors between the lobby and the bank proper are not only unlocked but are sometimes propped open; day gates are left open because it is inconvenient for employees to unlock them when it is necessary to enter the vault; money-safes and securities chests are unlocked for the reason that it takes time for the tellers to run combinations. The careful locking of all of these would not defeat a holdup, but it might influence the advance man, who is looking for the largest haul along the line of least resistance, to pass the bank which is exercising caution in these particulars because, we repeat, the success of this form of banditry depends upon the elements of surprise and speed, and even light locks militate against both of these. So it is well for the banker to take stock of his institution with a view of making it physically as resistant as practicable and to ascertain if the customs are such as to not menace its safety.

It is a question if some banks do not rely too much upon the protection of the police, sheriffs, and the law. It is proper that there should be confidence in these ministrations, but bankers are lacking in their full duty when they fail to give every aid within their power toward their own protection. The sheriff's office was designed to protect the county in the horse and buggy days when a trip across a county was one measured in hours. Today a few minutes is ample, yet the sheriff's office remains in equipment, man power, and limitations much as it was originally set up. Usually towns are underpoliced. With approximately one officer to each one thousand population in the average small city, the police department is expected to regulate traffic, to protect thousands of homes, scores of factories and places of business, and cannot give an undue amount of time to the few banks. Therefore the banker must accept a certain responsibility in his own protection; nor can he rest secure in the knowledge that his funds are adequately covered by insurance, for, in addition to the money loss, there is the more vital thing, the potential danger to employees and customers, which should make him more determined to wipe out the evil which has assailed his business. Insurance rates have been advanced and if losses justify, further increases will be made. It is within the range of possibility that the cost of this protection will reach a figure that will be prohibitive for some of the smaller banks. When this occurs then, indeed, will the needs of the community, which has been deprived of banking facilities, have been sacrificed because the many cannot protect themselves against the few. Such a condition could not or would not exist in America if those most interested would awaken to the need of aggressive action.

There is a way to put an end to these bank attacks and the answer will be found if bankers will acknowledge the responsibility that is theirs and undertake the solution with the same energy that they have brought to other problems which they have worked out to successful conclusions. If it becomes necessary for a customer to have a passport before being allowed to enter a bank it might seriously hamper the operations of financial institutions. To avoid this it may be necessary for banks in the afflicted areas to maintain armed guards so located and so protected that they would, without danger to themselves, be able to control any situation that might arise.

Banks should encourage their employees to learn to shoot, not with a view of putting up armed resistance in case of a holdup. In fact, if the other man has the drop on the best shooter in the world, that best shooter would be a very foolish person if he didn't throw his hands up just as high as he could reach and do everything else he is told to do. But if an employee is a trained shooter, is fast and accurate with a gun, and an opportunity presents itself, he is then in a position to do something for the protection of himself, his institution, and the banking business in general. The robber is no superman,—he makes mistakes. Within the week in our state one made a very serious error. He tried to handle too many men and a courageous banker, who was in the group he was herding into a back room, grappled with him, took the gun away from him and according to the latest newspaper reports the body is still in the morgue unclaimed. But while this robber was making the mistake of his life an accomplice climbed over the counter in an effort to get away and one of the tellers had time to empty a revolver at him, but nothing resulted except a loud noise and he got into an automobile and drove away. If the teller had been a trained shot at least two of the band would have remained among those present. and several rounds of ammunition would have been saved.

One of the indispensable pieces of bank furniture is the revolver. Regardless of size perhaps a banking institution would be as likely to attempt to carry on its business without an adding machine as without a revolver, and usually one is found at every window and the banker is serene in his belief that he has armed his force. As a matter of fact he may have provided a bunch of nondescript weapons, including various calibers in varying states of preservation, with possibly a few cheap foreigners and a scattering of the pot metal variety never intended to *handle the modern powders.*

There is only one kind of gun that is worthy of consideration if there is any chance of it being used for defense, and that is a good gun, and to go into action with one that is not dependable is to court disaster. A good gun in the hands of one incapable of handling it is more a source of danger than protection. Messenger policies require that one or more armed guards accompany the messenger. In the actual carrying out of this provision several employees, who could not hit the ground with their hats, put guns in their pockets and imagine they are armed; whereas, in fact, they constitute a menace to the safety of themselves and others for the reason that if they were to encounter the holdup man and attempted to use the weapons with which they are wholly unfamiliar it would unquestionably cause the yegg to start shooting, possibly resulting in the loss of lives as well as the valuables they have undertaken to guard.

With very small expenditure banks can establish shooting ranges in their basements or elsewhere and provide for the teaching of their employees to shoot. Then, when the opportunity comes, if it does come, they will be effective. The National Rifle Association, the Arms Companies, the Ammunition Manufacturers, men like our good friend Fitz, the author of this book, and others high up in the shooting game are always glad to lend assistance in teaching marksmanship and the safe handling of firearms to the right kind of people.

Generally in every community there is to be found a shooter or two who will advise and aid an institution which desires to undertake such an activity.

If every banker was as expert with a hand gun as he is with an interest table bank holdups would be a lost art. How many times have the marines been stuck up and made to lie face down on the floor while their money has been gathered up? So long as the robber knows that a fast car, a big gun, and a little "hop" with a banker ready to offer no resistance will yield him rich reward, just so long will holdups continue and with increasing boldness.

Bankers should give thoughtful consideration to the subject of anti-firearms legislation. This is especially invidious for the reason that arguments of its proponents are apparently so reasonable to one who is not well versed in the subject. Many well-intentioned persons have the honest, though mistaken, belief that if laws were passed that would prohibit the manufacture, sale and possession of hand guns, crimes with these weapons would cease. Such laws would result in the disarmament of the law-abiding citizen, leaving him unprotected against the criminal who has no regard for law. The enforcement of such laws would greatly aid the crook, so the banker should be especially interested in preventing their passage.

The answer to the holdup challenge may lie in an extension of the state police system, in providing armed guards according to the needs of the individual bank, or it may not lie in force. It may be more severe and more certain punishment for offenders or in the wiping out of organized crime by the forces of the government itself. But whatever the answer is, if the powerful bankers' group will tackle it with the spirit of "Whatever it takes we have" the solution will be found.

SECTION 62

THE ARMORED CAR, PASSENGER CAR AND GUARDS

Bank Protection

In tracing conditions back for many years we find that in the days when banks and trust companies delivered money and valuable papers by one or two guards on foot, holdups were frequent; with the horse and wagon the same conditions prevailed, and now, in the automobile age, the automobiles aiding the get-away, we are having more payroll robberies than ever before. Even the armored car does not always prevent the robbery.

The armored car, while a preventive against robbery between the bank and place of delivery, does not prevent it either while money is placed in the car or delivered at the end of the journey. Experienced guards is the answer whether money is delivered by armored car or on foot. Its safety rests with the guards and not the conveyance.

I have noticed many times a clerk or paymaster carrying a bag at his side containing the money, the guard walking along hands at side, and if a revolver is carried it is in the hip pocket. Usually both men are inexperienced in the use of firearms and if trouble came neither would know where to begin. If they were experienced they would never walk side by side; the guard would walk at least ten feet behind (closer in a crowd). Two guards are better than one, one ahead and one behind. Whether the money is to be carried two blocks or ten, it is best to use a car for delivery.

If a passenger car is used, the principal thing to watch for is some one jumping upon the running-board on either side or another car forcing the money car toward the side of the street or road. In this case wreck the car, if possible, blocking the get-away. Four properly instructed guards are equal to ten of the so-called gunmen. Use the car for a shield, first getting out, if ordinary car is used, as the cramped position in a car does not allow for movement enough to protect against the opponent's fire. As long as you stay in the car you are in one of five positions easily and accurately gauged from the outside; if on the floor you cannot see or protect yourself; on the outside your actual position is in doubt. It is no disgrace or no act of cowardice to use any available protection in a gun fight; it is good judgment. In a case of this kind or in any case all guards should be dressed in uniform, that officers coming to their assistance may know them from the gunmen.

The armored car has eliminated most of the trouble between starting and stopping points, but the danger is the same, as money is placed in the car and taken out at the other end. Again four or five properly trained guards will never be molested. I have found that the properly protected bank is never held up.

The procedure of bank robbers is to go to a town or city, look over the situation, and, if bank is easy, study system of protection; spend four or five weeks; find out when big shipments are made; and, when final arrangements are made, take the money,—this in case the protection is inadequate. If bank is properly protected, after checking up the system the robbers move to the next town. Why should they take a chance when so many hundreds of banks throughout the country are not protected. Many could be held up successfully by one man.

Five men who know protection are practically unbeatable, as two would cover one side of the doorway and sidewalk, the other two cover the other, backs turned to each other, while the fifth man with money would walk up space between them. If in doubt, stop all traffic until money is safely in bank or car and then close up around entrance, having revolver under the hand ready to use.

Unless both men and arms are tried out on the range no bank official can say that his bank is protected. The banks in the United States owe it to their employees and their families to take all necessary precautions in the way of instructions and proper firearms to safely protect lives and property.

Bank and payroll protection must be instantaneous. By this I mean that success or failure to protect is settled inside of ten seconds. Our Crime Commissions will tell us that the revolvers and automatic pistols are the cause of daylight robberies. This is not true; the automobile that allows the get-away is to blame. If there were no automobiles there would be very few daylight robberies. We cannot dispense with the automobiles, but we can perfect ourselves in the one thing that makes the get-away in an automobile a hazardous undertaking, namely, accurate revolver and pistol shooting.

A VERY EFFECTIVE ARMORED CAR

SECTION 63
MY DAD AND I

In the course of my shooting experience I have heard many amusing stories relating to experiences with the revolver and pistol. Usually some relative of the storyteller is the performer, or, if he is endowed with more than normal courage, he tells of his own wonderful doings.

While visiting the Delaware State Police I found it necessary to purchase some lumber for target frames and visited a local lumber yard. After stating my needs, the foreman asked: "Say, you're the guy that's doing tricks with a revolver over to the State Police Range, ain't you? Well! I sure don't believe you can do what I used to do with a revolver. Why, man, before my eyes went bad I used to take my revolver and drive tacks four out of five at forty yards and my Dad could beat me any day. I've seen him stick his old stem-winding watch in the crotch of a tree and wind it up by hitting the edge of the stem with six bullets. And, say, you sure ought to have seen him shooting game. I saw him once get four deer at one hundred yards with three shots. You see the deer was going pretty fast and Dad shot the first three deer dead in their tracks. The last one in line went down with the rest and when we looked them over we found that the old man had pulled one wild shot. The bullet fired at that third deer went high and hit the horn, but 'twasn't such a bad shot after all, as the bullet split and half of it went down into the top of the deer's head and the other half hit that last deer in the eye killing both deer. The old man's eyesight ain't so good, or he never would a-pulled that high shot. Say, Mr., how good can you shoot?"

I don't think he ever heard my answer for I was several yards away when he asked the question.

One morning while in the Colt's Testing Range an old man, who claimed he was seventy-six years old, came to visit me. I performed a few tricks for him, such as cutting a card, hitting empty shells, etc., and the old man said: "That's nothing, any one who can hold a revolver steady can do that." I agreed with him. He showed me a target with one-inch bull's-eye and five bullet holes, either in or touching the black, and said: "What do you think of that?" I asked at what distance it had been made, and he said: "Can't you read?" I looked again and saw at the top of the target the following: "Shot at three hundred yards with Colt Officer's Model, seven and one-half inch barrel." I handed over my revolver and said: "I can't shoot for you, Mr.; you shoot for me." I finally induced him to fire a few shots and placed a twelve and one-half yard target at fifty yards, apologizing for the fact that I had no three hundred yard range available. He fired six shots and, of course, did not hit any part of the target. When the target was shown him, he said: "Well, I forgot I had an extra cup of coffee this morning, and I always make my best scores before breakfast."

While on a hunting trip several years ago I met a young man and his father and, while conversing with them, I noticed that the old man was looking very intently into the top of a near-by tree. His son asked him what he was looking at and he said: "Squirrel." The young man and I circled the tree, but could see no trace of the squirrel. The old man insisted it was there and finally the son discovered the reason. "Why Dad, that's no squirrel, that's a louse on your eyebrow."

Several years ago a young man came into a sporting goods store and said he wished to dispose of his rifle, and this is the conversation which took place: *Clerk:* "Is that an accurate rifle?" *Rifle Owner:* "Say, Mr., that is the best rifle in this state. Tell you what my Dad did with it yesterday. I set three clay pipes up at three hundred and fifty yards and the old man stood up and hit the first two pipes with his first two shots. The third pipe he refused to shoot at because he couldn't see the stem. The old man's eyes ain't what they used to be and we thought he must be mistaken. However, we went out to the pipe and found a small green snake looking into the bowl, his body covering the stem so my Dad couldn't see it; but, Mr., that wasn't the gun's fault and my Dad would sure have taken that snake's head off if he had fired that third shot." The salesman bought the rifle and managed to ask: "Does your father wear glasses?" The man answered: "No, but I guess he will have to before long. He sure was a great shot in his day."

SECTION 64
OUR FRIENDLY TALK

And now I feel that we have become sufficiently acquainted to have a little plain talk about the art of pistol and revolver practice. I have many times instructed a class in revolver shooting when some of the class gave a very sorry exhibition and this was due to carelessness. As I instructed in the proper way to line up the sight, they would carelessly allow the front sight to extend above or below the top of the rear sight, possibly thinking that a sixteenth or a thirty-second of an inch would make no difference. It does make a difference and a very great difference if you are shooting twenty, twenty-five or fifty yards. Try to do just as the instructor tells you and you will see an improvement almost from the start.

The same carelessness will cause the student to allow the arm to swing to the right or left and he will tell me he can't help it. There is no such word as "can't," and if he will try to put the same amount of energy and will power into learning to shoot as he does into any other sport or part of his profession he will become an expert shot.

In police work I am a firm believer in every officer being able to shoot quick and straight with right and left hand. Still in one of the most up-to-date departments in the United States I was told by the men that they could not shoot straight with the left hand. Before the course was over the men made better scores on the Colt Silhouette target with the left hand than they did with the right hand. It is very important in police work to know that you have a one hundred per cent left hand and know how to use it. This means, of course, that the arm must be carried where you can reach it with the left hand as well as the right.

Another very important thing in police work is to be able to scent danger. Certain conditions arise which should spell to the officer "get ready." An unlocked door found by an officer; how many officers have blundered in with gloves on and their revolvers under three or four coats and sweaters to be killed because they did not take proper precaution. Learn to take advantage of conditions as you find them. Learn to handle every emergency which may arise and handle it to the credit of your department and yourself. If you should find a door unlocked, first look around and see where the street lights are, whether they will throw your shadow into the store or building if you should enter, making a target of you for any one in the store to shoot at. A friend of mine once caught two burglars by trying an unlocked door and instead of opening it stepped along to the next doorway and waited. In a short time the two men came out. He got his men because he used his head.

Carelessness and heedlessness are the things to avoid when on the shooting range. I will cite an instance which happened in a class of two hundred officers. I drew the diagram of sights as seen by the officer when revolver was in firing position and told them that they would all be asked that question in their examination papers and explained the diagram to each one separately. One week later in the examination not twenty per cent of the officers had the right answer.

I was asked by a certain chief of police to try to hammer SAFETY into the heads of his men due to an accidental shooting a week before. I explained for forty minutes the safe handling of firearms; even pictured an accident: an officer accidently killed by a brother officer, the man lying dead on the floor, a few days later being carried to his grave, the misery of two families whose lives were wrecked by carelessness. I nearly started crying myself over my heart-rending description of the case; then wiped my eyes and called the first man to the firing line. Before he was ready to fire a shot, one of the officers behind us, for some unknown reason, drew his revolver, aimed it at a knot in the floor, and hit it plumb center in a range of sixty men. However old or experienced the shooter, he is not too old to have an accident when thinking of other things. Keep the hands away from the revolver or pistol until you can forget everything else; put your mind on the revolver and nothing else.

I have been asked after a week or two spent with a department if I considered the school a success. My answer was: "Yes; no one was injured."

Officers should not spend too much time in figuring out just what they would do in a gun fight. They should spend a little time each day in this way, but do not carry it to excess or they will be in the same condition as the deer hunter who goes out for the first time and sees a set of antlers behind every bush. I have known officers who have done just that; too much study on the subject is almost as bad as too little. This applies to all marksmen, and alcohol, revolvers, and cartridges make a cocktail that should be avoided.

While enjoying the advantages and pleasures of meeting old friends from North, East, South and West, and of shooting in the matches at Camp Perry and elsewhere, we must not forget the organization that has made all this possible.

Since 1871 the National Rifle Association of America have used their untiring efforts to promote the shooting game. Recently has been added a police division to promote the use of revolvers in police departments and to assist them in promoting matches among the different departments. All branches of the National Rifle Association are presided over by men well versed in the shooting game.

Another welcome addition is the Sales and Service Department of the National Rifle Association, 816 Barr Building, Washington, D. C. The National Rifle Association is worthy of the consideration of every red-blooded American citizen. May it increase in membership from year to year, thereby allowing us to more thoroughly enjoy our chosen pastime.

THE END.

A CORNER IN GUN ROOM OF MR. ALBERT W. FOSTER, JR.
405 Walton Road, South Orange, N. J.

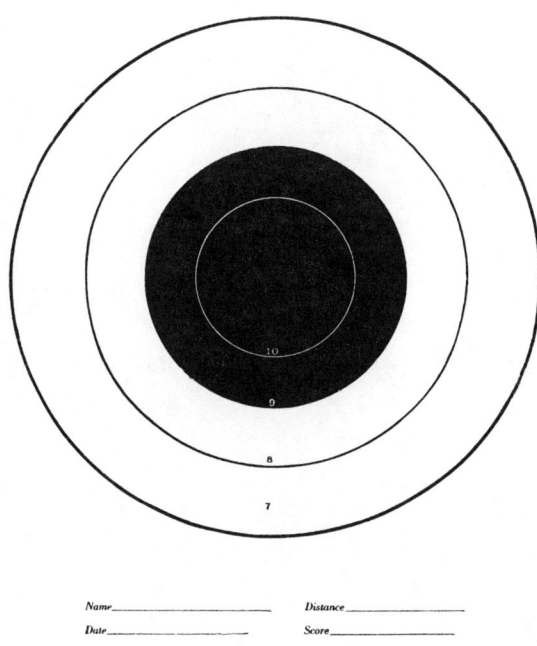

DRY SHOOTING TARGET
OR
10-YARD RAPID-FIRE TARGET